Pro Android Games

Third Edition

Massimo Nardone

Vladimir Silva

Pro Android Games, 3rd Edition

ISBN-13 (pbk): 978-1-4842-0588-4

ISBN-13 (electronic): 978-1-4842-0587-7

Managing Director: Welmoed Spahr
Lead Editor: Steve Anglin
Development Editor: Jody Larson
Technical Reviewer: Dante Pugliese
Editorial Board: Steve Anglin, Gary Cornell, Louise Corrigan, Jonathan Gennick, Robert Hutchinson, Michelle Lowman, James Markham, Matthew Moodie, Jeff Olson, Jeffrey Pepper, Douglas Pundick, Ben Renow-Clarke, Gwenan Spearing, Matt Wade, Steve Weiss
Coordinating Editor: Mark Powers
Copy Editor: Linda Seifert
Compositor: SPi Global
Indexer: SPi Global
Artist: SPi Global
Cover Designer: Anna Ishchenko

Distributed to the book trade worldwide by Springer Science+Business Media New York, 233 Spring Street, 6th Floor, New York, NY 10013. Phone 1-800-SPRINGER, fax (201) 348-4505, e-mail orders-ny@springer-sbm.com, or visit www.springeronline.com. Apress Media, LLC is a California LLC and the sole member (owner) is Springer Science + Business Media Finance Inc (SSBM Finance Inc). SSBM Finance Inc is a Delaware corporation.

For information on translations, please e-mail rights@apress.com, or visit www.apress.com.

Apress and friends of ED books may be purchased in bulk for academic, corporate, or promotional use. eBook versions and licenses are also available for most titles. For more information, reference our Special Bulk Sales–eBook Licensing web page at www.apress.com/bulk-sales.

Any source code or other supplementary material referenced by the author in this text is available to readers at www.apress.com/9781484205884. For detailed information about how to locate your book's source code, go to www.apress.com/source-code/.

I would like to dedicate this book to my family: my lovely wife, Pia, and my children, Luna, Leo, and Neve, as well as my mother, Maria, my father, Giuseppe, my brothers, Roberto and Mario, and finally Jani, Sanna, Hilla, and Lionel Irrmann. Thank you all for your love and support.

Contents at a Glance

Contents

About the Authors

Massimo Nardone holds a Master of Science degree in Computing Science from the University of Salerno, Italy. He worked as a PCI QSA and Senior Lead IT Security/Cloud/SCADA Architect for many years and currently works as Security, Cloud and SCADA Lead IT Architect for Hewlett Packard Finland. He has more than 20 years of work experience in IT, including Security, SCADA, Cloud Computing, IT Infrastructure, Mobile, and WWW technology areas for both national and international projects. Massimo has worked as a Project Manager, Cloud/SCADA Lead IT Architect, Software Engineer, Research Engineer, Chief Security Architect, and Software Specialist. He worked as visiting lecturer and supervisor for exercises at the Networking Laboratory of the Helsinki University of Technology (Aalto University). He has been programming and teaching how to program with Perl, PHP, Java, VB, Python, C/C++, and MySQL for more than 20 years. He is the author of *Beginning PHP and MySQL* (Apress, 2014) and *Pro Android Games* (Apress, 2015).

He holds four international patents (PKI, SIP, SAML, and Proxy areas).

Vladimir Silva holds a master's degree in computer science from Middle Tennessee State University. He worked for four years at IBM as a research engineer, where he acquired extensive experience in distributed and grid computing research. Vladimir is a highly technical, focus-based individual and team player. He belongs to two national honor societies, has published many computer science articles for IBM, and is author of *Grid Computing for Developers* (Charles River Media, 2005) and *RCP Practical Projects* (Apress, 2008).

About the Technical Reviewer

Dante Pugliese, Ph.D., is an engineer who works in the area of the Industrial Knowledge Management and as a university researcher. His competencies include techniques for Knowledge Acquisition, PLM, Engineering Knowledge Management, product configuration, Knowledge Based Engineering, Best Practices and Company procedures automation. He has also served as a lecturer at Politecnico di Milano and the University of Parma.

He has been developing Java, C/C++, and various mobile applications for Android, Windows Phone, and iOS for many years. His clients include universities such as Politecnico di Milano and software vendors such as Siemens PLM.

Additionally, he has developed projects in the following industrial fields: HVAC and renewable energy, filling and packaging, pressure plants, ventilation equipment, automation (control and switchboards), machine tools, oil and gas, and electrical grids for railways.

In his spare time, he runs a small Italian cuisine import company in Finland.

Acknowledgments

Many thanks go to my wonderful family—my lovely wife, Pia, and my children, Luna, Leo, and Neve, for supporting me when working on this book although I had less time to be with them. You are the beautiful reasons for my life.

I want to thank my parents, Maria and Giuseppe, for helping me to achieve my computer science dreams when I was a young student. This book is also dedicated to my brothers, Mario and Roberto, for always being there when I needed them, as well as to Lionel Irrmann who wants to become a software engineer one day. May this book be an inspiration for you.

I also want to thank my wonderful editorial staff at Apress. Big thanks go to Steve Anglin for giving me the opportunity to work as writer for this book. Steve had faith in my ability to write about this subject.

A special thanks to Mark Powers for doing a fantastic job of helping me through the editorial process as well as helping me with all the issues I had during the writing. He was fantastic.

Also, many thanks to Jody Larson, the Apress development editor, as well as to Dante Pugliese, the technical reviewer, for helping me to make a better book.

Introduction

Welcome to *Pro Android Games*, *Third Edition*. This book will help you create great games for the Android platform. You can find plenty of books out there that tackle this subject, but this book gives you a unique perspective by showing you how easy it is to bring native PC games to the platform with minimum effort.

To get the most out of this book, you must have a solid foundation in Java and ANSI C. However, even the most complicated concepts have been explained as clearly and as simply as possible using a combination of graphics and sample code. The real-world examples and source code provided for each chapter will help you understand the concepts in detail so you can excel as a mobile game developer.

The Green Robot Has Taken Over

It is hard to believe that only a few years have passed since Android came into the smartphone scene—and it has taken off with a vengeance. Take a look at the worldwide Smartphone OS Market Share[1] shown in Figure 1. In Q2 2014 Android lead with 84.7% and the stats just keep getting better and better. This opens a new frontier for developers looking to capitalize on the rocketing smartphone segment. This book will help you quickly build cutting-edge games for the Android platform.

---

[1]"IDC: Android has a heady 84.7% percent of world smartphone share," `http://www.idc.com/prodserv/smartphone-os-market-share.jsp`

Wolrdwide Smartphone OS Market Share

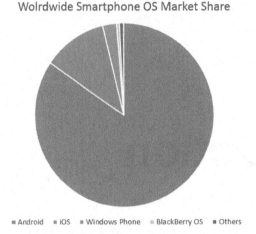

■ Android ■ iOS ■ Windows Phone ■ BlackBerry OS ■ Others

Figure 1. Worldwide smartphone market share 2014

Target Audience

This book targets seasoned game developers, not only in Java, but also in C. This makes sense, as performance is critical in game development. Other audiences include:

- *Business apps developers*: This book can be a valuable tool for business developers, especially those working on native applications.

- *Scientific developers*: In the science world, raw performance matters. The chapters dealing with JNI and OpenGL can help you achieve your goals.

- *Computer science students learning new mobile platforms*: Android is open and fairly portable, thus this book can be helpful for working on many platforms (iPhone, BlackBerry, Meego, and others).

- *Anyone interested in Android development*: Android has taken over the mobile market space at a furious pace. You must expand your skill set to include games and graphics or you may be left behind.

Needed Skills to Make the Most of This Book

The required skill set for Pro Android Games includes C/C++ and Java, plus some basic Linux shell scripting. Java provides elegant object-oriented capabilities, but only C gives you the power boost that game development needs.

A Solid Foundation of Android

This book assumes that you already know the basics of Android development. For example, you need to understand activities, views, and layouts. Consider the following fragment. If you understand what it does just by looking at it, then you are in good shape.

```
public class MainActivity extends Activity
{
public void onCreate(Bundle savedInstanceState) { super.onCreate(savedInstanceState);
setContentView(R.layout.main);
}
}
```

This fragment defines the main activity or class that controls the life cycle of the application. The onCreate method will be called once when the application starts, and its job is to set the content layout or GUI for the application.

You should also have a basic understanding of how GUIs are created using XML. Look at the next fragment. Can you tell what it does?

```
<?xml version="1.0" encoding="utf-8"?>
<RelativeLayout xmlns:android="http://schemas.android.com/apk/res/android"
android:layout_width="fill_parent" android:layout_height="fill_parent">


<ImageView android:id="@+id/doom_iv" android:layout_width="fill_parent"
android:layout_height="fill_parent" android:background="@drawable/doom"
android:focusableInTouchMode="true" android:focusable="true"/>


<ImageButton android:id="@+id/btn_upleft" android:layout_width="wrap_content"
android:layout_height="wrap_content" android:layout_alignParentBottom="true"
android:layout_alignParentLeft="true" android:src="@drawable/img1" />
</RelativeLayout>
```

This code defines a relative layout. In a relative layout, widgets are placed relative to each other (sometimes overlapping). In this case, there is an image view that fills the entire screen. This image displays as the background the file called doom.png stored in the res/drawable folder of the project, and it receives key and touch events. In the lower left of the screen, overlapping the image view, an image button with the ID btn_upleft is displayed.

Android development requires understanding of many concepts, and it is impossible to remember every detail about activities, views, and layouts. A handy place to access this information quickly is the Android tutorial at http://developer.android.com/.

The ultimate guide for Android developers—the latest releases, downloads, SDK Quick Start, version notes, native development tools, and previous releases—can be found at http://developer.android.com/sdk/index.html.

Throughout this book (especially in the chapters dealing with native code), I make extensive use of the Android software development kit (SDK) command tools (for system administrator tasks). Thus, you should have a clear understanding of these tools, especially the Android Debug Bridge (ADB). You should know how to implement the following tasks:

- *Create an Android Virtual Device (AVD)*: An AVD encapsulates settings for a specific device configuration, such as firmware version and SD card path. Creating an AVD is really simple and can be done from the integrated development environment (IDE) by using the AVD Manager (accessed by clicking the black phone icon in the toolbar).

- *Create an SD card file*: Some of the games in later chapters have big files (5MB or more). To save space, the code stores all game files in the device SD card, and you should know how to create one. For example, to create a 100MB SD card file called sdcard.iso in your home directory, use this command:

  ```
  $ mksdcard 100M $HOME/sdcard.iso
  ```

- *Connect to the emulator*: You need to do this for miscellaneous system administration, such as library extraction. To open a shell to the device, use this command:

  ```
  $ adb shell
  ```

- *Upload and pull files from the emulator*: These tasks are helpful for storing and extracting game files to and from the device. Use these commands:

  ```
  $ adb push <LOCAL_FILE> <DEVICE_FILE>
  $ adb pull <DEVICE_FILE> <LOCAL_FILE>
  ```

> **Note** Make sure the SDK_HOME/tools directory is added to your system PATH variable before running the commands to create an SD card file, connect to the emulator, or upload and pull files.

A Basic Knowledge of Linux and Shell Scripting

All the chapters in this book (except Chapter 1) use a hybrid combination of Java/C development, which requires knowledge about native development. In these chapters, you do the work within a Linux-like shell dubbed Cygwin, so dust off all those old Unix skills. You should know the basic shell commands, such as those for listing files, installing software components (this can be tricky, depending on your Linux distribution), and basic system administration. There are a few very simple shell scripts in this book. A basic knowledge of the bash shell is always helpful.

> **Tip**   If you need a refresher on your Linux and shell scripting, check out the following tutorial
> by Ashley J.S Mills: http://supportweb.cs.bham.ac.uk/documentation/tutorials/
> docsystem/build/tutorials/unixscripting/unixscripting.html.

Required Hardware and Software

The following sections cover the tools you will need to make the most of this book.

A Windows or Linux PC with a Java SDK, Properly Installed

This requirement is probably obvious, since most development for Android is done in Java.
Note that I mentioned a Java SDK, not JRE. The SDK is required because of the JNI header
files and command line tools used throughout the latter chapters.

Android Studio, Eclipse ADT, and Android SDK, Properly Installed

Android Studio is the de facto IDE for Android development. I used both the Eclipse Android
Development Tools (ADT) and Android Studio with Android SDK for Windows. The reason
for using both Eclipse ADT and Android Studio was that when this manuscript was updated
Android Studio did not fully support NDK.

Even though Eclipse ADT as well as Android Studio was used to create the code workspace,
you can use your favorite IDE. Of course that will require a bit of extra setup. You can get
Eclipse from www.eclipse.org/.

For instructions on how to setup the Android SDK with other IDEs go to
http://developer.android.com/tools/workflow/index.html. Refer to Chapter 1 for details
about configuring the Android SDK in your PC.

Native Development Kit (NDK)

The NDK is the essential tool for any serious game developer out there. It provides the
compiler chain, header files, and documentation required to bring your cutting-edge games
to the mobile landscape. By using the NDK, developers can escape the shackles of the
Java memory heap and unleash their creativity to build the most powerful C/C++ engines,
limited only by what the hardware can provide. In *Pro Android Games*, you'll use the NDK
extensively, thus a solid foundation of C programming is required to fully understand the
concepts presented in each chapter. For this book, the NDK Revision 10d was used. Refer
to Chapter 1 for details about setting up the latest NDK in your PC.

Chapter Source

This is an optional tool but it will help you greatly in understanding the concepts as you move along. I have made my best effort to describe each topic as simply as possible; nevertheless some of the games (especially Quake I and II) have very large core engines written in C (100,000 lines for Doom), which are poorly commented and very hard to understand. All in all, you will see how easily these great languages (Java and C) can be combined with minimal effort. You can download the companion source for the book from www.apress.com. It was built using the latest Eclipse SDK, Eclipse ADT, and Android Studio.

What Makes This Book Unique?

Even though Java is the primary development language for Android, Google has realized the need for hybrid Java/C development if Android is to succeed as a gaming platform—so much so that they released the NDK. I think that Google has been wise to support C development; otherwise it would have been overtaken by the overwhelming number of native games written for other mobile platforms such as the iPhone. PC games have been around for decades (mostly written in C); by using a simple ARM C compiler, you can potentially bring thousands of PC games to the Android platform.

This is what makes this book unique: why translate 100,000 lines of painfully complicated code from C to Java if you can just combine both languages in an elegant manner and save yourself lots of time and money in the process? In addition, this book provides plenty of examples about Android implementations such as Android Wear and Android TV, powered by the new SDK 5 version. Finally, this book does include chapters of pure Java games in a well-balanced layout to satisfy both the Java purist and the C lover in you.

What's Changed Since the Last Edition?

With the relentless pace of Android updates, many things have changed since the last iteration of *Pro Android Games*, including the following:

- *Updates*: This book includes the latest version of the Android SDK, NKD, OpenGL ES, the latest Eclipse ADT, and Android Studio.

- *Android Wear*: This edition helps you to understand how to build Android wearable applications to be tested with Android emulator and real Android Wear devices.

- *Android TV*: You'll learn all about how to start building TV apps or extend your existing app to run on TV devices.

Android SDK Compatibility

As a developer, you may wonder about the SDK compatibility of the code in this book, as new versions of the Android SDK come out frequently. At the time of this writing, Google released the Android SDK version 5.0 API 21. The code in this book has been fully tested with the following versions of the Android SDK:

- SDK version 5.0
- SDK version 4.4

The bottom line is that the code in this book will run in any version of the SDK, and that was my intention all along.

Chapter Overview

Here's a summary of what you'll find in *Pro Android Games*, Third Edition.

Chapter 1

This chapter provides the first steps to setting up a Windows system for hybrid game compilation, including

- Fetching the Android source
- Setting up the Eclipse ADT as well as Android Studio for development
- Installing the latest NDK
- Creating an emulator for testing or configuring a real device
- Importing the book's source into your workspace, which is critical for understanding the complex topics

Chapter 2

In this chapter you'll see how to combine Java and C code in an elegant manner by building a simple Java application on top of a native library. You'll learn exciting concepts about the Java Native Interface (JNI) and the API used to combine Java and C in a single unit, including how to load native libraries, how to use the native keywords, how to generate the JNI headers, plus all about method signatures, Java arrays versus C arrays, invoking Java methods, compiling and packing the product, and more.

Chapter 3

This chapter deals with 3D graphics with OpenGL. It presents a neat trick I stumbled upon that allows for mixing OpenGL API calls in both Java and C. This concept is illustrated by using the 3D cubes sample provided by Google to demonstrate OpenGL in pure Java and hybrid modes. This trick could open a new frontier of 3D development for Android with the potential to bring a large number of 3D PC games to the platform with enormous savings in development costs and time.

Chapter 4

This chapter tackles efficient graphics with OpenGL 2.0. It starts with a brief description of the most important features in OpenGL 2, including shaders, GLSL, and how they affect the Android platform. Then it takes a deeper look into GLSL by creating a neat Android project to render an icosahedron using OpenGL ES 2.0. As a bonus, it shows you how you can use single- and multi-touch functionality to alter the rotation speed of the icosahedron, plus pinching for zooming in or out.

Chapter 5

Chapter 5 takes things to the next level with the ground-breaking game for the PC: Doom. Doom is arguably the greatest 3D game ever created, and it opened new frontiers in 3D graphics. The ultimate goal of this chapter is not to describe the game itself, but to show you how easy it is to bring a complex PC game like Doom to the Android platform. The proof? Doom is over 100,000 lines of C code, but it was ported to Android with less than 200 lines of extra JNI API calls plus the Java code required to build the mobile UI. This chapter shows that you don't have to translate thousands of lines of C into Java; you can simply marry these two powerful languages in an elegant application. A must-read chapter!

Chapter 6

Here is where things start to get really exciting! This chapter brings you a first-person shooter (FPS) gem: Quake. You'll see how a powerful PC engine of this caliber can be brought to the Android platform with minimum effort—so much so that 95% of the original C code is kept intact! It only requires an extra 500–1000 lines of new, very simple Java wrapper code. Start playing Quake in all its glory on your smartphone now!

Chapter 7

This chapter builds upon the previous one to deliver the Quake II engine to your fingertips. It is remarkable how the highly complex OpenGL renderer of the Quake II engine can be kept intact thanks to a wonderful tool called NanoGL. NanoGL allows the developer to translate the complexity of the OpenGL immediate mode drawing into OpenGL ES transparently, keeping your original code intact. The chapter also shows how to make the Quake II engine behave properly in Android by creating custom audio and video handlers, at the same time demonstrating the great reusability features of the Java language. All in all, 99% of the original Quake II C code is kept intact, plus the thin Java wrappers of the previous chapter are reused without change.

Chapter 8

This chapter deals with Bluetooth controllers. You know it's difficult to play games (such as first-person shooters) with a touch screen interface or a tiny keyboard. Some games really require a gamepad controller. The hardcore gamer in you will smile at how easy is to integrate two popular gaming controllers, Wiimote and Zeemote, into your game. In the process, you'll also learn about the Bluetooth API, gain an insight into the inner workings of the Wiimote and Zeemote, pick up a little about JNI, asynchronous threads, and more.

Chapter 9

This chapter tackles two interesting new subjects coming soon to your mobile device and living room: augmented reality (AR) and Android TV. The future of casual gaming seems to be headed the AR way. Other platforms like the PS Vita are already taking the first step by providing a solid foundation of AR games out of the box. There is a lot of hype surrounding augmented reality, and Android developers are taking notice. This chapter shows you how to use the popular ARToolkit to build an AR-capable application/game using OpenGL and JNI. This chapter also looks at the rise of smart TVs, specifically Android TV. Android TV is powered by Android 5.0 and thus is fully compatible with the games you may be planning to create.

Chapter 10

This chapter covers deployment and compilation tips for Android applications. In addition to many time-saving goodies, this chapter includes tips for signing your application manually or using Android Studio, creating a key store for signature of your application package, and installing your signed application into a real Android device, as well as the most important tips you should remember when building hybrid games that use both Java and C/C++.

Chapter 11

This chapter introduces you to Android Wear. You'll learn what you need to install and configure to develop your first Wear application using the Android SDK 5.0 API 21.

More specifically you'll see how Android Wear works, the Android libraries needed for a Wear application, how to create a Wear Emulator with Android AVD Manager, and finally, how to create and run your first Wear application. After this chapter you'll find it easier to understand Android Wear apps and implement new ones, now that you know the basics.

Welcome to Android Gaming

This chapter kicks things off by explaining how to set up your environment to compile hybrid (C/Java) games, including the engines described in the later chapters of the book. It also explains how to set up the latest versions of the integrated development environment (IDE), which is Android Studio 1.0.1 with SDK for Windows, plus the native development kit (NDK). These tools are required to build powerful games for Android. They let you combine the elegant object-oriented features of Java with the raw power of C for maximum performance. The chapter ends by showing how to import the workspace for the game engines included in the source code of this book (which can be obtained at www.apress.com). Let's get started.

Preparing the development environment includes having the following software installed on your desktop:

- *Android IDE*: This is the development IDE used to create your projects. I have used the Android Studio with SDK for Windows in this manuscript.

- *Android SDK (properly configured)*: At the time of this writing, the latest version of the SDK is 5.0.1 (API 21).

- *Java JDK 7*: This is required to run Android Studio with SDK itself (JRE alone is not sufficient).

- Apache Ant 1.8 or later

The next section tells you how to set up your machine step by step.

Setting Up Your Machine

In this book I will install and use Android SDK 5.0.1 for Windows 7.

There are a few steps to be completed before you can get to the nitty-gritty stuff of building games for Android. Follow these steps:

1. The first and most basic thing you need is a current Java JDK 7. Make sure you have the proper version installed before proceeding. This book uses JDK version 8 64-bit.

2. Download and install the Android SDK 5.0.1. The SDK contains the core resources to develop for Android.

3. Configure Android Studio 1.0.1.

4. Install the NDK if you don't have it. This is a critical component for any kind of game that uses native APIS such as OpenGL. At the time of this writing, I used r10c Windows 64-bit. All in all, keep in mind that Android 5.0 is not binary compatible with older NDK versions, which means that if you have an old NDK, you have to update it.

5. Create an emulator. This is an optional step that will help you with testing your games in many API versions and screen sizes.

6. Configure a real device. I prefer to work in a real device because it is so much faster than using an emulator and is the best way to work if you use OpenGL.

Download and Install the SDK

Download the latest version of the Android Studio 1.0.1 for Windows from `http://developer.android.com/sdk/index.html#win-bundle` and install it (in my case named android-studio-bundle-135.1641136.exe).

> **Note**   Some of the code included in this book was developed, compiled and tested using the Eclipse IDE for Java Developers and Android SDK Tools instead of Android Studio 1.0.1 since when this manuscript was written, NDK and JNI were not supported by Android Studio.

Configure Android Studio

The very first step will be to run the Android SDK Manager to update all the needed APIs and libraries.

To run the SDK Manager from Android Studio, select Tools ➤ Android ➤ SDK Manager (see Figure 1-1).

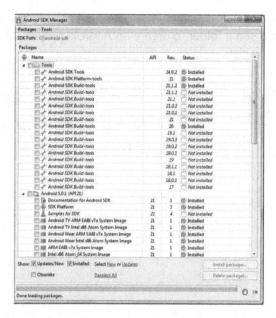

Figure 1-1. Installing the SDK 5 API and Libraries

To use Android SDK, you should install as a minimum the latest Android SDK tools and Android platform such as:

■ Android SDK Platform-tools (ARM EABI v7a System Image)

■ Android SDK Build-tools (highest version)

The Android Support Library provides an extended set of APIs that are compatible with most versions of Android such as:

■ Android Support Repository

■ Android Support Library

For the examples you also need to install the support library for additional APIs required for:

■ Android Wear

■ Android TV

■ Google Cast

Finally, to develop with Google APIs, you need the Google Play services package such as:

■ Google Repository

■ Google Play services

Select all the packages just described, click Install packages, and follow the instructions. After installation completes, close the SDK Manager.

You are ready to get your Android Studio up and running with the Android development kit.

Click File ➤ New Project wizard to make sure the Android plug-in has been successfully installed. If so, you should see a folder to create an Android project, as shown in Figure 1-2.

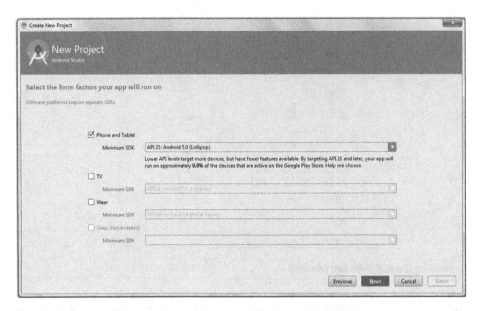

Figure 1-2. New Project wizard showing the Android options after final configuration

Android Studio 1.0.1 is ready for use. Now let's install the NDK.

Installing the Native Development Kit

The NDK is the critical component for creating great games. It provides all the tools (compilers, libraries, and header files) to build apps that access the device hardware natively.

As we said earlier in this chapter, when this manuscript was written, NDK and JNI were not supported by Android Studio so NDK and JNI must be used with the Eclipse IDE for Java Developers and Android SDK Tools.

> **Note**   The NDK site is a helpful resource to find step-by-step instructions, API descriptions, changes, and all things related to native development. It is a must for all C/C++ developers. Go to `http://developer.android.com/sdk/ndk/index.html`.

The NDK installation requires two simple steps: downloading the NDK and installing Cygwin (a free tool to emulate a Linux-like environment on top of Windows, but more on this in the next sections).

NDK Install

Download and unzip the latest NDK from http://developer.android.com/sdk/ndk/index.html into your work folder (in this case C:\eclipse-SDK).

You now need to configure Eclipse so that it knows where the NDK is in order to use it when building your native application. Follow these steps to set the location of the NDK:

1. Launch Eclipse.

2. Open the Preferences window and select Android ➤ NDK to see the directory of the NDK we just installed (see Figure 1-3).

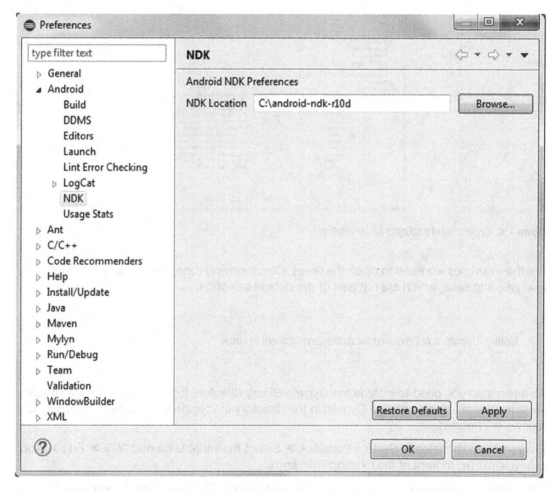

Figure 1-3. Preferences window showing where NDK is located

To verify the installation in the Project Explorer pane, right-click the project name; the context menu should appear. Then, when selecting Android Tools, if you see the Add Native Support option, it means that NDK is fully installed and configured.

Install Cygwin

Android is built on top of Linux, which is not compatible with Windows. Enter Cygwin (version 1.7.9-1 or later). I have used the version 1.7.32 in this manuscript. This is a tool that provides a Linux environment and very useful software tools to do Linux-like work on Windows (such as building a program). It is necessary to run the NDK compilation scripts, and it is required if you are doing any type of native development.

For this manuscript I installed the Windows version of the 1.7.33 development packages such as Devel/make and Shells/bash.

Figure 1-4. *Cygwin list of packages for installation*

For the examples we need to open the Devel (Development) category and at least select gcc, g++, gdb, and make, which are not part of the default selection.

Note   Cygwin is not required for native development in Linux.

As a last step you need to include the Cygwin Binary directory (bin) in the PATH environment variable. Because you installed Cygwin in the directory c:\cygwin you will need to select as follows in Windows:

Environment: Variables ➤ System Variables ➤ Select the variable named PATH ➤ Edit ➤ Add c:\cygwin\bin; in front of the existing PATH entry.

Let's verify Cygwin works properly by running the Cygwin Command shell (bash or sh) cygwin.bat. Cygwin Command shell information can be found at https://cygwin.com/cygwin-ug-net/using-utils.html. You should see the command prompt $ as shown in Figure 1-5.

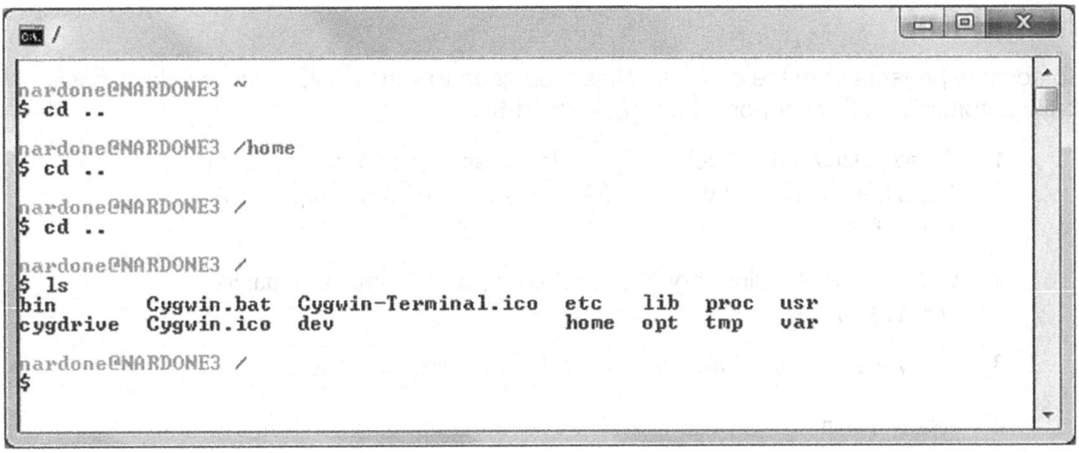

Figure 1-5. Cygwin console

Install MinGW

MinGW, which stands for Minimalist GNU for Windows, is a tool that can be used when developing native Microsoft Windows applications which do not depend on any third-party C-Runtime DLLs. You can download MinGW for Windows from the site http://sourceforge.net/projects/mingw/files/Installer/.

To verify that MinGW works properly run the MinGW executable file mingw-get.exe which is my case is located in C:\MinGW\bin. You should see the MinGW console as shown in Figure 1-6.

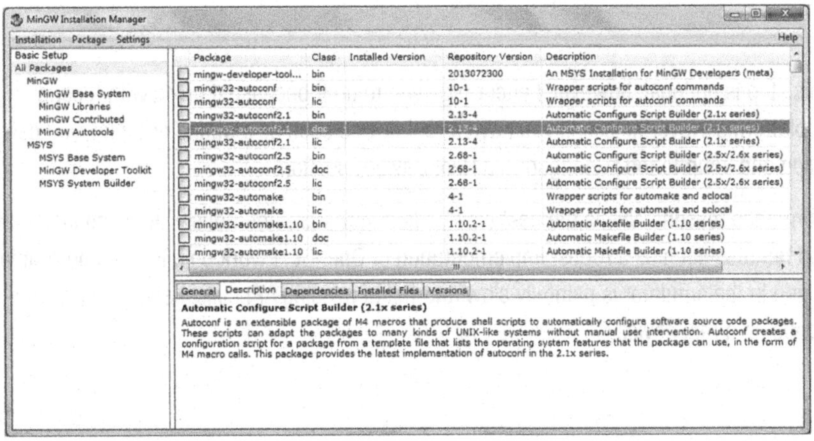

Figure 1-6. MinGW console

Install Ant

To compile projects from the command line, you need to install Ant, which is a Java-based build automation utility supported by the Android SDK.

1. Go to `http://ant.apache.org/bindownload.cgi` and download the Ant binaries, packed within a ZIP archive. In our case `apache-ant-1.9.4-bin.zip`.

2. Unzip Ant in the directory of your choice (for example, `C:\apache-ant-1.9.4`).

3. Verify the Ant installation by typing the following command:

```
ant -version
```

If properly installed you will see something like this:

```
Apache Ant(TM) version 1.9.4 compiled on April 29 2014
```

We can proceed to create the AVD to run the platform you just installed.

Creating an Android Emulator

Before you can start building your apps, you must create an Android Virtual Device (AVD), but you also need an SDK platform to run the AVD on. In this section you will learn how to do the following:

- Install the Android platform needed to test your apps
- Create the Virtual Device (emulator) that will run the above platform

> **Tip** This step is optional; however, I encourage you to do it because it helps with testing on multiple platforms. Nevertheless, if you have a real device such as a phone or tablet, you can skip this section and jump to the "Configuring a Real Device" section.
>
> For performance reasons, this is the best way to do it. AVDs are notoriously slow and lack many advanced features such as a robust implementation of OpenGL. I work on a laptop and running an OpenGL app in the emulator is painfully slow and full of missing API calls. I encourage you to test all of your code on a real device.

Creating an AVD

With version 1.5 and later of the SDK, Google introduced the concept of virtual devices (AVDs). An AVD is simply a set of configuration attributes applied to an emulator image that allows the developer to target a specific version of the SDK.

Follow these steps to create your AVD.

1. Click the AVD button on the Android Studio toolbar (see Figure 1-7).

Figure 1-7. Android toolbar in Android Studio

The AVD Manager is shown in Figure 1-8. The AVD Manager provides everything you need to:

- Create virtual devices (emulators)
- Delete/edit/start emulators

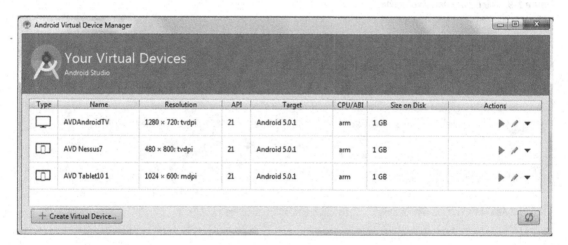

Figure 1-8. The AVD Manager

2. To create an emulator, simply press the Create Virtual Device. . . button.

3. In the new device dialog, enter the device name and complete the following settings (Figure 1-9):

    - Select the device model you want to emulate. In this case the device Nexus model S was selected.

    - In the target box, select Android 5.0 – API Level 21 in this case.

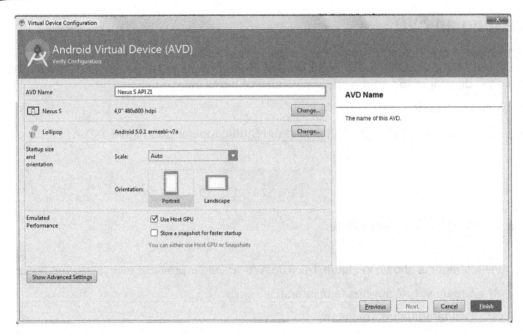

Figure 1-9. The Create new AVD dialog

4.   Click Finish.

Now the emulator is ready for use (Figure 1-10).

Type	Name	Resolution	API	Target	CPU/ABI	Size on Disk	Actions
	AVDAndroidTV	1280 × 720: tvdpi	21	Android 5.0.1	arm	1 GB	▶ ✎ ▾
	AVD Nessus7	480 × 800: tvdpi	21	Android 5.0.1	arm	1 GB	▶ ✎ ▾
	AVD Tablet10 1	1024 × 600: mdpi	21	Android 5.0.1	arm	1 GB	▶ ✎ ▾
	Nexus S API 21	480 × 800: hdpi	21	Android 5.0.1	arm	650 MB	▶ ✎ ▾

Figure 1-10. AVD Manager with brand new Nexus S device

Tip   You can create as many devices in as many versions or resolutions as you wish. This is helpful for testing in multiple API versions or screen sizes.

5.   Run the emulator by selecting the device and pressing Start ➤ Launch. The emulator should boot up, and after a while you will be able to start playing with it (see Figure 1-11).

Figure 1-11. Google Nexus S emulator (API level 21)

In the same way we can create many other emulators, such as a 10.1 inch tablet for instance (see Figure 1-12).

Figure 1-12. A 10.1-inch tablet (API level 21)

Configuring a Real Device

Personally, I think using a real device is the best way to develop games and apps that use OpenGL. The emulator is painfully slow, plus not all the OpenGL API calls are implemented. A real device has many advantages the emulator does not, namely speed and API reliability. The only caveat is that the emulator gives you the chance to test multiple screen sizes and API versions. All in all, a real device is the way to go if you are building an OpenGL game; use the emulator as a backup test tool to check your game.

Before Android Studio can recognize your device, you need to install a USB driver required for communications.

> **Note**   Before installing the USB driver, try to plug in in the device to your PC and see if it shows up in the Android Studio devices view (because the required driver may already be installed in your computer). If the device won't show up, then you need to install the USB driver.

MORE ON THE USB DRIVER

Notice that the Google USB driver is required for Windows only to perform Android Debug Bridge (ADB) debugging with any of the Google Nexus devices. The one exception is the Galaxy Nexus: the driver for Galaxy Nexus is distributed by Samsung (listed as model SCH-I515). Please take a look to the OEM USB drivers document at `http://developer.android.com/tools/extras/oem-usb.html`.

Windows drivers for all other devices are provided by the respective hardware manufacturer, as listed in the OEM USB Drivers document.

Here are some of the devices compatible with Google's USB driver:

- ADP1 / T-Mobile G1
- ADP2 / Google Ion / T-Mobile myTouch 3G
- Verizon Droid
- Nexus One, Nexus S, Nexus 4, Nexus 5, Nexus 7, and Nexus 10
- Galaxy Nexus
- PandaBoard (Archived)
- Motorola Xoom (U.S. Wi-Fi)
- Nexus S
- Nexus S 4G

Using the Nexus 7 that was originally sold with 4.1.2 or newer is not recommended. If you have other devices, you'll need to contact your vendor. A list of OEMs and more details on the USB driver for Windows is available at `http://developer.android.com/sdk/win-usb.html`.

To install the driver in your Windows host, follow these steps:

1. Connect your device to your computer's USB port. Windows detects the device and launches the Hardware Update Wizard.

2. Select Install from a list or select a specific location and click Next.

3. Select Search for the best driver in these locations, uncheck "Search removable media," and check "Include this location in the search."

4. Click Browse and locate the USB driver folder within your Android SDK installation (PATH-TO-SDK\android-sdk-windows\extras\google\usb_driver\).

5. Click Next to install the driver.

Tip   The USB driver can be downloaded or upgraded from the Android AVD Manager. To install Google, for instance, select Available Packages ➤ Google Inc ➤ Google USB Driver and click Install Selected, as shown in Figure 1-13.

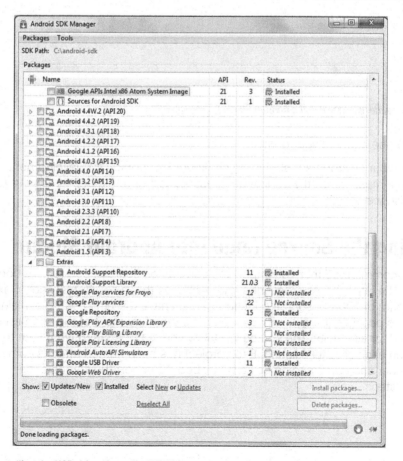

Figure 1-13. Installing the USB driver from the AVD Manager

6. After you have the USB driver properly installed, simply plug your phone into the USB port of your computer. Eclipse recognizes and displays it in the Android devices and log views, just as it does with the emulator.

The real device I used for this book was the Samsung Galaxy Grand 2, which, once the USB drivers are installed, will be listed as shown in Figure 1-14.

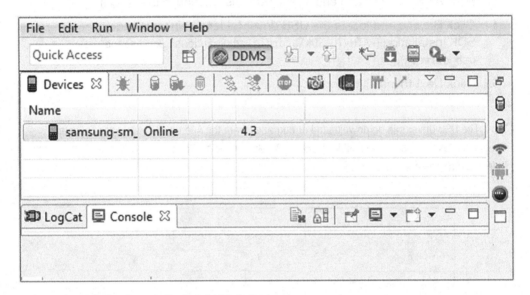

Figure 1-14. A real device shown in the Android Studio Device view

You can now use it to test your games!

At this point, your environment should be configured and ready for development, but before you finish, you must import the source code associated with this book into your Android Studio workspace.

Importing the Source Code into Android Studio

It is highly recommended that you import the companion source code for this book into your workspace. The later chapters describe game engines that are extremely complex, each with a minimum of 100K of source code in C/Java. I have tried my best to explain as simply and cleanly as possible the difficult concepts, and therefore most of the code listings have been stripped for simplicity. The source will allow you to understand what I am trying to emphasize on each chapter's listing. Each project has been named after its corresponding chapter number and game engine being described. To import the source code, follow these steps.

1. Obtain the source package (usually in ZIP format) from the Source Code/Download tab of the book's information page (www.apress.com/xxxxxxxxxxxxx) and decompress it into your working folder (in my case C:\workspace).

2. In the Android Studio main menu, click File ➤ Import Project. . . Point to the project you want to import from source package and click Ok.

3. The chapter project will be then loaded into Android Studio.

Each project in the source is named after a chapter number and engine being described. Look around each project to familiarize yourself with the project layout. You'll find that most projects have a large base of C code wrapped around thin Java wrappers. This workspace helps immensely for understanding the later chapters that describe native engines, which are big and difficult to explain.

Summary

Congratulations! You have taken the first step toward your mastery of Android game development. In this chapter, you learned how to set up your system to compile hybrid games, which included the following tasks:

- Installing the Android Studio 1.0.1

- Installing and configuring the Android NDK

- Creating emulators or real devices

This chapter has provided the foundation to compile the games described throughout this book. In Chapter 2, you will learn how to write and compile a basic native program (or shared library) and call it within a Java application.

## Chapter 2

Gaming Tricks for Phones or Tablets

In this chapter, you will get your feet wet with development in Android. You'll learn how easy it is to build a simple Android app that loads a native library and executes methods written in C within Java. You'll also learn how to call back Java methods within C, so the communication goes both ways between the languages. Next you'll learn how to cascade audio, video, key, and touch events from Java to C by using thin Java wrappers that simply pass event information to the native library. And finally, you'll tackle multi-touch, which is a useful subject for advanced games such as first person shooters and others. Multi-touch can be a tricky subject, so check it out. But first, you'll learn how to add native code to your Android project.

> **Note** All the code included in this chapter was developed, compiled and tested using Eclipse IDE for Java Developers instead of Android Studio 1.0.1 since, when this manuscript was written, NDK and JNI were not supported by Android Studio.

Let's get started by setting up the Windows environment.

Setting Up Windows

For the examples in this chapter we will be using the following tools:

- The JDK (Java Development Kit)
- The Android SDK (Software Development Kit)
- The Android NDK (Native Development Kit)
- An IDE (Integrated Development Environment): Eclipse
- Cygwin

All components in this list were installed as shown in Chapter 1 so let's install Ant to complete the installation of the tool needed.

Windows System Environment Variables

Let's configure the Windows system environment variables needed in this chapter.

1. Open the Windows System Environment Variables
2. Create the following:
   - `%ANDROID_NDK%`
   - `%ANDROID_SDK%`
   - `%ANT_HOME%`
   - `%JAVA_HOME%`
3. Finally edit PATH and add the following to the existing path:

   %JAVA_HOME%\bin;%ANDROID_SDK%\tools;%ANDROID_SDK%\
   platform-tools;%ANDROID_NDK%;%ANT_HOME%\bin;
4. Save and close the window (see Figure 2-1).

Figure 2-1. Windows system environment variables

Configuring Cygwin

After you have installed Cygwin, to run any of its command you need to write the paths like this:

/cygdrive/<Drive letter>/<Path to your directory>.

So for instance, because I installed Ant in c:\ apache-ant-1.9.4, then the path must be indicated as /cygdrive/c/ apache-ant-1.9.4.

We can solve this by going to the Cygwin/home directory and editing the file named .bash_profile.

Edit the file and add the following at the end of the file:

```
export ANDROID_SDK='cygpath–u "$ANDROID_SDK"'
export ANDROID_NDK='cygpath–u "$ANDROID_NDK"'
export ANT_HOME='cygpath–u "$ANT_HOME"'
export JAVA_HOME='cygpath–u "$JAVA_HOME"'
```

Now you can call any of the tools included in those directories without having to add all the directory path. For instance, if you try to call ant -version from the Cygwin directory you can see that it runs properly:

```
nardone@NARDONE3$ ant -version
Apache Ant(TM) version 1.9.4 compiled on April 29 2014
```

Now you have configured all you need and can start creating the Android NDK project.

Creating the Android Project with Native Support

Now you'll create a simple Android project to apply the concepts you learned in the previous section. The project consists of the following components:

- *An Android activity*: This is the main entry point for the application. Its job is to load a native library and call a C function optionally sending an array of strings as arguments.

- *A native library*: This library implements a simple C log function to extract a string argument from the Java activity and print the message to the Android log console.

Now, let's create the project for this section.

1. In Eclipse, click the New Android Project icon on the main toolbar or press CTRL-N and select Android ➤ Android project. This opens the New Android Project dialog box.

2. In the dialog box, enter a project name (ch02.Project in this example).

3. Enter an application name (ch02.Project in this example).

4. Enter a package name (ch02.project in this example).

5. Enter an activity name (ProjectActivity in this example).

6. Specify a minimum SDK version can be 4.4 API 19 in this example but I use the Android 5.0.1 API 21 as Target SDK. Figure 2-2 shows the completed New Android Application dialog box for this example.

7. Click Finish.

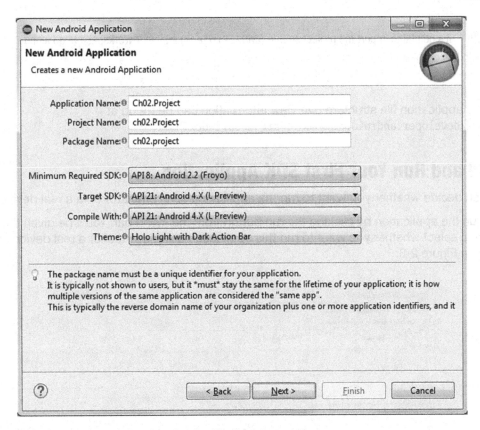

Figure 2-2. New Android Application dialog box for this chapter's example

Now that you have your project skeleton, let's look at how this application is architected. You'll start with a basic layout (architecture) of the components of the app including the Java main activity, a native interface (also written in Java), and the C implementation. Next, you'll see how to compile the native code, and finally you'll test on the emulator. Let's get started.

Application Architecture

Let's consider what you want to accomplish with this application: you want to create the basic Android application. When run in the emulator, the app will create a default view with the title "Hello Chapter2! My first Android NDK/JNI Project." Within the project, you will create a native folder with files to accomplish these tasks:

- Create a native library with a main subroutine that will be called from the Android main activity using JNI.

- The main library subroutine invokes a Java method (using JNI) within the Android project, sending a text message back to the Android Java layer.

> **Tip**   It's helpful to import the project source (ch02.Project) into your workspace to go along with this chapter.

Android application file structure overview information can be found at https://developer.android.com/tools/projects/index.html.

Build and Run Your First SDK Application

You can decide whether you want to run the application in an emulator or in a real device.

Let's run the application by clicking the run button from the menu bar. You'll be given the option to select whether you want to run this application using a virtual or a real device as shown in Figure 2-3.

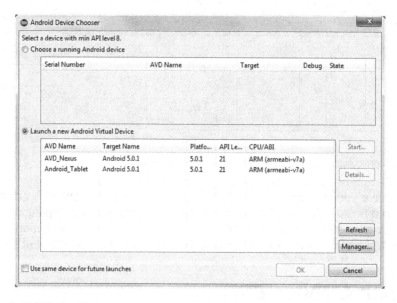

Figure 2-3. The Android Device Chooser

To use the virtual device "AVD_Nexus," just select it and click OK. The output will be then shown in the AVD_Nexus emulator as shown in Figure 2-4.

Figure 2-4. The Android Virtual Device (AVD)

Add Android Native Support

Now that you have created the Android application, the next step is to learn how to add Android Native support. You'll first create C/C++ source files. Then you'll compile them into a native library named "ch02," and finally let Java run the code. Let's start by adding Android Native Support.

Right-click Ch02.Project and select Android tools ➤ Add Native Support (see Figure 2-5).

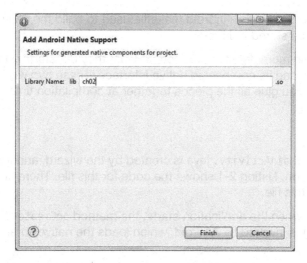

Figure 2-5. New Android project native support

This creates the NDK library named ch02 as well as the Android Native directory jni/ (see Figure 2-6).

Figure 2-6. Android native support directories

The jni folder contains the native code, including the following (see Figure 2-6):

- ch02.cpp: This is the main library code. It contains all the necessary JNI system calls to cascade information back and forth between Android and C.

- Android.mk: This is the Android makefile used to build the native library which will be stored in libs/.

Let's look at the files in more detail to understand what they do, starting from the top with the Java main activity and its companion native interface. These two work together with the native library. Finally, you glue all the pieces together at compilation time.

Main Activity

The file ch02.project.MainActivity.java is created by the wizard, and it is the entry point to the phone application. Listing 2-1 shows the code for this file. There are some remarkable things to note about this file.

As you should know, when the application starts, the method onCreate(Bundle savedInstanceState) is invoked by Android, which loads the native library using System. loadLibrary(name).

Listing 2-1. Main Activity for This Chapter's Example

```java
package ch02.project;

import android.support.v7.app.ActionBarActivity;
import android.os.Bundle;
import android.view.Menu;
import android.view.MenuItem;

public class ProjectActivity extends ActionBarActivity {

    static {
        System.loadLibrary("ch02");
        }

    public native String getMyData();

    @Override
    protected void onCreate(Bundle savedInstanceState) {
        super.onCreate(savedInstanceState);
        setContentView(R.layout.activity_project);
        setTitle(getMyData());
    }

    @Override
    public boolean onCreateOptionsMenu(Menu menu) {
        // Inflate the menu; this adds items to the action bar if it is
        // present.
        getMenuInflater().inflate(R.menu.project, menu);
        return true;
    }

    @Override
    public boolean onOptionsItemSelected(MenuItem item) {
        // Handle action bar item clicks here. The action bar
        // automatically handles clicks on the Home/Up button, so long
        // as you specify a parent activity in AndroidManifest.xml.
        int id = item.getItemId();
        if (id == R.id.action_settings) {
            return true;
        }
        return super.onOptionsItemSelected(item);
    }
}
```

You updated the `ProjectActivity.java` file by declaring the native method with the native keyword and no method body:

```
public native String getMyData();
```

Then you must load the native library that contains the "getMyData" method. Include this in the static initialization block and make sure it is called before the activity instance will be initialized:

```
static {
System.loadLibrary("ch02");
}
```

As last step you need to call the native method so that the screen content will be updated with the new value.

Add within "onCreate" the following:

```
setTitle(getMyData());
```

In the next step, update the file named `Android.mk` as follows:

```
LOCAL_PATH := $(call my-dir)
include $(CLEAR_VARS)
LOCAL_MODULE     := ch02
LOCAL_SRC_FILES := ch02.cpp
include $(BUILD_SHARED_LIBRARY)
```

Compiling the Java Application

As the next step you must compile the updated file `ch02.project.MainActivity.java`.

Follow these steps to compile the java file:

1. In Eclipse, select Run ➤ External Tools ➤ External Tools
    Configurations (see Figure 2-7).

2. Create a new "run configuration" with:

    ▪ Name: `Ch02 Project javah`.

    ▪ Location: `C:\Program Files\Java\jdk1.8.0_20\bin\javah.exe`

    ▪ Working directory: `${workspace_loc:/Ch02.Project/bin}`

    ▪ Arguments: `-d ${workspace_loc:/Ch02.Project/jni} -classpath`
      `${workspace_loc:/Ch02.Project/src} ch02.project.ProjectActivity`

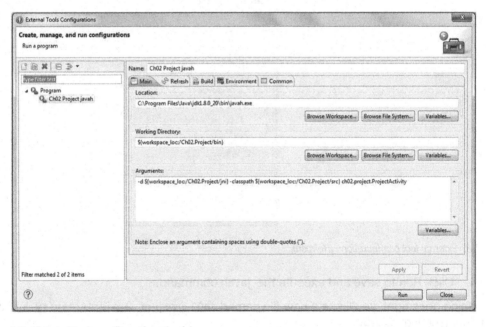

Figure 2-7. External tools configurations (main)

3. On the Refresh tab, check Refresh resources upon completion. Select Specific resources and select the jni folder (see Figure 2-8).

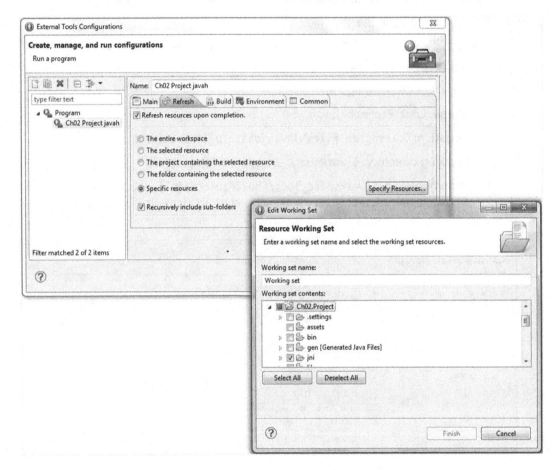

Figure 2-8. *External tool configurations (Refresh)*

4. Click Run to save and execute the javah command.

If everything goes right, you'll see a new file named ch02_project_ProjectActivity.h in the jni/ folder (see Figure 2-9).

Figure 2-9. External tools configurations (Refresh)

The file ch02_project_ProjectActivity.h is shown in Listing 2-2.

Listing 2-2. File ch02_project_ProjectActivity.h

```
/* DO NOT EDIT THIS FILE - it is machine generated */
#include <jni.h>
/* Header for class ch02_project_ProjectActivity */

#ifndef _Included_ch02_project_ProjectActivity
#define _Included_ch02_project_ProjectActivity
#ifdef __cplusplus
extern "C" {
#endif
/*
 * Class:      ch02_project_ProjectActivity
 * Method:     getMyData
 * Signature: ()Ljava/lang/String;
 */
JNIEXPORT jstring JNICALL Java_ch02_project_ProjectActivity_getMyData
  (JNIEnv *, jobject);

#ifdef __cplusplus
}
#endif
#endif
```

Your last step will be to create the C file ch02.ccp and compile it.

Native Library

Here is where all the work takes place. The implementation is provided in ch02.ccp
(see Listing 2-3). This file lives in the jni folder within the project.

> **Note**   Native libraries in Linux (also known as shared objects) are the equivalents of dynamic link
> libraries (DLLs) in Windows. By convention, shared objects are named as lib<NAME><VERSION>.so.

Listing 2-3. Native library implementation (ch02.ccp)

```
#include "ch02_project_ProjectActivity.h"
JNIEXPORT jstring Java_ch02_project_ProjectActivity_getMyData
(JNIEnv* pEnv, jobject pThis)
{
return pEnv->NewStringUTF("Hello Chapter2! My first Android NDK/JNI Project");
}
```

Compiling the Shared Library

Before you can run your native Android app, you need to compile the native C library. For that, the file Android.mk was created as we saw earlier in the jni folder of the project. You can decide to build the library using the Cygwin tool or using Eclipse.

Using the Cygwin tool to build the library:

1. Open your Cygwin console and change to the folder containing the project files.

   ```
   cd <root folder of the project>/
   ```

2. Run the following command: <path_where_NDK_is_placed>/ ndk-build

   In the case of your ch02.Project:

   ```
   $cd [PATH_TO]/ch02.Project
   ```

3. Then call the helpful NDK build script ndk-build (see Figure 2-10).

   ```
   $ ndk-build
   ```

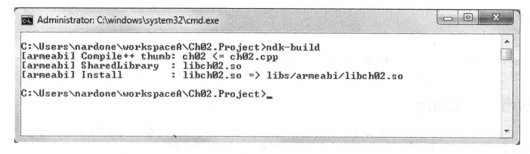

Figure 2-10. Native library compilation with Cygwin

Note The path to the NDK install directory must be included in your system Path variable; otherwise Cygwin won't be able to locate the ndk-build command.

To build the library using Eclipse:

1. Right-click ch02.Project.

2. Add C/C++ nature to the project via the Eclipse menu New ➤ Other ➤ C/C++ ➤ Convert to a C/C++ Project (see Figure 2-11).

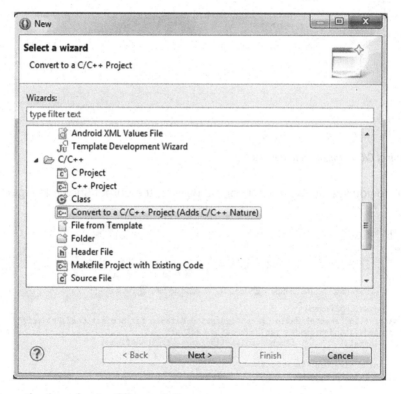

Figure 2-11. Converting the project to a C/C++ project

3. After the project is configured, right-click the project and select Properties. Now you can configure the C++ Builder (see Figure 2-12).

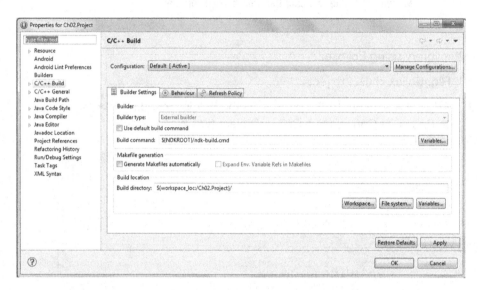

Figure 2-12. *Project C/C++ Builder configurations*

When compiling you see, in the console of the project, the output shown in Figure 2-13.

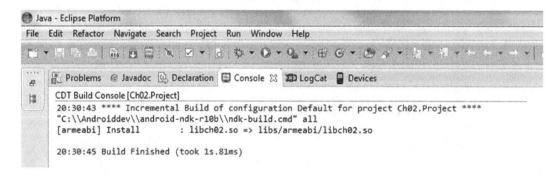

Figure 2-13. *Project library building output*

Now, start your emulator and let's test the library.

The new native library will be compiled in the libs/armeabi directory and named libch02.so.

Testing the App on a Device

To run your app on the device, you must create a Run configuration and fire up the emulator. Follow these steps:

1. Select Run Configurations from the main menu.

2. In the Run Configurations dialog box, right-click Android Application in the left list and choose New.

3. Enter a configuration name (ch02.Project) and select a project (ch02.Project), as shown in Figure 2-14. Then click Run.

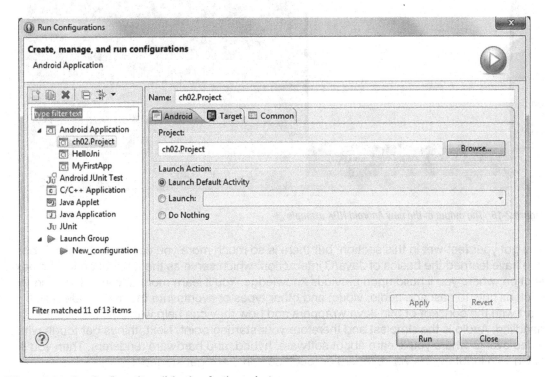

Figure 2-14. Run Configurations dialog box for the project

The application runs in the emulator and displays the text "Hello Chapter2! My first Android NDK/JNI Project" There is nothing out of the ordinary here (see Figure 2-15). You must look at the logcat view to see the messages from the native layer.

In the output, notice the following lines:

```
Trying to load lib /data/data/ch02.project/files/libch02.so ...
Added shared lib /data/data/ch02.project/files/libch02.so ...
```

These are JNI messages that tell you the library loaded successfully and the native methods can now be invoked within Java.

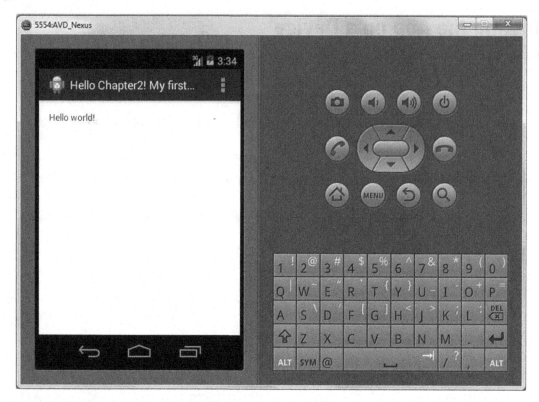

Figure 2-15. The output of the new Android NDK example

You got your feet wet in this section, but there is so much more you can do with native apps. You have learned the basics of Java/C interaction, which serve as the foundation for the next section, where you'll build upon previous knowledge. You'll learn more advanced techniques such as how to cascade audio, video, and other types of events into the native side. You'll start with the concept of thin Java wrappers and how they can help with efficient event handling. Audio is the simplest and therefore your starting point. Next, things get tough with video events where you'll learn about software, hybrid, and hardware renderers. Then you'll finish with input events via keyboard or touch screen. Let's get started.

Java Wrappers for C/C++ Event Handling

As a game developer in your organization, you probably have to build your code to support multiple platforms. Java is an elegant object-oriented language, but when it comes to max performance, it simply stinks. Many people would disagree with this statement, claiming that the Just in Time (JIT), a.k.a. dynamic compilation, nature of the Java language puts it at par with C performance-wise. This is simply not true. Any game developer who has worked in both languages and is concerned with squeezing every single bit of speed into a device will tell you that Java code is at least six times slower than raw native C, especially if you work in advanced OpenGL graphics. As a matter of fact, if you take a look at the underpinnings of the Android source, you'll find out that most of the Java APIs are simply JNI wrappers to a bunch of C libraries, especially when it comes to audio/video, which has been improved greatly with Android SDK 5.0.1.

All in all, because of the multiplatform nature of today's mobile landscape (iPhone, Android, Blackberry, Symbian, and others), most game developers build their engines in portable C. Then they simply build wrappers to target a specific platform, be it Objective-C for the iPhone or Java in Android. Keeping that in mind, in this section you will learn how to cascade the most important events for gaming—audio, video, key, and touch—by using thin Java wrappers. Let's start with audio.

Handling Audio Independently

Google has made it difficult in Android to handle audio directly on the native side. Before version 2.x of the SDK, it was simply not worth it to try to implement audio handling natively. Google used a very obscure audio implementation in the early days (Enhanced Audio System or EAS), although slowly but surely it has been turning to open standards such as OpenAL (Audio Library). Nevertheless, I still find it simpler just to read the native audio buffer and play it using the standard Android AudioTrack API.

> **Tip**   The MediaTrack API gives you the power of handling audio independently of the format. Behind the scenes, the API will detect the binary format and call the appropriate audio driver for any format supported by the platform: WAV, MP3, OGG, etc.

The process of handling audio directly on the native side can be summarized as follows:

1. The game engine loads audio assets typically from game files. Audio assets are simply audio files such as wave (wav) and Ogg Vorbis (ogg).

2. The game engine typically initializes the audio hardware and defines the overall audio properties, such as frequency (in Hz), audio resolution (16- vs. 32- bit), and number of channels (2 for stereo, 1 for mono).

3. Whenever an audio event occurs in the game, such as the player fires a gun or jumps, the engine plays the specific raw audio assets by writing an audio buffer to the device hardware.

> **Warning**   Handling audio in the native side only via OpenAL is not supported in Android versions prior to 3. Nevertheless, it is the most efficient way of doing it. On the other hand, using a thin Java wrapper works in all Android versions. It is a bit slower, however.

By using a thin Java wrapper to the Mediatrack API, you can work around Android's lack of support of popular audio standards such as OpenAL and others. With a wrapper you can read the audio buffer from the native library and render it using the AudioTrack API. Thus, the preceding steps get slightly modified as follows.

1. The native game engine loads audio assets. This step remains unchanged.

2. The game engine initializes the audio hardware. This step can be used not to initialize the audio hardware, but rather to tell the Android Java code that audio has been initialized with a specific frequency, resolution, and number of channels.

3. The thin Java wrapper then uses a thread to read bytes from the native audio buffer and render them to the hardware using an AudioTrack.

This may not be the best way of doing things but it works quite well, as you'll see in the chapters dealing with the 3D Quake engines later on in this book. To illustrate the preceding steps, let's consider a Java class dubbed `NativeAudio` (see Listing 2-4), which performs the following tasks:

- It defines a native audio painter, `PaintAudio(ByteBuffer buf)`, that reads the audio buffer from the native library.

- It implements the following methods for audio playback:

  - `start(freq, channels, bits, bufferSize)`: Here is where the good stuff happens. This method starts a thread that reads the audio buffer from the native engine (by calling PaintAudio). The thread will loop continuously until it is told to stop using a `boolean` flag. The arguments to this sub are: sound frequency in Hertz, the number of channels (1 for mono, 2 for stereo), sound resolution in bits, and the size of the buffer.

  - `stop()`: This subroutine is used to stop the audio thread from Java.

  - `OnInitAudio(freq, channels, bits)`: This is one of a series of magic subs called from C that tell the Java code it is time to start playing. This function will be called whenever the native library initializes the audio. It receives the frequency, number of channels, and resolution. It then calls the start method with those arguments.

  - `OnLockAudio()/OnUnlockAudio()`: These methods are used to lock/unlock the audio when the user pauses the game for example. They simply tell the main thread when to read data.

  - `OnCloseAudio()`: This function is fired from the native side to close the audio and cleanup resources.

Listing 2-4. A Java Class to Read Audio Data from a Native Library

```java
public class NativeAudio {
    private static boolean mDone = false;
    private static boolean mAudioLocked = false;
    private static boolean mAudioRunning = false;
    private static boolean mNativeAudioInitialized = false;

    // Native audio painter
    native int PaintAudio(ByteBuffer buf);

    // Audio will start from C
    private static void start(final int freq, final int channels,
            final int bits, final int bufferSize) {
        if (isRunning()) {
            Log.w(TAG, "WARNING: Java Audio thread already running!!");
            return;
        }

        // Must be direct for JNI to work!
        // Native BUFFERS MUST BE DIRECT!!! ByteBuffer
        final ByteBuffer audioBuffer = ByteBuffer.allocateDirect(bufferSize);
        final byte[] audioData8 = new byte[bufferSize];

        Thread t = new Thread(new Runnable(){
            public void run(){
                AudioTrack mTrack = new AudioTrack(
                        android.media.AudioManager.STREAM_MUSIC,
                        freq, // frequency in Hz
                        channels == 1 ? AudioFormat.CHANNEL_CONFIGURATION_MONO
                                : AudioFormat.CHANNEL_CONFIGURATION_STEREO,
                        bits == 16 ? AudioFormat.ENCODING_PCM_16BIT
                                : AudioFormat.ENCODING_PCM_8BIT,
                        4 * (freq / 5),
                        AudioTrack.MODE_STREAM);

                Log.d(TAG, "Audio thread start. Freq=" + freq + " Channels="
                        + channels + " Bits=" + bits + " Buf Size="
                        + bufferSize);

                mDone = false;
                mAudioRuning = true;

                try {
                    mTrack.play;
                } catch (Exception e) {
                    Log.e(TAG, e.toString());
                    mDone = true;
                }
```

```java
            while (!mDone) {
                if (!mAudioLocked) {
                    // Read audio buffer from C
                    PaintAudio(audioBuffer);

                    // set the buffer position
                    audioBuffer.position(0);

                    // get bytes
                    audioBuffer.get(audioData8);

                    // Write the byte array to the track
                    mTrack.write(audioData8, 0, audioData8.length);
                } else {
                    // sleep for a while if au locked
                    sleep(50);
                }
            }

            // Audio thread loop done
            mAudioRuning = false;
        }
    });
    // start thread
    t.start();
}

public static void stop(){
    // signal stop
    mDone = true;

    // wait until au thread quits
    while (mAudioRuning) {
        Log.d(TAG, "Waiting for audio thread...");
        sleep(200);
    }
}

public static boolean isRunning(){
    return mAudioRuning;
}
```

```
/*****************************************************************
 * C - CALLBACKS - Entry points
 *****************************************************************/
private static void OnInitAudio(int freq, int channels, int bits) {
    Log.d(TAG, "NATIVE THREAD::OnInitAudio Au Start -> freq:" + freq
            + " channels:" + channels + " bits:" + bits);
    // start audio
    start(freq, channels, bits);
}

private static void OnLockAudio() {
    mAudioLocked = true;
}

private static void OnUnLockAudio(){
    mAudioLocked = false;
}

private static void OnCloseAudio(){
    stop();
}
}
```

Now you need a C implementation of PaintAudio (see Listing 2-5). Notice the third argument: jobject buf, which encapsulates a reference to the ByteBuffer used to store the audio data. You can access a Java ByteBuffer memory address and capacity directly from C by calling the JNI functions: GetDirectBufferAddress and GetDirectBufferCapacity, respectively. The prototype paint_audio defines the C function that writes the audio data into the game audio buffer. PaintAudio calls this subroutine to fill the Java ByteBuffer with data from the native audio buffer. The final result is a Java thread that receives a sequence of audio bytes, which in turn are sent to the Android AudioTrack for playback.

Listing 2-5. C Companion for NativeAudio.java

```
// engine audio renderer
extern int paint_audio (void *unused, void * stream, int len);

JNIEXPORT jint JNICALL Java_ NativeAudio_PaintAudio
 ( JNIEnv* env, jobject thiz, jobject buf )
{
    void *stream;
    int len;

    stream = (*env)->GetDirectBufferAddress(env,  buf);
    len = (*env)->GetDirectBufferCapacity (env, buf);

    return paint_audio ( NULL, stream, len );
}
```

```
// Init audio
void jni_init_audio(int freq, int channels, int bits)
{
    JNIEnv *env;

    (*g_VM)->AttachCurrentThread ( g_VM, &env, NULL);

    jmethodID mid  = (*env)->GetStaticMethodID(env
        , jNativesCls
        , "OnInitAudio", "(III)V");

    if ( mid) {
        (*env)->CallStaticVoidMethod(env, jNativesCls, mid , freq, channels, bits);
    }
}
```

Listing 2-5 also shows how you can call a Java method within C to initialize the audio. The function jni_init_audio will be called by the engine on audio startup, which in turn calls the Java method OnInitAudio with three arguments: frequency, number of channels, and audio resolution. Note that this function is called from a separate thread (the game thread), therefore it must attach to the current (Java) thread by calling.

```
(*g_VM)->AttachCurrentThread ( g_VM, &env, NULL);
```

Here g_VM is a global reference to the Java virtual machine, which must be saved the first time you call JNI (when you call the game main function, for example). jNativesCls is a class reference that points to the NativeAudio Java class obtained by doing a JNI class lookup with FindClass and NewGlobalRef in the same spot, like so:

```
jclass clazz = (*env)->FindClass(env, "NativeAudio");
jNativesCls = (jclass)(*env)->NewGlobalRef(env, clazz);
```

Finally, jni_init_audio calls OnInitAudio in NativeAudio.java using JNI's CallStaticVoidMethod with the three arguments: frequency, channels, and bits. You have effectively created a C to Java callback.

```
(*env)->CallStaticVoidMethod(env, jNativesCls, mid , freq, channels, bits);
```

This is the technique used to play audio in the Quake and Quake II engines demonstrated in this book. More details will be explained in those chapters. Now, let's tackle video buffers.

Cascading Video Events

When it comes to handling video, game engine designers typically decouple the rendering process from the actual drawing. This keeps the engine modularized and makes it easy to port to multiple platforms. For example, low-end devices may not support a graphics processing unit (GPU), and thus decoupling the drawing and rendering will allow developers to use a software renderer. On the other hand, if a device does have a GPU, a hardware renderer could be used, all the while keeping the drawing pipeline intact. With that in mind, video handling can be classified in three groups, as described in the following sections.

Pure Software Renderer

A pure software renderer is good for low-end devices with poor quality or no GPUs. This renderer is typical on simple games that don't require a lot of horsepower. The Wolfenstein 3D in Chapter 5 in this book has used a software renderer. The process is simple; at the end of every interaction of the game loop, an image buffer is drawn with all the sprites for that state in the game. The image buffer is then sent to the Android activity, which renders it in a specific view (see Figure 2-16).

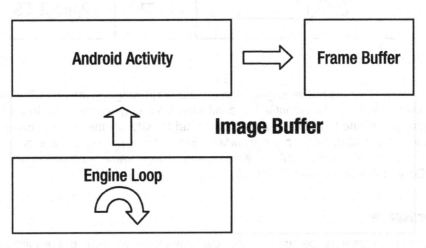

Figure 2-16. Pure software renderer

The drawback of this technique is that it is the slowest and can consume the most memory and CPU power of the three.

Mixed or Hybrid Renderer

In a mixed renderer, the drawing of the sprites is performed in software, but the actual rendering is performed in hardware (typically by using OpenGL ES). Figure 2-17 shows the component interactions of this technique. The benefits? It is faster than the previous one (by orders of magnitude). The caveats? It requires a GPU to implement an OpenGL ES renderer.

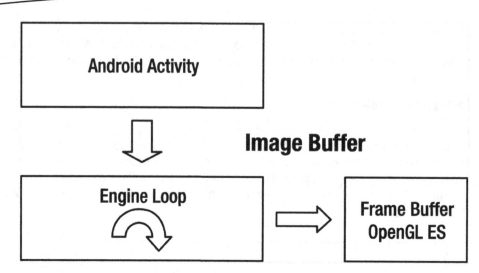

Figure 2-17. Mixed renderer

Figure 2-17 shows that the native engine is in charge of drawing the image buffer into the hardware. Depending on how OpenGL ES is initialized, the engine may have to tell the Android activity it is time to draw. Usually the Android activity will take care of initializing the OpenGL context and obtaining a display surface; in this case, however, the engine must tell Android it is time to draw (swap buffers) whenever an image frame is rendered. This renderer is used in Doom for Android (see Chapter 5).

Pure Hardware

A pure hardware renderer is the fastest and most powerful of them all, but requires a device with a GPU. It can be painful to program for Android, where there is a lot of hardware fragmentation. Many people have made a lot of fuss about version fragmentation, but the real problem (for game developers at least) resides in all the different types of GPUs in today's Android devices. I can attest to the pain of trying to deal with the big three GPU OEMs:

- PowerVR: From experience, I can tell you this is a hell of a GPU. It's the best and most powerful one out there (the iPhone uses this type of GPU; there's no wonder why). Devices that use this GPU are the Motorola Droid and Samsung Galaxy S family.

- Qualcomm: Commonly used by HTC smartphones. This is probably the worst GPU I've dealt with. It really is substandard compared with PowerVR. The drivers are buggy and it's very limited when there are a lot of polygons and textures in your game.

- Tegra: The new kid in the block by NVIDIA. Certainly powerful and fast.

Figure 2-18 shows the components of the pure hardware renderer. The chapters dealing with the Quake I/II engines in this book use this type of rendering.

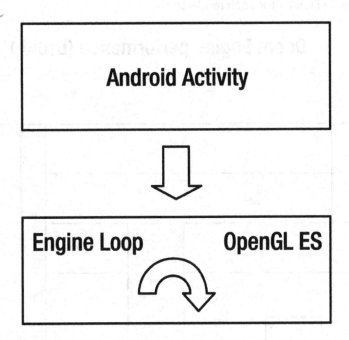

Figure 2-18. *Pure hardware renderer*

So you can have an idea of the difference in performance for these rendering techniques Figure 2-19 shows the number of frames per second (FPS) rendered by the Doom engine running in a Motorola Droid 1 for each renderer.

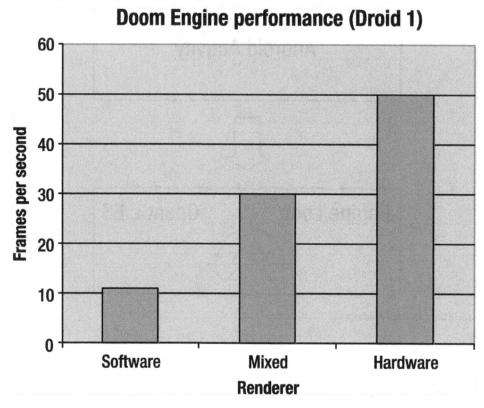

Figure 2-19. Renderer performance for the Doom engine

As you can see from Figure 2-19, the hardware renderer is many times faster than the software or hybrid; but, it is much harder to program, plus you will have to deal with all the GPU types out there. The mixed renderer is slower than the hardware one (because it draws using the CPU), but it offers less GPU fragmentation as the GLES rendering is really simple and should work in any GPU. The software renderer is awfully slow, but it offers the highest degree of compatibility (it will run anywhere, from the oldest Android version to the most obscure phone/device you can find). It is up to you to decide. You must weigh performance versus. version compatibility.

Next, let's look at key events.

Cascading Key Events

Cascading key events from Android to a native engine involves these steps:

1. Listening for key presses or releases from the Android activity.

2. Translating the Android keys to ASCII (or whatever format the engine uses to encode keys).

3. Calling the native methods keyPress or keyRelease for presses and releases, respectively.

Note that Android uses its own format to encode key values; thus the tricky part is to translate the Android key codes to a format understood by the engine (ASCII is the format for most portable engines). Listing 2-6 shows a simple way of doing this. You start by defining two Java native methods: keyPress and keyRelease in the Android activity. Both take an ASCII code as the argument.

When the user presses/releases a key on the device, Android fires the events onKeyDown and onKeyUp, respectively. These events receive an Android key value and a KeyEvent containing detailed information about the event. You then use the Android built-in function queueEvent to queue a runnable to be run on the GL rendering thread. This can be used to communicate with the renderer on the rendering thread in the game engine. The function keyCodeToASCIICode is used to translate the Android key code to a portable ASCII code. Finally, the native engine must implement the Java methods keyPress/keyRelease as Java _keyPress and Java _keyPress, respectively. These methods will receive the ASCII code and push it to the event queue (in this case, the event queue for the Quake engine).

Listing 2-6. Cascading Keys from Java to C

```
// In Java
public static native int keyPress(int key);
public static native int keyRelease(int key);

public boolean onKeyDown(final int keyCode, final KeyEvent event)
{
    queueEvent(new Runnable() {
        public void run() {
            keyPress(keyCodeToASCIICode(keyCode));
        }
    });

    return true;
}

public boolean onKeyUp(final int keyCode, final KeyEvent event)
{
    queueEvent(new Runnable() {
        public void run() {
            keyRelease(keyCodeToASCIICode(keyCode));
        }
    });
    return true;
}
```

```c
// In C
// Push key to the event queue in Quake
extern void Key_Event (int key, qboolean down);

/*
 * C Implementation of Java native int keyPress(int key);
 */
JNIEXPORT jint JNICALL Java _keyPress
  (JNIEnv * env, jclass cls, jint key)
{
    Key_Event((int)key, 1);
    return key;
}

/*
 * C Implementation of Java native int keyRelease(int key);
 */
JNIEXPORT jint JNICALL Java _keyRelease
  (JNIEnv * env, jclass cls, jint key)
{
    Key_Event((int)key, 0);
    return key;
}
```

Cascading Touch Events

Touch events work in a similar way as key events. When the user touches the device screen, the Java activity overrides onTouchEvent, which receives a MotionEvent. The event contains the coordinates of the pointer where the top-left corner of the device represents the origin (0,0). The type of event, ACTION_DOWN, ACTION_UP or ACTION_MOVE, can be obtained by calling event.getAction(). Based on this value, you save the start XY coordinates.

Finally, when you drag a finger, the XY increments (dx, dy) are calculated and sent to the native layer for consumption. When the finger is lifted, the start XY coordinates are reset, as shown in Listing 2-7. The final effect is a sequence of delta XY increments, which the native engine can use to either move a character in 3D space or look around the surroundings. This is how Quake handles movement.

Listing 2-7. Cascading Touch Events Between Java and C

```java
// Java: Natives to be implemented in C
public static native int mouseLook(int deltaX, int deltaY);
public static native int mouseMove(int deltaX, int deltaY);

// down coordinates
float startX = -1, startY = -1;

public boolean onTouchEvent(MotionEvent event)
{
```

```
    int action = event.getAction();
    if ( action == MotionEvent.ACTION_DOWN ) {
        startX = event.x;
        startY = event.y;
    }
    else if ( action == MotionEvent.ACTION_UP ) {
        startX = startY = 0;
    }
    else if ( action == MotionEvent.ACTION_MOVE)
    {
        final float dx = event.x - startX;
        final float dy = event.y - startY;

        // decide to move or look
        mouseLook(dx , dy );
        //mouseMove (dx, dy);
    }
    return true;
}

// C implementation of int mouseLook(int deltaX, int deltaY)
JNIEXPORT jint JNICALL Java_Natives_mouseMove
  (JNIEnv * env, jclass cls, jint dx, jint dy)
{
    LOGD("Mouse Move %d, %d", dx, dy);
}

// C implementation of int mouseLook(int deltaX, int deltaY)
JNIEXPORT jint JNICALL Java_Natives_mouseLook
  (JNIEnv * env, jclass cls, jint dx, jint dy)
{
    LOGD("Mouse Look %d, %d", dx, dy);
}
```

In the previous section you looked at single touch events, which may not be adequate for some types of games, such as first-person shooters where the player needs to move and aim at the same time. The next section can help. Multi-touch is a technique that expands on the touch API to provide more fingers you can use around your game for more complex interactions.

Multi-touch Tricks

The multi-touch capabilities of Android are an extension of MotionEvent. With these capabilities, you have all the information you need to implement a multi-touch scheme. For example, let's assume that you have a game where sweeping a finger on the left side moves a character forward or sideways in 3D space, and sweeping on the right side looks around. Using the Android MotionEvent, you can easily implement such a scheme. Consider three sample classes, MultiTouchGesture, MultiTouchScreen, and TestActivity, all of which are discussed in the following sections.

MultiTouchGesture

MultiTouchGesture is a class that encapsulates a gesture type such as a character move or look (see Listing 2-8). It also defines the bounds on the screen where this gesture is valid (by using the Rect Android class). When the gesture is valid, it will execute some action (sending the move or look increments to the native engine, for example).

Listing 2-8. MultiTouchGesture

```
package com.touch;

import android.graphics.Point;
import android.graphics.Rect;
import android.view.MotionEvent;

public class MultiTouchGesture {
  public enum eGestureType {  MOVE, LOOK };

  Rect bounds;
  eGestureType type;

  public MultiTouchGesture(eGestureType type, Rect bounds) {
    this.type = type;
    this.bounds = bounds;
  }

  /**
   * Execute gesture
   * @param action
   *            {@link MotionEvent} action: ACTION_UP, ACTION_MOVE,...
   * @param p
   *            Finger point XY coordinates
   */
  public boolean execute(int action, Point p) {
    switch (type) {
    case MOVE:
      doMove(action, p);
      break;

    case LOOK:
      doLook(action, p);
      break;

    default:
      break;
    }
    return true;
  }
```

```
public void reset() {
  switch (type) {
  case MOVE:

    break;
  case LOOK:
    break;

  default:
    break;
  }
}

private void doMove(int action, Point p) {
  // Tell the native engine to move
}

private void doLook(int action, Point p) {
  // Tell native engine to look
}
}
```

MultiTouchGesture executes by checking its type (in this case MOVE or LOOK). Depending on the type, a native method could be fired to send the XY coordinates to the game engine. The action argument tells the gesture what kind of MotionEvent has fired. It can be one of the following:

```
MotionEvent.ACTION_DOWN (first finger)
MotionEvent.ACTION_UP (first finger)
MotionEvent.ACTION_MOVE (first finger)
ACTION_POINTER_1_DOWN (second)
ACTION_POINTER_1_UP (second)
ACTION_POINTER_2_DOWN (third)
ACTION_POINTER_2_UP (third)
ACTION_POINTER_3_DOWN (fourth)
ACTION_POINTER_3_UP (fourth)
```

Tip   Android supports up to four simultaneous pointers/fingers on screen.

MultiTouchScreen

MultiTouchScreen is in charge of storing a list of gestures, checking their bounds, and interacting with the main activity (see Listing 2-9).

Listing 2-9. MultiTouchScreen

```
package com.touch;

import java.util.ArrayList;
import android.graphics.Point;
import android.view.MotionEvent;

public class MultiTouchScreen {

  private ArrayList<MultiTouchGesture> mGestures;

  /**
   * Constructor
   * @param gestures
   */
  public MultiTouchScreen(ArrayList<MultiTouchGesture> gestures) {
    mGestures = gestures;
  }

  /**
   * Touch Event. Events with bogus pressure pop up when using 1 finger
   * @param e
   */
  public void onTouchEvent(MotionEvent e) {
    final int action = e.getAction();
    int count = e.getPointerCount();

    Point[] points = new Point[count];

    // for each finger extract coords
    for (int i = 0; i < points.length; i++) {
      points[i] = new Point((int) e.getX(i), (int) e.getY(i));
    }

    // for each gesture
    for (MultiTouchGesture g : mGestures) {
      // for each finger (pointer)
      for (int j = 0; j < count; j++) {
        if (g.bounds.contains(points[j].x, points[j].y)) {
          g.execute(action, points[j]);
        }
      }
    }

    // reset when finger goes up
    if (action == MotionEvent.ACTION_UP) {
      for (MultiTouchGesture g : mGestures) {
        g.reset();
      }
    }
  }
}
```

The class `MultiTouchScreen` receives the `MotionEvent` from the main activity and checks each gesture to see if the XY coordinates of the finger fall within the bounds of the gesture. If so, then the gesture is executed. You can get the number of pointers from the `MotionEvent` by calling

```
int count = e.getPointerCount();
```

Then, the coordinates for each pointer can be obtained by looping through the number of pointers and extracting their XY coordinates, like so:

```
Point[] points = new Point[count];

// for each finger extract coords
for (int i = 0; i < points.length; i++) {
  points[i] = new Point((int) e.getX(i), (int) e.getY(i));
}
```

Finally, you can check whether the pointer falls within the gesture bounds by looping through each gesture and checking if each pointer XY coordinates falls within the gesture bounding rectangle.

```
for (MultiTouchGesture g : mGestures) {
  // for each finger (pointer)
  for (int j = 0; j < count; j++) {
    if (g.bounds.contains(points[j].x, points[j].y)) {
      g.execute(action, points[j]);
    }
  }
}
```

TestActivity

The last thing you need is an activity that will initialize the multi-touch screen and the gesture bounds, and listen for touch events (see Listing 2-10).

Listing 2-10. TestActivity for the MultiTouchScreen Class

```
public class TestActivity extends Activity {

  MultiTouchScreen mtScreen;

  @Override
  public void onCreate(Bundle savedInstanceState) {
    super.onCreate(savedInstanceState);
    setContentView(R.layout.main);
```

```
// init multi touch screen
ArrayList<MultiTouchGesture> gestures = new ArrayList<MultiTouchGesture>();

int w = getWindow().getWindowManager().getDefaultDisplay().getWidth();
int h = getWindow().getWindowManager().getDefaultDisplay().getHeight();

// move: left half of the screen
gestures.add(
 new MultiTouchGesture(eGestureType.MOVE, new Rect(0, 0, w / 2, h)));

// look right half
gestures.add(
    new MultiTouchGesture(eGestureType.LOOK, new Rect(w / 2, 0, w, h)));

mtScreen = new MultiTouchScreen(gestures);
}

@Override
public boolean onTouchEvent(MotionEvent event) {
  mtScreen.onTouchEvent(event);
  return true;
}
}
```

TestActivity initializes the gestures coordinates by obtaining the display width and height
(using getWindow() getWindowManager() getDefaultDisplay()). It then initializes two types
of gestures: MOVE with bounds on the left half of the screen, and LOOK with bounds on the
right half. The gestures are passed to the MultiTouchScreen constructor. Finally, when a
single or multi-touch event fires, onTouchEvent in the main activity will be called and the
event relayed to MultiTouchScreen for consumption. This will allow your game character
to move and look simultaneously in 3D space. This technique will be put to the test in the
Quake I and II chapters of this book.

FINAL THOUGHTS ABOUT MULTI-TOUCH

Before you think about implementing complex multi-touch schemes on your game, you should be aware that
the Android Multitouch API can be buggy (full of bogus pointers and false coordinates) in old devices such as
the Motorola Droid 1 and first-generation phones. For example, when you touch and slide two fingers across
the screen and simply dump the MotionEvent coordinates on screen, you will get a ton of false coordinates
and bogus pointers, which can be very frustrating, especially for 3D shooters such as Quake. This is probably
due to cheap hardware or buggy kernel drivers. I am happy to report that in second- and third-generation
devices, such as the Droid 3, things have improved dramatically. In the latest Android SDK, multi-touch drivers
have improved even further to the point that if you have a device with decent hardware, you will probably not
encounter this type of multi-touch issue. More info about multi-touch can be found at
http://developer.android.com/training/gestures/multi.html.

You have seen some neat tricks for handling audio, video, and input using keyboard, single, and multi-touch.
Let's wrap things up and see what is coming up in the next chapter.

Summary

In this chapter, you took the first steps toward building a hybrid game using JNI by learning how to create the main Java activity and loading a native library within it. Next, you learned about Java native methods using the `native` keyword plus the C header file required to implement them. You also learned some useful C tricks, such as converting Java arrays to C arrays, getting the size of a Java array, and invoking Java methods within C.

You then learned how to cascade audio, video, key, and touch events from Java to C by using thin Java wrappers that simply pass event information to the native library. Plus, you learned about the Multitouch API, and how you can track multiple pointers across the screen reacting accordingly.

This and the previous chapter have provided the basic foundation if you are planning to port a game that has significant Linux C code to the Android platform. In Chapter 3, you will tackle native OpenGL in more detail.

## Chapter 3

More Gaming Tricks with OpenGL and JNI

Chapter 2 provided a solid introduction to some basic gaming techniques for Android, including handling audio/video and I/O events Now it's time to ramp things up..

In this chapter, you will learn a neat trick using OpenGL code in Java. Any game developer knows that OpenGL is the Holy Grail of advanced game development. You won't find any powerful games that are not written with this API, because it takes advantage of hardware acceleration, which is infinitely superior to any kind of software renderer.

OpenGL can be a scary subject to the newcomer due to its complexity. But you don't have to be an OpenGL guru to understand what it does and how to draw elements with this API. All you need is the desire to learn a powerful and exciting tool for gaming.

> **Note**   The goal of this chapter is not to teach you OpenGL (a whole book wouldn't be enough for that), but to show you how to take the Android OpenGL sample provided by Google and modify it in a completely different way by mixing OpenGL API calls in Java for maximum reusability.

The chapter starts by showing a simple OpenGL project displaying a simple triangle. Then we introduce a project to create an OpenGL tumbling cubes sample to expose how OpenGL works in Java. The final section discusses some of the limitations of the OpenGL Embedded System when it comes to advanced 3D games. And, as in the previous chapter, all material discussed within this one is compatible with Android 4 (and later). During the writing of this manuscript the Android SDK version 5.0.1 API 21 was used.

For this manuscript I used the OpenGL ES version 3.0. This API specification is supported by Android 4.3 (API level 18) and higher. You need to be aware that the support of the OpenGL ES 3.0 API on a device requires an implementation of this graphics pipeline provided by the device manufacturer. Even a device running Android 4.3 or higher may not support the OpenGL ES 3.0 API so I suggest checking what version of OpenGL ES is supported at runtime; see "Checking OpenGL ES Version" at `http://developer.android.com/guide/topics/graphics/opengl.html#version-check`.

> **Note**   All the code included in this chapter was developed, compiled and tested using Eclipse IDE for Java Developers instead of Android Studio 1.0.1 since, when this manuscript was written, NDK and JNI were not supported by Android Studio.

Let's get started.

NEED AN OPENGL REFRESHER?

For this chapter, you'll need a basic understanding of OpenGL. If your OpenGL is a bit rusty, I suggest referring to the best tutorials I have found on the Web:

- The Android Developer web site provides a good starting point about OpenGL and Android.

  `http://developer.android.com/guide/topics/graphics/opengl.html`

- The OpenGL Coding Resources:

  `https://www.opengl.org/resources/`

- I do recommend you have a good look at the OpenGL 4.5 specification released publicly by Khronos. It brings the very latest functionality to the industry's most advanced 3D graphics API while maintaining full backward compatibility, enabling applications to incrementally use new features.

  `https://www.khronos.org/opengl/`

- Greg Sidelnikov's tutorial about the OpenGL coordinate system covers the basics, such as perspectives, orthographic projections, 3D camera, graphics pipeline, variable and function naming conventions, and more. It is a good place to start.

  `www.falloutsoftware.com/tutorials/gl/glo.htm`

- If you are confused about OpenGL projections, MathWorld has some good information about all kinds of 3D projections used in OpenGL.

  `http://mathworld.wolfram.com/OrthographicProjection.html`

- NeHe Productions has compiled a comprehensive set of tutorials that cover pretty much everything you need to write an OpenGL application. They are very popular.

  `http://nehe.gamedev.net/`

The Power of Mobile Devices

Mobile Android devices have become pretty powerful for graphics development. Check out the following hardware stats for the Samsung Galaxy S:

- *Processor*: 1 GHz ARM Cortex-A8 based CPU core

- *GPU*: 200 MHz PowerVR SGX 540

- *Memory*: 394 MB RAM

- *Display*: 4.0 in (100 mm) Super AMOLED with RBGB-Matrix (Pentile) 800×480 pixels WVGA (233 ppi)

To make good use of the GPU, Google has included the OpenGL Embedded System (ES) within Android. OpenGL ES provides the software API to make high-performance, hardware-accelerated games possible. This is a Java API, which is good news for Java developers who want to create 3D games from scratch, but bad news for C developers who want to reuse 3D engines written in C. 3D game engines are very complex and large, and are mostly written in C. Rewriting these engines in Java would be a difficult task, consuming significant development and time resources.

Please refer to this link to read about the OpenGL ES specifications and documentation: https://www.khronos.org/registry/gles/.

A HEAD START: THE SOURCE CODE FOR THIS CHAPTER

In this chapter, you'll use the Android 3D cubes sample in its original Java language. This sample is available from the Android site; however, the sample is composed of many resources, which are bundled as part of the overall Android samples pack. To make things simpler, I have packed the required files, plus the changes described throughout this chapter, in the chapter source code.

If you wish, you can import the project into your workspace. To do so, select File ➤ Import. In the dialog box, select Existing Projects into Workspace. Next, navigate to the chapter source ch03.OpenGL. Optionally, check Copy project into workspace. When you click Finish, the automated build will load.

OpenGL the Java Way

Let's look at how OpenGL graphics are done in Java. You'll start by creating a project for your sample application. Then you'll look at the classes that make up the project: the main activity used to launch the app, the surface view used to render graphics, the GL thread used to perform drawing operations in the background, the cube renderer used to draw the actual cube, and the cube class that has information such as dimensions, color, and others.

Creating Your First OpenGL Project

Your first OpenGL project simply displays a white triangle in the center of your Watch device.

1. Click the New Android Application Project button.

2. In the New Android Project dialog box, enter a project name, such as
    FirstOpenGL as project name, FirstOpenGLApp as application name,
    and opengl.test.as package name. Click Next.

3. Specify the minimum SDK version, which can be 4.4 API 20, but
    we want to show this example using the SDK API version 21 and
    show this example using the tablet device. Figure 3-1 shows the first
    wizard dialog for this example.

4. Select Create Activity and enter **JavaGLActivity**.

5. Click Finish.

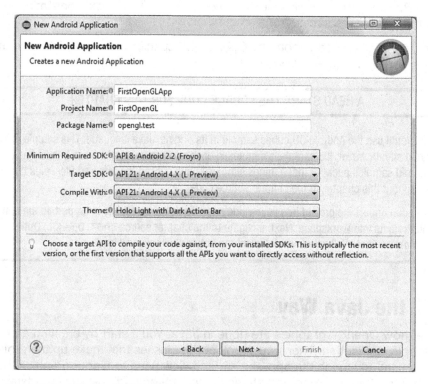

Figure 3-1. New Android project for the OpenGL sample

Listing 3-1 shows the JavaGLActivity.java file.

Listing 3-1. Main Activity for the OpenGL Sample

```
package opengl.test;

import opengl.test.MyGLRenderer;

import android.support.v7.app.ActionBarActivity;
import android.os.Bundle;
import android.opengl.GLSurfaceView;

public class JavaGLActivity extends ActionBarActivity {

private GLSurfaceView glView;

@Override
protected void onCreate(Bundle savedInstanceState) {
super.onCreate(savedInstanceState);
glView = new GLSurfaceView(this);
glView.setRenderer(new MyGLRenderer(this));
this.setContentView(glView);
    }

@Override
protected void onPause() {
super.onPause();
glView.onPause();
    }

@Override
protected void onResume() {
super.onResume();
glView.onResume();
    }
  }
```

The JavaGLActivity.java overrides onCreate(), onPause(), and onResume(). Then, override onCreate() to allocate the GLSurfaceView, set the view's renderer to a custom renderer, and finally, set this activity to use the view.

The next step is to create two new Java classes such as MyGLRenderer.java and Mytriangle.java.

Listing 3-2 shows the MyGLRenderer.java file.

Listing 3-2. The Renderer Class for the OpenGL Sample

```
package opengl.test;

import javax.microedition.khronos.egl.EGLConfig;
import javax.microedition.khronos.opengles.GL10;
import android.content.Context;
import android.opengl.GLSurfaceView;
import android.opengl.GLU;

public class MyGLRenderer implements GLSurfaceView.Renderer {

Mytriangle mytriangle;
public MyGLRenderer(Context context) {
mytriangle = new Mytriangle();
    }

@Override
public void onSurfaceCreated(GL10 gl, EGLConfig config) {
gl.glClearColor(0.0f, 0.0f, 0.0f, 1.0f);
    gl.glClearDepthf(1.0f);
    gl.glEnable(GL10.GL_DEPTH_TEST);
    gl.glDepthFunc(GL10.GL_LEQUAL);
    gl.glHint(GL10.GL_PERSPECTIVE_CORRECTION_HINT, GL10.GL_NICEST);
    gl.glShadeModel(GL10.GL_SMOOTH);
    gl.glDisable(GL10.GL_DITHER);
    }
@Override
public void onSurfaceChanged(GL10 gl, int width, int height) {
    if (height == 0) height = 1;
    float aspect = (float)width / height;

    gl.glViewport(0, 0, width, height);
    gl.glMatrixMode(GL10.GL_PROJECTION);
    gl.glLoadIdentity();
    GLU.gluPerspective(gl, 45, aspect, 0.1f, 100.f);
    gl.glMatrixMode(GL10.GL_MODELVIEW);
    gl.glLoadIdentity();
    }

@Override
    public void onDrawFrame(GL10 gl) {
        gl.glClear(GL10.GL_COLOR_BUFFER_BIT | GL10.GL_DEPTH_BUFFER_BIT);
        gl.glLoadIdentity();
        gl.glTranslatef(-1.5f, 0.0f, -6.0f);
        mytriangle.draw(gl);
        gl.glTranslatef(3.0f, 0.0f, 0.0f);
    }
}
```

The rendering class implements the interface GLSurfaceView.Renderer, which is responsible for making the OpenGL calls to render a frame. It declares three methods to be called back by the Android graphics sub-system upon specific GL events, such as:

1. onSurfaceCreate: Called when the surface is first created or re-created.

2. onSurfaceChanged: Called when the surface is first displayed and after window's size changes.

3. onDrawFrame: Called to draw the current frame.

The last step is to create the white triangle you want to show.

Listing 3-3 shows the Mytriangle.java file.

Listing 3-3. The Triangle Class for the OpenGL Sample

```
package opengl.test;
import java.nio.ByteBuffer;
import java.nio.ByteOrder;
import java.nio.FloatBuffer;

public class Mytriangle {
    private FloatBuffer vertexBuffer;
    private ByteBuffer indexBuffer;

    private float[] vertices = {
        0.0f,  1.0f, 0.0f,
        -1.0f, -1.0f, 0.0f,
        1.0f, -1.0f, 0.0f
    };
    private byte[] indices = { 0, 1, 2 };

    public Mytriangle() {
        vbb.order(ByteOrder.nativeOrder());
        vertexBuffer = vbb.asFloatBuffer();
        vertexBuffer.put(vertices);
        vertexBuffer.position(0);
        indexBuffer = ByteBuffer.allocateDirect(indices.length);
        indexBuffer.put(indices);
        indexBuffer.position(0);
    }

    public void draw(GL10 gl) {
        gl.glEnableClientState(GL10.GL_VERTEX_ARRAY);
        gl.glVertexPointer(3, GL10.GL_FLOAT, 0, vertexBuffer);
        gl.glDrawElements(GL10.GL_TRIANGLES, indices.length, GL10.GL_UNSIGNED_BYTE,
indexBuffer);
        gl.glDisableClientState(GL10.GL_VERTEX_ARRAY);
    }
}
```

In OpenGL ES, we have to use a vertex array to define a group of vertices. So, you will:

1. Define the (x, y, z) location of the vertices in a Java array.

2. Allocate the vertex-array buffer, and transfer the data into the buffer.

To render from the vertex-array, you need to enable the client-state vertex-array, which is done in gl.glEnableClientState(GL10.GL_VERTEX_ARRAY); and then render the triangle in the draw() method by doing the following:

1. Enable vertex-array client states:
   gl.glEnableClientState(GL10.GL_VERTEX_ARRAY);

2. Define the location of the buffers: gl.glVertexPointer
   (3, GL10.GL_FLOAT, 0, vertexBuffer)

3. Render the primitives using glDrawElements(), using the index array to reference the vertex and color arrays. gl.glDrawElements
   (GL10.GL_TRIANGLES, numIndices, GL10.GL_UNSIGNED_BYTE, indexBuffer)

Now you can run the project and see the result in Figure 3-2.

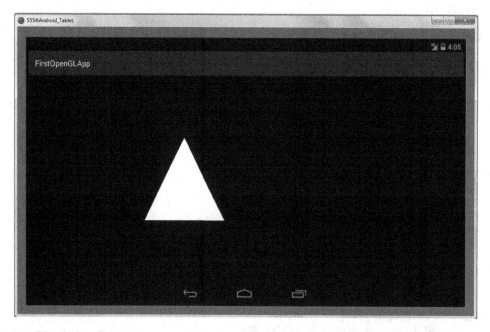

Figure 3-2. Triangle OpenGL sample

Creating an OpenGL and JNI Project

For this exploration, you'll create a project to hold the GL tumbling cubes application from the Android samples. Follow these steps:

1. Click the New Android Application Project button.

   In the New Android Project dialog box, enter a project name, such as ch03.OpenGL as project name, Ch03.OpenGL as application name, and opengl.test as package name. Click Next.

2. Enter an application name, such as Ch03.OpenGL.

3. Enter a package name, such as opengl.test.

4. Select Create Activity and enter JavaGLActivity.

5. Specify the minimum SDK version. I have chosen version API 21 for Android 5. Please note that all versions of Android are binary compatible; therefore, this project should run fine in the version that best suits your needs. Figures 3-3, 3-4, and 3-5 show all the wizard dialogs for this example.

6. Click Finish.

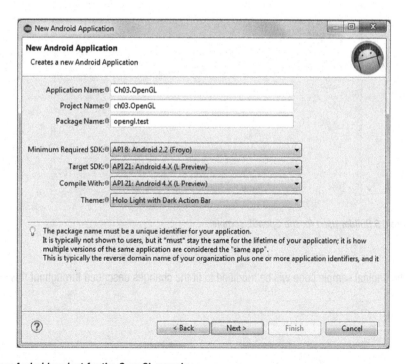

Figure 3-3. New Android project for the OpenGL sample

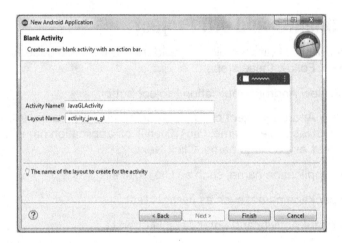

Figure 3-4. New Android Activity for the OpenGL sample

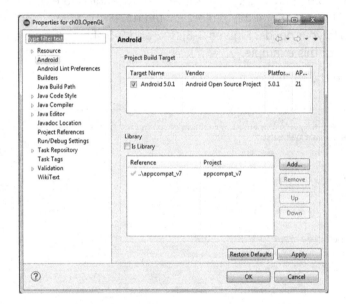

Figure 3-5. Android 5 Builder used for the OpenGL sample

Note   The original sample code will be modified to fit the changes described throughout this chapter.

The Android cubes sample consists of the following Java classes (see Figure 3-6):

- GLSurfaceView: This is an implementation of SurfaceView that uses a dedicated surface for displaying an OpenGL animation. The animation runs in a separate thread (GLThread).

- GLThread: This is a generic thread with a loop for GL operations. Its job is to perform resource initialization. It also delegates rendering to an instance of the Renderer interface.

- Renderer: This is a generic interface for rendering objects. In this case, you are rendering two tumbling cubes.

- EglHelper: This is a GL helper class used to do the following:

  - Initialize the EGL context.

  - Create the GL surface.

  - Swap buffers (perform the actual drawing).

- CubeRenderer: This is an implementation of the Renderer interface to draw the cubes.

- Cube: This class encapsulates a GL cube, including vertices, colors, and indices for each face.

Because the sample needs to be slightly modified to illustrate the concepts of the chapter, the following classes have been added for this purpose:

- JavaGLActivity: This is the Android activity that starts the Java-only version of the application.

- NativeGLActivity: This activity starts the hybrid version of the sample (with Java/C/JNI code).

- Natives: This class defines the native methods used by this sample.

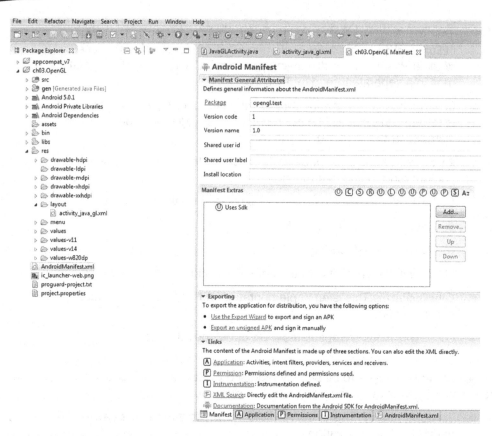

Figure 3-6. Resource list for the OpenGL sample

The Android manifest needs to be updated to include the new activities defined in the previous paragraph, as shown in bold in Listing 3-4.

Listing 3-4. Manifest File for This Chapter's Example

```xml
<?xml version="1.0" encoding="utf-8"?>
<manifest xmlns:android="http://schemas.android.com/apk/res/android"
      package="opengl.test"
      android:versionCode="1"
      android:versionName="1.0">
   <application android:icon="@drawable/icon"
      android:label="@string/app_name">
      <activity android:name=".JavaGLActivity"
                android:label="OpenGL Java">
         <intent-filter>
            <action android:name="android.intent.action.MAIN" />
            <category android:name="android.intent.category.LAUNCHER" />
         </intent-filter>
      </activity>
```

```
    <activity android:name=".NativeGLActivity"
            android:label="OpenGL Native">
        <intent-filter>
            <action android:name="android.intent.action.MAIN" />
            <category android:name="android.intent.category.LAUNCHER" />
        </intent-filter>
    </activity>
</application>
<uses-sdk android:minSdkVersion="3" />
</manifest>
```

The following lines tell Android to create two application launchers in the device launchpad;
one for each of the activities, OpenGL Java and OpenGL Native:

```
<action android:name="android.intent.action.MAIN" />
<category android:name="android.intent.category.LAUNCHER" />
```

Let's start with the Java-only implementation. Figure 3-7 defines the basic workflow of the
OpenGL application. The figure shows the main activity (JavaGLActivity), which creates
the rendering surface (GLSurfaceView). The surface creates a renderer (CubeRenderer) that
contains a thread (GLThread). GLThread in turn contains the loop that invokes the renderer
draw() method that draws the tumbling cubes seen on the device display.

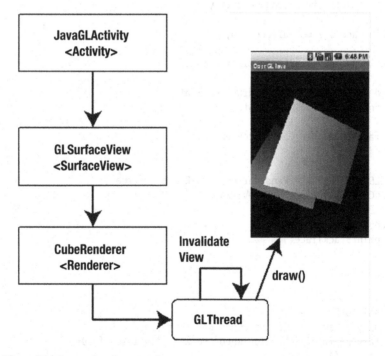

Figure 3-7. Workflow of the Java-only cubes sample

Java Main Activity

When the user starts the application, the JavaGLActivity.onCreate() method will be called (see Listing 3-5). Here is where the surface view (mGLSurfaceView) is initialized and set as the application content:

```
mGLSurfaceView = new GLSurfaceView(this);
mGLSurfaceView.setRenderer(new CubeRenderer(true));
setContentView(mGLSurfaceView);
```

Note that the GL surface view must use a renderer (CubeRenderer in this case), which implements the Renderer interface and takes a Boolean argument, indicating whether a translucent background should be used.

Listing 3-5. Main Activity for the Java-Only Version of the GL Cubes Sample

```
package opengl.test;

import opengl.scenes.GLSurfaceView;
import opengl.scenes.cubes.CubeRenderer;
import android.app.Activity;
import android.os.Bundle;

public class JavaGLActivity extends Activity
{
    private GLSurfaceView mGLSurfaceView;

    /** Called when the activity is first created. */
    @Override
    public void onCreate(Bundle savedInstanceState) {
        super.onCreate(savedInstanceState);

        mGLSurfaceView = new GLSurfaceView(this);

        try {
            mGLSurfaceView.setRenderer(new CubeRenderer(true));
            setContentView(mGLSurfaceView);

        } catch (Exception e) {
            e.printStackTrace();
        }
    }

    @Override
    protected void onPause() {
        // Ideally a game should implement onResume() and onPause()
        // to take appropriate action when the activity loses focus
        super.onPause();
        mGLSurfaceView.onPause();
    }
```

```
    @Override
    protected void onResume() {
        super.onResume();
        mGLSurfaceView.onResume();
    }
}
```

When the application loses focus or resumes, the onPause() or onResume() method will be called, respectively. These methods delegate to the surface view (GLSurfaceView) to take the appropriate action, such as saving application state or suspending/resuming the rendering process.

Surface View

The class GLSurfaceView (see Listing 3-6) defines the surface where the tumbling cubes animation will take place. The class constructor starts by initializing a callback to receive notifications when the surface is changed, created, or destroyed.

```
mHolder = getHolder();
mHolder.addCallback(this);
mHolder.setType(SurfaceHolder.SURFACE_TYPE_GPU);
```

By implementing SurfaceHolder.Callback and calling SurfaceHolder.addCallback(), the class will receive the events:

- surfaceCreated(SurfaceHolder holder): This is called immediately after the surface is first created. In this case, the surface delegates to the inner thread GLThread.surfaceCreated().

- surfaceDestroyed(SurfaceHolder holder): This method is called immediately before a surface is being destroyed. After returning from this call, the surface should not be accessed. In this case, the method delegates to the rendering thread GLThread.surfaceDestroyed().

- surfaceChanged(SurfaceHolder holder, int format, int w, int h): This method is called immediately after any structural changes (format or size) have been made to the surface. Here is where you tell the inner thread that the size has changed. This method is always called at least once, after surfaceCreated(). The second argument of this method (format) is the pixel format of the graphics defined in the PixelFormat class.

Listing 3-6. Surface View for the GL Cubes Sample

```
package opengl.scenes;

import opengl.jni.Natives;
import android.content.Context;
import android.util.AttributeSet;
import android.view.SurfaceHolder;
import android.view.SurfaceView;
```

```java
/**
 * An implementation of SurfaceView that uses the dedicated surface for
 * displaying an OpenGL animation. This allows the animation to run in a
 * separate thread, without requiring that it be driven by the update
 * mechanism of the view hierarchy.
 *
 * The application-specific rendering code is delegated to a GLView.Renderer
 * instance.
 */
public class GLSurfaceView extends SurfaceView
  implements  SurfaceHolder.Callback
{
    public GLSurfaceView(Context context) {
        super(context);
        init();
    }

    public GLSurfaceView(Context context, AttributeSet attrs) {
        super(context, attrs);
        init();
    }

    private void init() {
        // Install a SurfaceHolder.Callback so we get notified when the
        // underlying surface is created and destroyed
        mHolder = getHolder();
        mHolder.addCallback(this);
        mHolder.setType(SurfaceHolder.SURFACE_TYPE_GPU);
    }

    public SurfaceHolder getSurfaceHolder() {
        return mHolder;
    }

    public void setRenderer(Renderer renderer) {
        mGLThread = new GLThread(renderer, mHolder);
        mGLThread.start();
    }

    public void surfaceCreated(SurfaceHolder holder) {
        mGLThread.surfaceCreated();
    }

    public void surfaceDestroyed(SurfaceHolder holder) {
        // Surface will be destroyed when we return
        mGLThread.surfaceDestroyed();
    }
```

```java
public void surfaceChanged(SurfaceHolder holder, int format, int w,
        int h) {
    // Surface size or format has changed. This should not happen in
    // this example.
    mGLThread.onWindowResize(w, h);
}

/**
 * Inform the view that the activity is paused.
 */
public void onPause() {
    mGLThread.onPause();
}

/**
 * Inform the view that the activity is resumed.
 */
public void onResume() {
    mGLThread.onResume();
}

/**
 * Inform the view that the window focus has changed.
 */
@Override
public void onWindowFocusChanged(boolean hasFocus) {
    super.onWindowFocusChanged(hasFocus);
    mGLThread.onWindowFocusChanged(hasFocus);
}
/**
 * Queue an "event" to be run on the GL rendering thread.
 *
 * @param r
 *            the runnable to be run on the GL rendering thread.
 */
public void queueEvent(Runnable r) {
    mGLThread.queueEvent(r);
}

@Override
protected void onDetachedFromWindow() {
    super.onDetachedFromWindow();
    mGLThread.requestExitAndWait();
}

private SurfaceHolder mHolder;
private GLThread mGLThread;

}
```

Other important methods in the surface view include the following:

- setRenderer(): This method creates the inner thread that does all the work and starts it. The thread keeps a reference to the surface holder available by calling getHolder().

```
public void setRenderer(Renderer renderer) {
    mGLThread = new GLThread(renderer, mHolder);
    mGLThread.start();
}
```

- queueEvent(Runnable r): This method sends an event to be run by the inner thread.

- onDetachedFromWindow(): This method is called when the view is detached from a window. At this point, it no longer has a surface for drawing.

The surface view provides the drawing canvas for the next component, the GL thread. A thread is required to perform tasks in the background, thus offloading processing time from the main application thread to make the application run seamlessly. Let's see what it does.

GL Thread

The main loop of the animation is performed by GLThread. When started, this thread performs the following steps:

1. It creates a semaphore.

```
sEglSemaphore.acquire();
guardedRun(); // Only 1 thread can access this code
sEglSemaphore.release();
```

2. It runs the critical animation loop. Within the loop, the actual drawing is delegated to the CubeRenderer.

3. When asked to quit, the loop terminates and the OpenGL resources are released.

Note   A *semaphore* is an object often used to restrict the number of threads that can access the OpenGL context. When the Android framework launches a second instance of an activity, the new instance's onCreate() method may be called before the first instance returns from onDestroy(). A semaphore ensures that only one instance at a time accesses the GL API. You must do this because OpenGL is a single-threaded API (which means that only one thread can access the GLContext at a time).

Listing 3-7 shows a fragment of the GLThread class taken from the GL cubes sample. When the thread starts, the run() method is invoked, and a semaphore is used to ensure that guardedRun() can be accessed by one thread only. guardedRun() performs other important steps, such as the following:

- Initializes the OpenGL ES for a given configuration specification. The configuration specification defines information, such as pixel format and image depth.

- Creates the OpenGL surface and tells the renderer about it.

- Checks whether the size of the surface has changed and tells the renderer about it.

- Queues and gets events to be run on the GL rendering thread.

Listing 3-7. Rendering Thread for the GL Cubes Sample

```java
package opengl.scenes;

// ...

/**
 * A generic GL Thread. Takes care of initializing EGL and GL.
 * Delegates to a Renderer instance to do the actual drawing.
 */
public class GLThread extends Thread
{
    public GLThread(Renderer renderer, SurfaceHolder holder) {
        super();
        mDone = false;
        mWidth = 0;
        mHeight = 0;
        mRenderer = renderer;
        mHolder = holder;
        setName("GLThread");
    }

@Override
    public void run() {
        try {
            try {
                sEglSemaphore.acquire();
            } catch (InterruptedException e) {
                return;
            }
            guardedRun();
        } catch (Exception ex) {
            ex.printStackTrace();
        } finally {
            sEglSemaphore.release();
        }
    }
```

```java
private void guardedRun() throws InterruptedException {
    mEglHelper = new EglHelper();

    // Specify a configuration for the OpenGL session
    int[] configSpec = mRenderer.getConfigSpec();
    mEglHelper.start(configSpec);

    GL10 gl = null;
    boolean tellRendererSurfaceCreated = true;
    boolean tellRendererSurfaceChanged = true;

    // This is the main activity thread's loop
    while (!mDone) {

        // Update the asynchronous state (window size)
        int w, h;
        boolean changed;
        boolean needStart = false;
        synchronized (this) {
            Runnable r;
            while ((r = getEvent()) != null) {
                r.run();
            }
            if (mPaused) {
                mEglHelper.finish();
                needStart = true;
            }
            if (needToWait()) {
                while (needToWait()) {
                    wait();
                }
            }
            if (mDone) {
                break;
            }
            changed = mSizeChanged;
            w = mWidth;
            h = mHeight;
            mSizeChanged = false;
        }
        if (needStart) {
            mEglHelper.start(configSpec);
            tellRendererSurfaceCreated = true;
            changed = true;
        }
        if (changed) {
            // Create the surface
            gl = (GL10) mEglHelper.createSurface(mHolder);
            tellRendererSurfaceChanged = true;
        }
```

```
            if (tellRendererSurfaceCreated) {
                mRenderer.surfaceCreated(gl);
                tellRendererSurfaceCreated = false;
            }
            if (tellRendererSurfaceChanged) {
                mRenderer.sizeChanged(gl, w, h);
                tellRendererSurfaceChanged = false;
            }
            if ((w > 0) && (h > 0)) {
                /* draw a frame here */
                mRenderer.drawFrame(gl);

                // Call swapBuffers() to instruct the system to display
                mEglHelper.swap();
            }
        }

        // Clean up...
        mEglHelper.finish();
    }

    // ...
    private static final Semaphore sEglSemaphore = new Semaphore(1);
    private EglHelper mEglHelper;
}
```

The GL thread makes use of the next two sections: the cube renderer to perform drawing, rotation, and the positioning operations on the cube and the cube class, which has information about the cube itself. Let's look at the renderer in more detail.

CubeRenderer Class

CubeRenderer is the class that renders the pair of tumbling cubes (see Listing 3-8). It implements the Renderer interface and does some very interesting things.

The void drawFrame(GL10 gl) method does the actual drawing and gets called many times per second. The method starts by setting the matrix mode to GL_MODELVIEW. This essentially says to render things in a 3D perspective (model view). Next, it clears all screen buffers by calling glLoadIdentity().

```
gl.glMatrixMode(GL10.GL_MODELVIEW);
gl.glLoadIdentity();
```

Next, the perspective is translated in the z axis by three units toward the eye viewpoint (also known as the camera).

```
gl.glTranslatef(0, 0, -3.0f);
```

The next two instructions tell the pipeline to rotate the perspective in the y and x axes by an angle given in radians (0–6.28, 0 meaning zero degrees and 6.28 meaning 360 degrees).

```
gl.glRotatef(mAngle, 0, 1, 0);
gl.glRotatef(mAngle * 0.25f, 1, 0, 0);
```

Next, CubeRenderer requests that vertices and colors be rendered. These are defined within the Cube class like so:

```
gl.glEnableClientState(GL10.GL_VERTEX_ARRAY);
gl.glEnableClientState(GL10.GL_COLOR_ARRAY);
```

Then the cube is drawn.

```
mCube.draw(gl);
```

The perspective is rotated again in the y and z axes, and translated half a unit away from the eye.

```
gl.glRotatef(mAngle * 2.0f, 0, 1, 1);
gl.glTranslatef(0.5f, 0.5f, 0.5f);
```

The second cube is drawn, and the angle of rotation is increased for the next iteration.

```
mCube.draw(gl);
mAngle += 1.2f;
```

The int[] getConfigSpec() method initializes the pixel format and the depth of the display. The pixel format describes the size of the ARGB values used to describe a pixel. The depth indicates the maximum number of colors used. For example, the following integer array requests 32 bits per pixel (ARGB 32 bpp) with a depth of 16 (2^{16} colors):

```
int[] configSpec = {
EGL10.EGL_RED_SIZE,      8,
EGL10.EGL_GREEN_SIZE,    8,
EGL10.EGL_BLUE_SIZE,     8,
EGL10.EGL_ALPHA_SIZE,    8,
EGL10.EGL_DEPTH_SIZE,   16,
EGL10.EGL_NONE
};
```

The following are two other interesting methods in the cube renderer:

- void sizeChanged(GL10 gl, int width, int height): This method fires when the size of the viewport changes. It scales the cubes by setting the ratio of the projection matrix and resizing the viewport.

- void surfaceCreated(GL10 gl): This method fires when the surface is created. Here, some initialization is performed, such as setting a translucent background (if requested) and miscellaneous OpenGL renderer tweaking.

When the code in drawFrame() is executed many times per second, the result is two tumbling cubes (see Figure 3-8).

Listing 3-8. Cube Renderer for the Pair of Tumbling Cubes

```
package opengl.scenes.cubes;

import javax.microedition.khronos.egl.EGL10;
import javax.microedition.khronos.opengles.GL10;

import opengl.jni.Natives;
import opengl.scenes.Renderer;

/**
 * Render a pair of tumbling cubes.
 */
public class CubeRenderer implements Renderer {

    public CubeRenderer(boolean useTranslucentBackground) {
        mTranslucentBackground = useTranslucentBackground;
        mNativeDraw = nativeDraw;
        mCube = new Cube();
    }

    public void drawFrame(GL10 gl) {
        /*
         * Usually, the first thing one might want to do is to clear
         * the screen. The most efficient way of doing this is
         * to use glClear().
         */
        gl.glClear(GL10.GL_COLOR_BUFFER_BIT | GL10.GL_DEPTH_BUFFER_BIT);

        /*
         * Now we're ready to draw some 3D objects
         */
        gl.glMatrixMode(GL10.GL_MODELVIEW);
        gl.glLoadIdentity();
        gl.glTranslatef(0, 0, -3.0f);
        gl.glRotatef(mAngle, 0, 1, 0);
        gl.glRotatef(mAngle * 0.25f, 1, 0, 0);

        gl.glEnableClientState(GL10.GL_VERTEX_ARRAY);
        gl.glEnableClientState(GL10.GL_COLOR_ARRAY);

        mCube.draw(gl);

        gl.glRotatef(mAngle * 2.0f, 0, 1, 1);
        gl.glTranslatef(0.5f, 0.5f, 0.5f);

        mCube.draw(gl);

        mAngle += 1.2f;
    }
```

```
public int[] getConfigSpec() {
    if (mTranslucentBackground) {
        // We want a depth buffer and an alpha buffer
        int[] configSpec = { EGL10.EGL_RED_SIZE, 8,
                EGL10.EGL_GREEN_SIZE, 8, EGL10.EGL_BLUE_SIZE, 8,
                EGL10.EGL_ALPHA_SIZE, 8, EGL10.EGL_DEPTH_SIZE, 16,
                EGL10.EGL_NONE };
        return configSpec;
    } else {
        // We want a depth buffer, don't care about the
        // details of the color buffer.
        int[] configSpec = { EGL10.EGL_DEPTH_SIZE, 16,
                EGL10.EGL_NONE };
        return configSpec;
    }
}

public void sizeChanged(GL10 gl, int width, int height) {
    gl.glViewport(0, 0, width, height);

    /*
     * Set our projection matrix. This doesn't have to be done each time we
     * draw, but usually a new projection needs to be set when the viewport
     * is resized.
     */
    float ratio = (float) width / height;
    gl.glMatrixMode(GL10.GL_PROJECTION);
    gl.glLoadIdentity();
    gl.glFrustumf(-ratio, ratio, -1, 1, 1, 10);
}

public void surfaceCreated(GL10 gl) {
    /*
     * By default, OpenGL enables features that improve quality but reduce
     * performance. One might want to tweak that especially on software
     * renderer.
     */
    gl.glDisable(GL10.GL_DITHER);

    /*
     * Some one-time OpenGL initialization can be made here probably based
     * on features of this particular context
     */
    gl.glHint(GL10.GL_PERSPECTIVE_CORRECTION_HINT
        , GL10.GL_FASTEST);
    if (mTranslucentBackground) {
        gl.glClearColor(0, 0, 0, 0.5f);
    } else {
        gl.glClearColor(1, 1, 1, 0.5f);
    }
```

```
        gl.glEnable(GL10.GL_CULL_FACE);
        gl.glShadeModel(GL10.GL_SMOOTH);
        gl.glEnable(GL10.GL_DEPTH_TEST);
    }

    private boolean mTranslucentBackground;
    private Cube mCube;
    private float mAngle;
}
```

The final piece of this puzzle is the cube itself, which has information such as dimensions, colors, and other specifications. It works in tandem with the previous two components. Let's see what the cube does.

Cube Class

CubeRenderer delegates drawing to the Cube class (see Listing 3-9). This class defines a 12-sided cube with 8 vertices (8 × x, y, and z coordinates), 32 colors (8 vertices × 4 ARGB values), and 36 indices for the x, y, and z coordinates of each side. The class consists of two methods:

- ▩ Cube(): This is the class constructor. It initializes arrays for the vertices, colors, and indices required to draw. It then uses direct Java buffers to place the data on the native heap where the garbage collector cannot move them. This is required by the gl*Pointer() API functions that do the actual drawing.

- ▩ draw(): To draw the cube, you simply set the vertices and colors, and issue a call to glDrawElements using triangles (GL_TRIANGLES). Note that a cube has 6 faces, 8 vertices, and 12 sides.

```
gl.glVertexPointer(3, GL10.GL_FIXED, 0, mVertexBuffer);
gl.glColorPointer(4, GL10.GL_FIXED, 0, mColorBuffer);
gl.glDrawElements(GL10.GL_TRIANGLES, 36
    , GL10.GL_UNSIGNED_BYTE,  mIndexBuffer);
```

Listing 3-9. Cube Class for the GL Cubes Sample

```
package opengl.scenes.cubes;

import java.nio.ByteBuffer;
import java.nio.ByteOrder;
import java.nio.IntBuffer;
import javax.microedition.khronos.opengles.GL10;

/**
 * A vertex shaded cube.
 */
```

```java
public class Cube {
    public Cube() {
        int one = 0x10000;
        // 8 vertices each with 3 xyz coordinates
        int vertices[] = { -one, -one, -one
                , one, -one, -one
                , one, one, -one
                , -one, one, -one
                , -one, -one, one
                , one, -one, one
                , one, one, one
                , -one, one, one };

        // 8 colors each with  4 RGBA values
        int colors[] = { 0, 0, 0, one
                , one, 0, 0, one
                , one, one, 0, one
                , 0, one, 0, one
                , 0, 0, one, one
                , one, 0, one, one
                , one, one, one, one
                , 0, one, one, one};
        // 12 indices each with 3 xyz coordinates
        byte indices[] = { 0, 4, 5, 0, 5, 1, 1, 5, 6, 1, 6, 2, 2, 6, 7,
                2, 7, 3, 3, 7, 4, 3, 4, 0, 4, 7, 6, 4, 6, 5, 3, 0, 1,
                3, 1, 2 };

        ByteBuffer vbb = ByteBuffer.allocateDirect(vertices.length * 4);
        vbb.order(ByteOrder.nativeOrder());
        mVertexBuffer = vbb.asIntBuffer();
        mVertexBuffer.put(vertices);
        mVertexBuffer.position(0);

        ByteBuffer cbb = ByteBuffer.allocateDirect(colors.length * 4);
        cbb.order(ByteOrder.nativeOrder());
        mColorBuffer = cbb.asIntBuffer();
        mColorBuffer.put(colors);
        mColorBuffer.position(0);

        mIndexBuffer = ByteBuffer.allocateDirect(indices.length);
        mIndexBuffer.put(indices);
        mIndexBuffer.position(0);
    }

    public void draw(GL10 gl) {
        gl.glFrontFace(GL10.GL_CW);
        gl.glVertexPointer(3, GL10.GL_FIXED, 0, mVertexBuffer);
        gl.glColorPointer(4, GL10.GL_FIXED, 0, mColorBuffer);
        gl.glDrawElements(GL10.GL_TRIANGLES, 36, GL10.GL_UNSIGNED_BYTE,
                mIndexBuffer);
    }
```

```
    private IntBuffer mVertexBuffer;
    private IntBuffer mColorBuffer;
    private ByteBuffer mIndexBuffer;
}
```

Figure 3-8 shows the sample in action. In the next section, you'll see how portions of this code can be implemented natively.

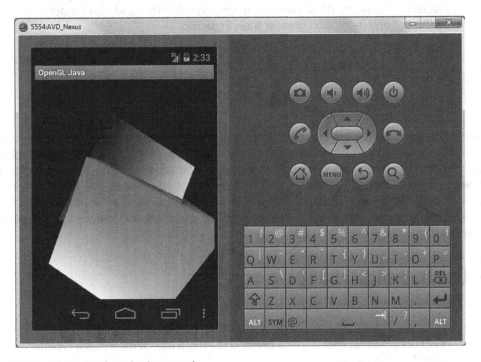

Figure 3-8. Tumbling cubes from the Java sample

So you have seen one way of tackling OpenGL rendering purely using Java. However, you can build the same example using the combination of a thin Java wrapper and a native renderer. Both are equally valid and can achieve the same results. However, the latter works better if you already have large portions of OpenGL code written in C and you wish to reuse them. The former is the way to go if you plan to write your code entirely in Java. Choosing the right rendering technique is difficult but not the only challenge you will face when creating your game. Video scaling is another difficult subject, and you'll tackle it in the next section.

Scaling Video Buffers with Hybrid OpenGL ES

One of the trickiest parts of working with software-based games is scaling the video buffer to fit the display size. It is even more troublesome when you have a multitude of resolutions, such as in an open environment such as Android. As a developer, you must try to achieve the right balance of performance versus display quality. As you saw in Chapter 2, video scaling can be one of three kinds, from slowest to the fastest.

■ *Software*: The slowest method but the easiest to implement. Best for old devices with no GPUs. However, most of today's phones are hardware accelerated.

■ *Hybrid*: Uses a mix of software drawing (to create an image buffer) and hardware rendering (to draw into the display). It is fast and can render images at any resolution greater than 256x256.

■ *Hardware only*: The fastest of the bunch but the hardest to implement. Depending on the complexity of your game, it may require a powerful GPU. If you have good hardware, it can create games with amazing quality and effects. It is a tough choice in hardware-fragmented platforms such as Android.

This section tackles the middle choice, hybrid scaling. It is the best choice for a fragmented platform where you have a software renderer and want to scale your game to any display resolution. It is perfect for games such as emulators, arcade, simple shooters, and others. It also works very well in low-, middle-, and high-power devices. First, you'll get a general overview of hybrid scaling and why it is the preferable method to scale video. Next, you'll dig into the implementation, including how to initialize a surface and draw into the texture to perform the actual scaling.

Why Use Hybrid Scaling?

The principle behind this scaling technique is simple.

■ Your game creates an image buffer (usually in pixel format RGB565, the most common for mobile) at a given size. You'll use 320x240, the typical size of an emulator.

■ The image 320x240 needs to be scaled to a tablet size (1024x768)—or any device for that matter. Here you could use a software scaler but it would be painfully slow. Instead you create an OpenGL ES texture and render the image (320x240) into the texture using a GL Quad.

■ By magic the texture will be scaled to the display size (1024x768) using hardware, thus offering a significant performance boost to your game.

From the implementation point of view, the process can be described as follows:

■ *Initialize the OpenGL ES texture*: At the stage of the game where the video gets initialized, a hardware surface must be created. This surface consists of a simple texture where the video image will be rendered (see Listings 3-10 and 3-11).

■ *Draw the image buffer into the texture*: At the end of your game loop, render the video image into the texture, which will be automatically scaled to fit any display size (see Listing 3-12).

Listing 3-10 shows `CreateEmptyTextureRGB565`, which creates an empty texture for drawing and has the following arguments:

- `w,h`: This is the size of the video image.

- `x_offset, y_offset`: These are the XY offset coordinates at which the image will be rendered into the texture. Read on to see why you may need this.

To create a texture in OpenGL, you simply call

```
glGenTextures(1, &mTextureID);
glBindTexture(GL_TEXTURE_2D, mTextureID);
```

where mTextureID is an integer that has stored the ID of your texture. Next, it sets the following texture parameters:

- `GL_TEXTURE_MIN_FILTER`: This texture-minifying function is used whenever the pixel being textured maps to an area greater than one texture element. The minifying function you use is `GL_NEAREST`, which returns the value of the texture element that is nearest (in Manhattan distance) to the center of the pixel being textured.

- `GL_TEXTURE_MAG_FILTER`: This texture-magnification function is used when the pixel being textured maps to an area less than or equal to one texture element. The magnification function you use is `GL_LINEAR`, which returns the weighted average of the four texture elements that are closest to the center of the pixel being textured.

- `GL_TEXTURE_WRAP_S`: This sets the wrap parameter for each texture coordinate S to `GL_CLAMP`, which causes the coordinates to be clamped to the range [0,1] and is useful for preventing wrapping artifacts when mapping a single image onto an object.

- `GL_TEXTURE_WRAP_T`: This sets the wrap parameter for each texture coordinate T to `GL_CLAMP`.

Finally, you specify a two-dimensional texture image with `glTexImage2D` with the following parameters:

- `GL_TEXTURE_2D`: Specifies the target texture.

- *Level*: Specifies the level-of-detail number. Level 0 is the base image level.

- *Internal format*: Specifies the color components in the texture, in this case RGB.

- *Width and height*: Size of the texture. It must be a power of two.

- *Format*: It specifies the format of the pixel data and must be the same as the internal format.

- *Type*: It specifies the data type of the pixel data, in this case RGB565 (16 bit).

- *Pixels*: It specifies a pointer to the image data in memory. It must be encoded as RGR656.

Note The size of the texture must be a power of two: 256, 512, 1024, etc.). However, the size of the video image can be arbitrary. This means the size of the texture must be a power of two equal to or greater than the size of the video. This is a caveat that will be explained later.

Listing 3-10. Create an Empty Texture as RGB656

```
// Texture ID
static unsigned int mTextureID;

// These are used to compute an XY offset of the image drawn into the texture
static int xoffset;
static int yoffset;

/**
 * Create an empty texture as RGB565
 * params: (w,h) width, height of the texture
 * (x_offsety_offset): XY offset of the image drawn into the texture
 */
static void CreateEmptyTextureRGB565 (int w, int h, int x_offset, int y_offset)
{
  int size = w * h * 2;

  xoffset = x_offset;
  yoffset = y_offset;

  // buffer
  unsigned short * pixels = (unsigned short *)malloc(size);

  memset(pixels, 0, size);

  // Init GL sate
  glDisable(GL_DITHER);
  glHint(GL_PERSPECTIVE_CORRECTION_HINT, GL_FASTEST);

  glClearColor(.5f, .5f, .5f, 1);
  glShadeModel(GL_SMOOTH);
  glEnable(GL_DEPTH_TEST);
  glEnable(GL_TEXTURE_2D);

  // Create texture
  glGenTextures(1, &mTextureID);
  glBindTexture(GL_TEXTURE_2D, mTextureID);
```

```
// texture params
glTexParameterf(GL_TEXTURE_2D, GL_TEXTURE_MIN_FILTER,GL_NEAREST);
glTexParameterf(GL_TEXTURE_2D, GL_TEXTURE_MAG_FILTER,GL_LINEAR);

glTexParameterf(GL_TEXTURE_2D, GL_TEXTURE_WRAP_S, GL_CLAMP_TO_EDGE);
glTexParameterf(GL_TEXTURE_2D, GL_TEXTURE_WRAP_T, GL_CLAMP_TO_EDGE);

// Texture is RGB565
glTexImage2D(GL_TEXTURE_2D, 0, GL_RGB, w, h, 0, GL_RGB, GL_UNSIGNED_SHORT_5_6_5 , pixels);

free (pixels);
}
```

Now, let's take a look at the actual implementation of the hybrid video scaler. The next two sections show you how to initialize a surface for scaling and how to perform the actual drawing.

Initializing the Surface

For this scaler to work, it is critical that the size of the texture is a power of two equal to or greater than the size of the video. If you don't make sure this rule applies, you will see a white or black screen whenever the image is rendered. In Listing 3-11, the function JNI_RGB565_ SurfaceInit makes sure this rule is obeyed. It takes the width and height of the image as arguments. It then calls getBestTexSize to obtain the closest texture size, and finally creates the empty texture by calling CreateEmptyTextureRGB565. Note that if the image is smaller than the texture, it will be centered on-screen by calculating XY offset coordinates.

Listing 3-11. Surface Initialization

```
// Get the next POT texture size greater or equal to image size (wh)
static void getBestTexSize(int w, int h, int *tw, int *th)
{
  int width = 256, height = 256;

  #define MAX_WIDTH 1024
  #define MAX_HEIGHT 1024

  while ( width < w && width < MAX_WIDTH) { width *= 2; }
  while ( height < h && height < MAX_HEIGHT) { height *= 2; }

  *tw = width;
  *th = height;
}

/**
 * Ini an RGB565 surface
 * params: (w,h) width, height of the image
 */
```

```
void JNI_RGB565_SurfaceInit(int w, int h)
{
  // min texture w&h
  int texw = 256;
  int texh  = 256;

  // Get texture size (must be POT) >= WxH
  getBestTexSize(w, h, &texw, &texh);

 // Center image on screen?
 int offx = texw > w ? (texw - w)/2 : 0;
 int offy = texh > h ? (texh - h)/2 : 0;

 if ( w > texw || h > texh)
   printf ("Error: Invalid surface size %sx%d", w, h);

  // Create the OpenGL texture used to render
  CreateEmptyTextureRGB565 (texw, texh, offx, offy);
}
```

Drawing into the Texture

Finally, to render into the display (also known as *surface flipping*), you call JNI_RGB565_Flip with
an array of pixel data (encoded as RGB565) plus the size of the image. JNI_RGB565_Flip draws
into the texture by calling DrawIntoTextureRGB565 and swaps the buffers. Note that the buffer
swapping is done in Java, not C, and therefore you need a way to tell Java it is time to swap. You
can do this using JNI to call some Java method to do the actual swapping (see Listing 3-12).

Listing 3-12. Drawing an Image Buffer into a Texture Using a Quad

```
// Quad vertices X, Y, Z
static const float vertices[] = {
    -1.0f, -1.0f, 0,
     1.0f, -1.0f, 0,
     1.0f,  1.0f, 0,
    -1.0f,  1.0f, 0
};
// Quad coords (0-1)
static const float coords[] = {
    0.0f, 1.0f,
    1.0f, 1.0f,
    1.0f, 0.0f,
    0.0f, 0.0f,
 };

// Quad vertex indices
static const unsigned short indices[] = { 0, 1, 2, 3};

/**
 * Draw an array of pixels in the entire screen using a Quad
 *  pixels: unsigned short for RGB565
 */
```

```
static void DrawIntoTextureRGB565 (unsigned short * pixels, int w, int h)
{
  // clear screen
  glClear(GL_COLOR_BUFFER_BIT | GL_DEPTH_BUFFER_BIT);

  // enable vetices & and texture coordinates
  glEnableClientState(GL_VERTEX_ARRAY);
  glEnableClientState(GL_TEXTURE_COORD_ARRAY);

  glActiveTexture(GL_TEXTURE0);
  glBindTexture(GL_TEXTURE_2D, mTextureID);

  glTexSubImage2D(GL_TEXTURE_2D, 0, xoffset, yoffset, w, h, GL_RGB, GL_UNSIGNED_SHORT_5_6_5,
pixels);

  // Draw quad
  glFrontFace(GL_CCW);
  glVertexPointer(3, GL_FLOAT, 0, vertices);
  glEnable(GL_TEXTURE_2D);
  glTexCoordPointer(2, GL_FLOAT, 0, coords);
  glDrawElements(GL_TRIANGLE_FAN, 4, GL_UNSIGNED_SHORT, indices);
}

// Flip surface (Draw into texture)
void JNI_RGB565_Flip(unsigned short *pixels , int width, int height)
{
  if ( ! pixels) {
    return;
  }
  DrawIntoTextureRGB565 (pixels, width, height);

  // Must swap GLES buffers here
  jni_swap_buffers ();
}
```

To render into the texture using OpenGL, follow these steps.

1. Clear the color and depth buffers using glClear(GL_COLOR_BUFFER_
   BIT | GL_DEPTH_BUFFER_BIT).

2. Enable the client state: vertex array and texture coordinates array for
   writing when glDrawElements is called.

3. Select active texture unit with glActiveTexture where the initial value
   is GL_TEXTURE0.

4. Bind a named texture to a texturing target. GL_TEXTURE_2D
   (a 2D surface) is the default target to which the texture is bound.
   mTextureID is the ID of a texture.

5. Specify a two-dimensional texture subimage using `glTexSubImage2D` with the following parameters:

    ▪ GL_TEXTURE_2D: It specifies the target texture.

    ▪ *Level*: It specifies the level of detail number. Level 0 is the base image level.

    ▪ *Xoffset*: It specifies a texel (texture pixel) offset in the x direction within the texture array.

    ▪ *Yoffset*: It specifies a texel offset in the y direction within the texture array.

    ▪ *Width*: It specifies the width of the texture subimage.

    ▪ *Height*: It specifies the height of the texture subimage.

    ▪ *Format*: It specifies the format of the pixel data.

    ▪ *Type*: It specifies the data type of the pixel data.

    ▪ *Data*: It specifies a pointer to the image data in memory.

6. Draw the Quad vertices, coordinates, and indices by calling the following:

    ▪ `glFrontFace`: It enables the front face of the Quad.

    ▪ glVertexPointer: It defines the array of the Quad's vertex data with a size of 3, of type GL_FLOAT, and a stride of 0.

    ▪ glTexCoordPointer: It defines the Quad's array of texture coordinates with a size of 2, of type GL_FLOAT, and a stride of 0.

    ▪ `glDrawElements`: It renders primitives from the data array using triangles (GL_TRIANGLES), with 4 elements (hence a Quad) of type short (GL_UNSIGNED_SHORT) plus a pointer to the indices.

In Listing 3-12 you see that the range of coordinates of the Quad is (–1, 1) in both axes. This is because the range of the OpenGL coordinate system is (–1, 1) where the origin (0,0) is the center (see Figure 3-9).

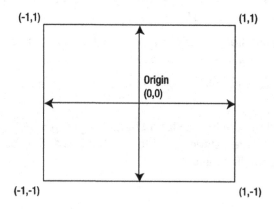

Figure 3-9. OpenGL coordinate system

In a perfect world you shouldn't have to worry much about the size of the video buffer (especially if using software-only scalers/renderers). This is not true, however, when scaling video using OpenGL in Android. In this case, the size of the buffer is crucial. In the next section, you will learn how to deal with arbitrary video sizes that don't work very well with OpenGL.

When the Image Is Not a Power of Two

As mentioned before, hybrid scaling works flawlessly when the size of the image is a power of two. However, your image buffer probably won't be a power of two. For example, the chapter dealing with the Doom engine has a video size of 320x240. In that case, the image will still be scaled, but to a percentage of the size of the texture. To see this effect in action, take a look at Figures 3-10 and 3-11.

Figure 3-10. Scaling a non-power-of-two image

In Figure 3-10 you have the following sizes:

- Device display: 859x480
- Texture: 512x256
- Image: 320x240

As you can see, the image is scaled but to 62% (320/512 × 100) of the texture width and 93% (240/256 × 100) of the height. Therefore, the image will be scaled to 62%x93% of any device resolution provided the resolution is greater than 256. Now let's take a look at Figure 3-11.

Figure 3-11. Scaling a power-of-two image

In Figure 3-11 you have the following sizes:

- Device display: 859x480
- Texture: 512x256
- Image: 512x256

Zoom and Draw

In Figure 3-11 you can see that the image will be scaled at 100% of any device resolution, which is what you want. But what do you do when the image is not a power of two? To get past this caveat, you could

1. Zoom the 320x240 image to the closest power of two (512x256 in this case) using a software scaler.

2. Convert the scaled surface into a RGB656 image, compatible with DrawIntoTextureRGB565 from the previous section.

3. Draw into the texture, thus performing hardware scaling to the display resolution.

This solution is a little slower than the one in the preceding section but still much faster than using a pure software scaler, especially if you run in high-resolution devices such as tablets. Listing 3-13 shows how to zoom an SDL surface using the popular SDL_gfx library.

Listing 3-13. Zooming an Image with SDL_gfx roto-zoom

```
void JNI_Flip(SDL_Surface *surface )
{
  if ( zoom ) {
    // if surface is 8bit scaled will be 8bit else surface is 32 bit RGBA!
    SDL_Surface * sized = zoomSurface( surface, zoomx, zoomy, SMOOTHING_OFF);

    JNI_FlipByBPP (sized);

    // Must clean up!
    SDL_FreeSurface(sized);
  }
  else {
    JNI_FlipByBPP (surface);
  }
}
```

Zoom and Draw Implementation

To zoom/scale an SDL surface, you simply call SDL_gfx zoomSurface with

1. An SDL surface

2. Horizontal zoom factor:(0–1)

3. Vertical zoom factor

4. SMOOTHING_OFF: This disables anti-aliasing for faster drawing

Next, you flip the SDL surface based on its resolution (bits per pixel). Listing 3-14 shows how this is done for an 8-bit RGB surface.

Listing 3-14. Flipping an SDL Surface by Resolution

```
/**
 * Flip SDL Surface by bits per pixel
 */
static void JNI_FlipByBPP (SDL_Surface *surface)
{
  int bpp = surface->format->BitsPerPixel;

  switch ( bpp ) {
    case 8:
      JNI_Flip8Bit (surface);
      break;
    case 16:
      // Flip 16bit RGB (surface);
      break;
    case 32:
      // flip 32 bit RGB (surface);
      break;
    default:
      printf("Invalid depth %d for surface of size %dx%d", bpp, surface->w, surface->h);
  }
}

/**
 * Flip 8bit SDL surface
 */
static void JNI_Flip8Bit(SDL_Surface *surface )
{
  int i;
  int size = surface->w * surface->h;
  int bpp = surface->format->BitsPerPixel;

  unsigned short pixels [size]; // RGB565

  SDL_Color * colors = surface->format->palette->colors;

  for ( i = 0 ; i < size ; i++ ) {
    unsigned char pixel =   ((unsigned char *)surface->pixels)[i];

    pixels[i] = ( (colors[pixel].r >> 3) << 11)
      | ( (colors[pixel].g >> 2) << 5)
      | (colors[pixel].b >> 3);    // RGB565

  }

  DrawIntoTextureRGB565 (pixels, surface->w,  surface->h);

  jni_swap_buffers ();
}
```

Given an SDL surface, you simply check the format's bits per pixel

```
surface->format->BitsPerPixel
```

and based on that value you create an RGB565 array of pixels that can be used by DrawIntoTextureRGB565.

```
for ( i = 0 ; i < size ; i++ ) {
    unsigned char pixel = ((unsigned char *)surface->pixels)[i];

    // RGB565
    pixels[i] = ( (colors[pixel].r >> 3) << 11)
      | ( (colors[pixel].g >> 2) << 5)
      | (colors[pixel].b >> 3);
  }
```

Each pixel consists of a Red, Green, and Blue value extracted from the surface color palette with

```
SDL_Color * colors = surface->format->palette->colors;
RED: colors[pixel].r
GREEN: colors[pixel].g
BLUE: colors[pixel].b
```

To build an RGB565 pixel, discard the least significant bits from each color component.

```
colors[pixel].r >> 3 (8 - 3 = 5)
colors[pixel].g >> 2 (8 - 2 = 6)
colors[pixel].b >> 3 (8 - 3 = 5)
```

Then shift each component into the proper position of a 16-bit value (5+6+5 = 16, hence RGB656).

```
pixels[i] = (RED << 11) | (GREEN << 5) | BLUE
```

Finally, you send the new array to DrawIntoTextureRGB565 along with the image width and height. For the final piece of the puzzle, you need a way to tell whether the surface requires zooming. This can be done at video initialization when the surface is created in the first place. Listing 3-15 shows how to create a software surface using SDL.

Listing 3-15. Zoom Surface Initialization

```
// Should be zoom?
static char zoom = 0;

// Zoom scales [0,1]
static double zoomx = 1.0;
static double zoomy = 1.0;
```

```c
/**********************************************************
 * Image Constructor
 * The image must be a power of 2 (256x256, 512x256,...)
 * to render full screen on the OpenGL texture. If the image
 * is not POT (320x240) it will be scaled
 **********************************************************/
SDL_Surface * JNI_SurfaceNew(int width, int height, int bpp, int flags)
{
  Uint32 rmask = 0, gmask = 0, bmask =0 , amask = 0;

  // texture size & offset
  int realw = 256, realh = 256, offx = 0, offy = 0;

  // Image must be a power of 2 for OpenGL to scale it.
  if ( width > 512 ) {
    Sys_Error("ERROR: INVALID IMAGE WIDTH %d (max POT 512x512)", width);
  }

  // REAL W/H must be the closest POT value to wxh
  // Will scale to 512x256
  // could be 256 but 512 gives better res (slower)
  if ( width > 256 ) realw = 512;

  // size not POT , zoom to closest POT. Choices are:
  // 256x256 (fastest/low res) 512x256 (better res/slower)
  // 512x512 slowest.
  if ( ( ( width != 512 && width != 256) || ( height != 256 ) ) {
    zoom = 1;
    zoomx = realw / (float)width;
    zoomy = realh / (float)height;

    offx = offy = 0;

    printf("WARNING Texture of size %dx%d will be scaled to %dx%d zoomx=%.3f zoomy=%.3f"
      , width, height, realw, realh, zoomx, zoomy);
  }

  // Create the OpenGL texture used to render
  CreateEmptyTextureRGB565 (realw, realh, offx, offy);

  // This is the real surface used by the client to render the video
  return SDL_CreateRGBSurface (SDL_SWSURFACE, width, height, bpp, rmask, gmask, bmask,
amask);
}
```

If the size of the image is not a power of two, then the zoom flag will be set to 1 and the horizontal and vertical zoom factors will be computed. Then, the empty texture will be created by calling `CreateEmptyTextureRGB565` with the width, height, and XY offset values of the texture. Finally, the SDL surface is created by calling `SDL_CreateRGBSurface` with:

- `SDL_SWSURFACE`: It tells SDL to create a software surface.

- *Width, height*: It defines the size of the surface.

- *Bpp*: It defines the bits per pixel (resolution) of the surface (8, 16, 24, or 32).

- *Rmask, gmask, bmask, amask*: These are mask values for the red, green, blue, and alpha (transparency) components of the pixel format. Set them to 0 to let SDL take care of it.

Hybrid Scaler Rules of Thumb

Always keep in mind the following rules of thumb when using a hybrid scaler like this in your games:

- Always set the video size, if you can, to a power of two, such as 256x256 or 512x56. Values above 512 are simply too big for this technique.

- If you cannot set the video size but still want a full screen display, use the SDL software scaler from the previous section to scale to the closest power of two resolution, then use the hardware scaler.

- This scaling technique may not be useful (performance wise) if your video size if greater than 512x512.

Summary

The veil has been lifted to reveal a new frontier of 3D development for Android. The techniques demonstrated in this chapter can help you to bring a large number of 3D PC games to the platform, at an enormous savings in development costs.

In this chapter, you learned a trick to mix OpenGL code in Java. You started by looking at a simple OpenGL example and then moving to a more complex tumbling cubes sample provided by Google. You saw that the sample's rendering process included EGL initialization, the main loop, drawing, buffer swap, and cleanup. Then you saw how to reimplement the cube rendering invoked within the main loop. You learned how to create the cube renderer and cube class used to render the cubes.

Finally, you looked at the limitations of OpenGL ES when it comes to advanced 3D games.

I hope this chapter will help you create your own 3D games for Android with minimal effort and maximum code reuse. This is a prelude to the next chapters, in which you will look at more details about the efficiency, graphics, and portability of the new OpenGL ES version 3.1.

Efficient Graphics and Portability with OpenGL ES

In this chapter, you will learn about portability or multiplatform support in today's mobile graphics development and also how to use the most common features of Open GL ES version 3.1. This is the latest version of OpenGL ES when this manuscript was written and fully supported by the Android SDK version 5.0.1 used in this book.

Today's organizations have vast amounts of code created for OpenGL on the PC, which is not compatible with OpenGL ES for mobile devices. The investment can be significant; some game engines can easily cost millions to develop and take many years of continuous R&D work. So it is only logical that companies want to leverage that code in mobile platforms. In the first part of this chapter you will learn some of the challenges of reusing the OpenGL code built for the PC in your mobile, plus some tricks you can use to save time and cost.

> **Note** All the code included in this chapter was developed, compiled and tested using Eclipse IDE for Java Developers instead of Android Studio 1.0.1 since, when this manuscript was written, NDK and JNI were not supported by Android Studio.

Let's get started.

Portability

Because most organizations have invested significant resources in PC development (including OpenGL and others), it makes no business sense to start from scratch to enter the mobile gaming arena. With a few tricks and tips, your engine PC code can work efficiently in mobile processors. In this section you'll learn these tricks and tips, plus some of the caveats about reusing graphics code in multiple platforms, including the following:

■ *Immediate mode*: This is a technique commonly used in OpenGL on the PC and Mac to render geometry in 3D space. The problem in mobile is that it has been removed for efficiency's sake. If you are reusing graphics code from the PC, it will probably be full of immediate mode calls.

■ *Other less critical issues*: Such as loading textures (which is slightly different in GL ES), display lists, handling attribute state, and others.

■ But first let's look at the issues surrounding immediate mode.

Handling Immediate Mode

Take a look at the following code fragment that renders a square in the XY plane (shown in Figure 4-1):

```
glBegin( GL_QUADS );           /* Begin issuing a polygon */
glColor3f( 0, 1, 0 );          /* Set the current color to green */
glVertex3f( -1, -1, 0 );       /* Issue a vertex */
glVertex3f( -1, 1, 0 );        /* Issue a vertex */
glVertex3f( 1, 1, 0 );         /* Issue a vertex */
glVertex3f( 1, -1, 0 );        /* Issue a vertex */
glEnd();                       /* Finish issuing the polygon
```

The code above is asking to draw 4 vertices (a rectangle or quad) and to fill this geometry with a green color. This code is typical in OpenGL but it will not compile in GL ES. Nevertheless it can be easily rendered in GL ES using arrays and glDrawArrays (which by the way are supported by both GL and GL ES), as you can see in the next fragment:

```
GLfloat q3[] = {
        -1, -1,0,
        -1, 1, 0,
         1, 1, 0,
         1, -1,0
    }; /* array of vertices */
glEnableClientState(GL_VERTEX_ARRAY); /* enable vertex arrays */
glColor3f( 0, 1, 0 );                 /* Set the current color to green */
glVertexPointer(2, GL_FLOAT, 0, q3);
glDrawArrays(GL_TRIANGLE_FAN,0,4);
glDisableClientState(GL_VERTEX_ARRAY);
```

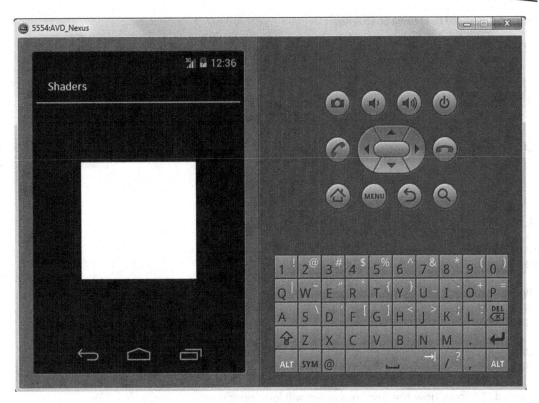

Figure 4-1. Rendering using glDrawArrays

Simple enough, but things get tricky when you need to apply image data to your geometry (also known as texturing). Let's see how this is done on the PC. The following fragment renders a textured quad with traditional OpenGL:

```
glBindTexture (GL_TEXTURE_2D, 13);
glBegin (GL_QUADS);
glTexCoord2f (0.0, 0.0);
glVertex3f (0.0, 0.0, 0.0);
glTexCoord2f (1.0, 0.0);
glVertex3f (10.0, 0.0, 0.0);
glTexCoord2f (1.0, 1.0);
glVertex3f (10.0, 10.0, 0.0);
glTexCoord2f (0.0, 1.0);
glVertex3f (0.0, 10.0, 0.0);
glEnd ();
```

Note that this fragment assumes that texturing has been enabled and that a texture has been uploaded with the ID of 13—perhaps with a call such as

```
glTexImage2D (GL_TEXTURE_2D, 0, GL_RGB, imageWidth, imageHeight, 0, GL_RGB, GL_UNSIGNED_BYTE, imageData)
```

where imageData is an array of unsigned bytes representing RGB values for the texture with ID 13. Listing 4-1 shows the previous fragment re-written using arrays for GL ES.

Listing 4-1. Textured Quad Using GL ES Arrays

```
GLfloat vtx1[] = {
    0, 0, 0,
    0.5, 0, 0,
    0.5, 0.5, 0
    0, 0.5, 0
};

GLfloat tex1[] = {
    0,0,
    1,0,
    1,1,
    0,1
};

glEnableClientState(GL_VERTEX_ARRAY);
glEnableClientState(GL_TEXTURE_COORD_ARRAY);

glVertexPointer(3, GL_FLOAT, 0, vtx1);
glTexCoordPointer(2, GL_FLOAT, 0, tex1);
glDrawArrays(GL_TRIANGLE_FAN,0,4);

glDisableClientState(GL_VERTEX_ARRAY);
glDisableClientState(GL_TEXTURE_COORD_ARRAY);
```

Figure 4-2 shows how the textured quad will look onscreen.

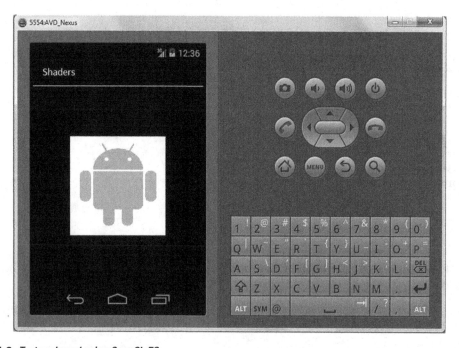

Figure 4-2. Textured quad using OpenGL ES

Drawing textured quads is the most common technique used in OpenGL ES. Furthermore, you can wrap Listing 4-1 in a function and reuse it anywhere you need to draw a textured quad, thereby avoiding the need to repeat Listing 4-1. Thus you have Listing 4-2.

Listing 4-2. Wrapping Textured Quad Drawing Functions

```
void GL_ES_DrawTexturedQuad ( int vertexSize, int texCoordSize
, GLfloat * vtx, GLfloat * texC)
{
  glEnableClientState(GL_VERTEX_ARRAY);
  glEnableClientState(GL_TEXTURE_COORD_ARRAY);

  glVertexPointer(vertexSize, GL_FLOAT, 0, vtx);
  glTexCoordPointer(texCoordSize, GL_FLOAT, 0, texC);

  glDrawArrays(GL_TRIANGLE_FAN,0,4);

  glDisableClientState(GL_VERTEX_ARRAY);
  glDisableClientState(GL_TEXTURE_COORD_ARRAY);
}
```

GL_ES_DrawTexturedQuad can be reused whenever you need a textured quad; thus Listing 4-1 can be rewritten as Listing 4-3.

Listing 4-3. A Simpler Way of Drawing Textured Quads

```
GLfloat vtx[] = {
    0, 0, 0,
    0.5, 0, 0,
    0.5, 0.5, 0
    0, 0.5, 0
};
GLfloat tex[] = {
    0,0,
    1,0,
    1,1,
    0,1
};
GL_ES_DrawTexturedQuad (3, 2, vtx, tex);
```

Listing 4-3 saves you some typing if your code draws a lot of textured quads. Next you'll look at other portability caveats.

Loading Textures

Loading textures is performed in both GL and GL ES with a call to `glTexImage2D`. However, there are differences in the way the image data needs to be handled. In GL ES, all textures must have dimensions in powers of 2. This is not necessarily the case in traditional GL. To overcome this, you could

- Resize the image assets of your game to be powers of 2. This should make startup times faster but can consume time depending on the number of assets.

- Resize images on the fly when loading. This may increase loading times but you won't have to manually resize those images. I would recommend resizing the files to speed up loading times.

When loading textures with `glTexImage2D`, the only supported formats are `GL_ALPHA`, `GL_RGB`, `GL_RGBA`, `GL_LUMINANCE`, or `GL_LUMINANCE_ALPHA` (traditional GL supports many more). Arguments for internal format and format (arguments 3 and 7) must be the same. This is not necessarily the case in GL and is often a common mistake made when porting between both platforms. Thus the correct way of loading pixels in GL ES is

```
glTexImage2D( target, 0, GL_RGBA, width, height, 0, GL_RGBA, GL_UNSIGNED_BYTE, pixels)
```

The bottom line when using `glTexImage2D` is to make sure the pixel format is correct and that it matches the format defined by arguments 3 and 7 of the call.

Display Lists, Server Attributes, and Others

When it comes to display lists and server attributes, there is some bad news: they are not supported by GL ES in any way or form, and there is no easy workaround.

Display lists are sequences of precompiled GL statements that can be called again and again to increase performance. They are commonly used when rendering fonts or repetitive shapes or objects (the pieces of a 3D chess game are commonly rendered using display lists). Fortunately, a display list is not something you will find in every 3D engine out there (3D chess, checkers, and so on. are the most common culprits). If they are used in your code, you must remove them manually.

Server attributes are handled by two calls: `glPushAttrib` and `glPopAttrib`. They don't exist in GL ES; therefore you'll have to manage these states yourself.

Another minor issue is that GL ES only supports `float`. `GLdouble` doesn't exist, so any `GLdouble` should be converted to `GLfloat`; plus all GL function calls ending with a "d" should have the d replaced with f. You can easily do this with

```
#define GLdouble     GLfloat
#define GL_CLAMP     GL_CLAMP_TO_EDGE
#define glClearDepth glClearDepthf
#define glOrtho      glOrthof
```

Also, GL ES only knows glColor4f as the function to create a color; glColor3f, glColor3d, glColor4d or any other color conventions must be converted to glColor4f, like so:

```
#define glColor4fv(a) glColor4f(a[0], a[1], a[2], a[3])
#define glColor3fv(a) glColor4f(a[0], a[1], a[2], 1.0f)
#define glColor3f(a,b,c) glColor4f(a, b, c, 1.0f)
```

These are the most common portability caveats you will find between GL and GL ES. The problem with the preceding approach is that you must change the code to fit the new platform, which, depending on the size of your engine, resources, and time constraints, may not be a viable solution. Here is where library wrappers can help.

Using Library Wrappers

In the previous section, you learned how to deal with GL–to–GL ES portability caveats by changing your code (basically adjusting the immediate mode to use gl arrays instead when running in a mobile processor). That may take time and consume valuable development resources. Another way to deal with PC or Mac game code that needs to be ported to mobile is to simply wrap the code with a GL library wrapper such as NanoGL. I love this library because it allows you to keep your engine code intact (and I mean zero changes to the original code). Then, by adding tiny wrappers, you can add support for I/O events such as screen touch, keyboard, and so on.

NanoGL is truly a life saver, and as a matter of fact, it was written to handle heavy-duty game engines such as Quake I and Quake II. As you will see in the later chapters of this book, you can get these engines running on your phone in no time with zero changes to the original engine code—all thanks to NanoGL. Sound too good to be true? It probably is. NanoGL has some of the caveats of the previous section. NanoGL cannot handle display lists or server state (glPushAttrib/glPopAttrib). Besides these caveats, NanoGL should be able to handle any OpenGL engine you throw at it.

OpenGL ES Compatibility

Android supports several versions of the OpenGL ES API such as:

- OpenGL ES 1.0/1.1: Supported by Android 1.0 and higher.
- OpenGL ES 2.0: Supported by Android 2.2 (API level 8) and higher.
- OpenGL ES 3.0: Supported by Android 4.3 (API level 18) and higher.
- OpenGL ES 3.1: Supported by Android 5.0 (API level 21) and higher.

In this chapter, we focus only on the new version 3.1.

OpenGL ES 3.0 and 3.1

Since August 2012 OpenGL ES 3.0 has been available in the 4.3 or later version of Android SDK and NDK. In June 2014, the OpenGL ES version 3.1 of was completed by Khronos Group. You can download the new version 3.1 specification document from this web page: https://www.khronos.org/registry/gles/#specs31. An introduction to the most important new features in OpenGL 3.1 can be found at: https://www.khronos.org/news/press/khronos-releases-opengl-es-3.1-specification.

> **Note**   Backward compatibility with OpenGL ES 2.0 and 3.0: programmers can add ES 3.1 functionality incrementally to working ES 2.0 and 3.0 applications.

Please refer to this link for the entire list of features: https://www.khronos.org/assets/uploads/developers/library/2014-gdc/Khronos-OpenGL-ES-GDC-Mar14.pdf

The Android Developer Preview "L" introduces support for 64-bit systems and other preview NDK APIs. To use this enhancement you need to download and install NDK Revision 10, such as the android-ndk64-r10 package for your target platform.

Here are the hardware and drivers needed by the Android (since version L) devices supporting OpenGL ES 3.1:

- Intel HD Graphics for Intel Atom Z7300 series

- Intel HD Graphics for Intel Celeron N and J series

- Intel HD Graphics for Intel Pentium N and J series

- Nvidia Tegra K1

Here are the Android devices (since version 4.3) supporting OpenGL ES 3.0:

- Nexus 7 (2013)

- Nexus 4

- Nexus 5

- Nexus 10

- HTC Butterfly S

- HTC One/One Max

- LG G2

- LG G Pad 8.3

- Samsung Galaxy S4 (Snapdragon version)

- Samsung Galaxy Note 3

- Samsung Galaxy Note 10.1 (2014 Edition)

- Sony Xperia Z/ZL

- Sony Xperia Z1

- Sony Xperia Z Ultra

- Sony Xperia Tablet Z

> **Note**   When this book was written, Android SDK version 5.0.1 fully supported the OpenGL ES version 3.1 used in this chapter.

If your application is exclusively for devices that support OpenGL ES 3.0/3.1, you can also specify this in your manifest:

```
<!-- Tell the system this app requires OpenGL ES 3.1. -->
<uses-feature android:glEsVersion="0x00030001" android:required="true" />
```

To use the OpenGL ES 3.0/3.1, the application needs to link to the following library:

- OpenGL ES 3.0/3.1 library: `libGLESv2.lib`

- Here is the OpenGL ES 3.0/3.1 file needed by the application:

    `#include <GLES3/gl3.h>`

Let's see what we can now do with OpenGL ES version 3.1.

Superb Efficiency with OpenGL ES 3.1

This section covers the cutting edge in graphics development: OpenGL ES 3.1. It begins with a brief description of the most important features OpenGL ES 3.1 can offer, including shaders, GLSL, and how they affect the Android platform. Then we take a deeper look into GLSL by creating a neat Android project to render an icosahedron using OpenGL ES 3.1. Let's get started.

OpenGL ES 3.1 emphasizes a programmable 3D graphics pipeline that can create shader and program objects and can write vertex and fragment shaders in the GLSL.

OpenGL ES 3.1 provides the following desirable qualities for current graphics programming:

- A wider range of precision options for use in embedded devices using shading language similar to the desktop OpenGL 2.0.

- Framebuffer objects to simplify surface management and offer a subset of functionality from the desktop FBO.

- One hundred percent backward compatible with OpenGL ES 1.x and built with the latest standards and most advanced ideas available for graphics development.

Android fully implements the OpenGL ES 3.1 specification. However, the following are some caveats you should consider before using this technology to build your games:

- OpenGL ES 3.1 is not supported in all versions of Android. If you are targeting the largest breadth of devices out there, you should stick with OpenGL ES 1.x.

- OpenGL ES 3.1 implements the slickest ideas and technology in graphics rendering; however, that doesn't necessarily mean that the code will be better or run faster.

It does provide a desirable characteristic, nevertheless: it is designed to reduce power consumption in embedded systems such as phones, so it could reduce your game's overall power requirements and provide more efficient graphics rendering. All in all, having a solid knowledge of OpenGL ES 3.1 is a good thing for your résumé. Chances are that if you are a graphics developer looking for a job, the very first thing you'll be asked about in a job interview is your knowledge about shaders and GLSL.

Shaders

A shader is a simple program that describes the traits of either a vertex or a pixel. At the low level, a shader defines a set of software instructions used to calculate rendering effects with a high degree of flexibility. Shaders were created to replace the traditional desktop OpenGL fixed-function pipeline that allowed only common geometry transformation and pixel-shading functions. They provide the following advantages over the traditional desktop OpenGL pipeline:

- Customized effects can be applied for rendering.
- A higher degree of flexibility.
- Simplicity and higher degree of reusability.

There are three basic types of shaders implemented in OpenGL ES 3.1: vertex, fragment, and geometry.

Vertex Shaders

Vertex shaders are run once for each vertex given to the GPU and transform the 3D position in virtual space to the 2D coordinate for on-screen rendering. They can manipulate properties such as position, color, and texture coordinates but cannot create new vertices.

Fragment Shaders

Fragment shaders (also known as pixel shaders) calculate the color of individual pixels. They are typically used for scene lighting and related effects, such as bump mapping and color toning, and are often called many times per pixel for every object that is in the corresponding space.

Geometry Shaders

Geometry shaders can add and remove vertices from a mesh. They are used to generate geometry or to add volumetric detail to existing meshes that would be too costly to process on the CPU.

GLSL

GLSL is the OpenGL ES 3.1 Shading Language for programming vertex and fragment shaders that has been adapted for embedded platforms. It is meant to work together with OpenGL ES 1.1 to minimize the cost and power consumption of embedded devices like smartphones.

> **Tip**   OpenGL ES 3.1 removes fixed-point functionality commonly used in desktop OpenGL and replaces it with shader for power savings critical on smartphones and other embedded systems.

At the implementation level, GLSL is actually two closely related languages: vertex shader and fragment shader.

Vertex Shader Language (VSL)

At its simplest, VSL is a C-style program to manipulate the attributes of a vertex. The following fragment defines a simple vertex shader to set the rendering position to the position of the current vertex:

```
void main(void)
{
  // This is a C++ style comment
 /* This is a C style comment */
  gl_Position = gl_Vertex;
}
```

As you can see, the shader has a C-style syntax with main function where you simply declare GLSL instructions. In this case, you use two built-in variables:

- gl_Position: Sets the position of the vertex to be rendered.
- gl_Vertex: Contains the position of the current vertex being processed.

Fragment Shader Language (FSL)

The FSL is used to change the color attributes (RGBA) of the current pixel. For example, the following fragment sets the color of the current pixel to red RGBA (1, 0, 0, 0):

```
void main(void)
{
   gl_FragColor = vec4(1.0, 0.0, 0.0, 0.0);
}
```

gl_FragColor is the built-in variable used to set the color of the current pixel. As with any programming language, GLSL provides all the things you would expect from a computer language, including:

- *Variables and functions*: All variables and functions must be declared before being used.

- *Basic types*: This includes void, bool, int, float, vec2 (two-component float point vector); boolean or integer 2, 3, or 4 component vectors; 2 × 2, 3 × 3, or 4 × 4 float matrices.

- *Declaration scope*: Determines where the declaration is visible. This includes global and local variables, name spaces, and re-declarations within the same scope.

- *Storage qualifiers*: Qualifiers specified in front of the type—pure traditional C-style—including local variables and constants.

New to GLSL are the following items:

- attribute: Defines the linkage between a vertex shader and OpenGL ES for per-vertex data.

- uniform: Tells that the value does not change across the primitive being processed. It also forms the linkage between a shader, OpenGL ES, and the application.

- varying: Defines that linkage between a vertex shader and a fragment shader for interpolated data.

- *Parameter qualifiers*: These are the qualifiers passed to the arguments of a function, including:

    - in: A parameter is passed into a function.

    - out: A parameter passed back out of a function, but not initialized.

    - inout: A parameter is passed both into and out of a function.

- *Precision qualifiers*: For floating point precision, including highp, mediump, and lowp for high, medium, and low precision, respectively.

- *Variance and the invariant qualifier*: These are used to handle the possibility of getting different values from the same expression in different shaders. It is possible, in independent compilation, that two identical shaders are not exactly the same when they run, in which case there are two qualifiers—invariant and varying—to prevent or allow this.

- *Operators and expressions*: All the common operators and expressions you would expect from your typical programming language (see the following sidebar for more details).

- *Many other powerful features*: These include built-in angle, trigonometry, exponential, matrix, and vector functions plus built-in variables and more.

NEED GLSL HELP?

There is so much to the GLSL language. The best source on GLSL is probably the OpenGL Software Development Kit at `https://www.opengl.org/sdk/docs/man4/index.php`. Another great source on the GLSL syntax is available from the Khronos Group at `www.khronos.org/files/opengles_shading_language.pdf`.

These sites can help you learn more about GLSL features and syntax, so make sure to check them out.

Now let's take a look at how to implement a shader and use it in an Android program.

Anatomy of a Shader

The anatomy of a shader is defined by the following steps:

1. *Create a program*: The first step is to create a shader program to be run within your main program—a program within a program, if you will.

2. *Load the shader*: Once you create the shader, you must load it from a string variable or file.

3. *Attach*: Next, you must attach the shader to the main program.

4. *Link*: This step compiles the shader code and checks for syntax errors.

5. *Optional validation*: It is always a good idea to validate the link status and handle errors appropriately.

6. *Enable and use*: Finally, you can enable it and use it against a set of vertices.

Creating the Shader Program

To create a shader object or program, use the glCreateShader API call. It takes as a parameter a shader type, either GL_VERTEX_SHADER or GL_FRAGMENT_SHADER for vertex or fragment, respectively. glCreateShader returns a non-zero value by which it can be referenced. The following fragment creates two shaders to load a vertex and fragment shaders to draw an icosahedron (described later in this chapter):

```
int          Shader[2]
 // Create 2 shader programs
   Shader[0] = glCreateShader(GL_VERTEX_SHADER);
   Shader[1] = glCreateShader(GL_FRAGMENT_SHADER);

   // Load VertexShader: It has the GLSL code
   LoadShader((char *)VertexShader, Shader[0]);

   // Load fragment shader: FragmentShaderBlue has the GLSL code
   LoadShader((char *)FragmentShaderBlue, Shader[1]);

   // Create the program and attach the shaders & attributes
   int Program  = glCreateProgram();
```

You also make an API call to glCreateProgram that creates an empty program object and returns a non-zero value by which it can be referenced. Shaders must be attached to a program. This provides a mechanism to specify the shader objects that will be linked to create a program. It also provides a means for checking the compatibility of the shaders that will be used to create a program. Next, you load it.

Loading the Shader

A shader object is used to maintain the source code strings that define a shader. For this purpose, you can create a load function that invokes glShaderSource and glCompileShader. glShaderSource takes as arguments the ID of the shader, the number of elements, a string containing the source code to be loaded, and an array of string lengths (NULL in this case). glCompileShader compiles the shader described by its reference ID. The following fragment describes the load function that will be used to draw the icosahedron for an upcoming project:

```
// Simple function to create a shader
void LoadShader(char *Code, int ID)
{
    // Compile the shader code
    glShaderSource  (ID, 1, (const char **)&Code, NULL);
    glCompileShader (ID);

    // Verify that it worked
    int ShaderStatus;
    glGetShaderiv(ID, GL_COMPILE_STATUS, &ShaderStatus);

    // Check the compile status
    if (ShaderStatus != GL_TRUE) {
        printf("Error: Failed to compile GLSL program\n");
        int Len = 1024;
        char Error[1024];
```

```
        glGetShaderInfoLog(ID, 1024, &Len, Error);
        printf("%s\n", Error);
        exit (-1);
    }
}
```

As a bonus, you can also check the compilation status using the API call glGetShaderiv. It takes as arguments a shader ID, a query constant (GL_COMPILE_STATUS, in this case, to check the compilation status), and the status of the query. If the status is not GL_TRUE, then the compilation errors can be extracted by calling glGetShaderInfoLog with the ID of the shader and a string buffer that described the nature of the error. The next step is to attach the shader to a program.

Attaching to the Shader

To attach your shader to the main program, use the API call glAttachShader. It takes as arguments the ID of the program object to which a shader object will be attached plus the shader object that is to be attached, as shown in the following fragment:

```
glAttachShader(Program, Shader[0]);
glAttachShader(Program, Shader[1]);
glBindAttribLocation(Program, 0, "Position");
glBindAttribLocation(Program, 1, "Normal");
```

You also use glBindAttribLocation to associate a user-defined attribute variable in the program object with a generic vertex attribute index. The name of the user-defined attribute variable is passed as a null-terminated string in the last argument. This allows the developer to declare variables in the master program and bind them to variables in the shader code.

Linking the Shader Program

To use the shaders, you must link the program that contains them by calling glLinkProgram with the reference ID of the program. Behind the scenes, OpenGL creates an executable that will run on the programmable fragment processor.

```
// Link
glLinkProgram(Program);
```

Getting the Link Status

The status of the link operation is stored as part of the program object's state. It is always a good idea to check for errors by getting the status of the link using glGetProgramiv, very similar to the way you checked the compilation status but using the GL_LINK_STATUS constant in this particular case. The following fragment demonstrates how to do so:

```
// Validate our work thus far
    int ShaderStatus;
    glGetProgramiv(Program, GL_LINK_STATUS, &ShaderStatus);
    if (ShaderStatus != GL_TRUE) {
```

```
        printf("Error: Failed to link GLSL program\n");
        int Len = 1024;
        char Error[1024];
        glGetProgramInfoLog(Program, 1024, &Len, Error);
        printf("%s\n", Error);
        exit(-1);
    }
```

Optional: Program Validation and Status

You should always validate program objects; it helps to see whether you have syntax errors in your shader code. To validate a program, use the API call glValidateProgram with the reference ID of the program. Next, call glGetProgramiv with the program validation constant GL_VALIDATE_STATUS. The result of the validation is returned in the last argument (ShaderStatus in this case). Then, simply check the status and handle the error accordingly, as shown in the following fragment:

```
glValidateProgram(Program);
glGetProgramiv(Program, GL_VALIDATE_STATUS, &ShaderStatus);

if (ShaderStatus != GL_TRUE) {
    printf("Error: Failed to validate GLSL program\n");
    exit(-1);
}
```

Finally, enable and use the program.

Enabling and Using the Program

To start things off, use glUseProgram with the program ID to install a program object as part of a current rendering state. A program object contains an executable that runs on the vertex processor if it contains one or more shader objects of type GL_VERTEX_SHADER that have been successfully compiled and linked.

```
// Enable the program
glUseProgram                (Program);
glEnableVertexAttribArray   (0);
glEnableVertexAttribArray   (1);
```

Remember the two local attributes (Position and Normal) you declared in the attach step? They must be enabled before they can take effect. By default, all client-side capabilities are disabled, including all generic vertex attribute arrays. If enabled, the values in the generic vertex attribute array will be accessed and used for rendering when calls are made to vertex array commands such as glDrawArrays, glDrawElements, glDrawRangeElements, glArrayElement, glMultiDrawElements, or glMultiDrawArrays.

Now let's put what you have learned so far into practice by building a neat Android project to draw an icosahedron using shaders.

Invoking OpenGL ES 3.1 in Android

Before you jump into the Android project, there are three steps that you should keep in mind when using OpenGL ES 3.1 in Android as opposed to old OpenGL ES versions.

1. The surface view Java class must use a custom context factory to enable 2.0 rendering.

2. The surface view class must use a custom EGLConfigChooser to be able to select an EGLConfig that supports 2.0. This is done by providing a config specification to eglChooseConfig() that has the attribute EGL10.ELG_RENDERABLE_TYPE containing the EGL_OPENGL_ES2_BIT flag set.

3. The surface view class must select the surface's format, then choose an EGLConfig that matches it exactly (with regards to red/green/blue/alpha channels bit depths). Failure to do so will result in an EGL_BAD_MATCH error.

Project Icosahedron

Now you can put your skills to the test with a cool Android project to draw an icosahedron using vertex and fragment shaders. The goals of the exercise are to

■ Demonstrate the use of vertex and fragment shaders using OpenGL ES 3.1.

■ Demonstrate the use of hybrid activities (both Java and C++) to perform the geometry rendering. The project launcher, surface, and rendering thread will be created in Java. All OpenGL ES 3.1 rendering will be performed in C++, using JNI to glue both parts together.

■ Demonstrate Android multi-touch functionality to manipulate the rotation speed (using swipes) and the zooming (using pinching) of the shape.

But before you start, let's take a closer look at an icosahedron.

Reviewing the Shape

An icosahedron is a regular polyhedron with 20 identical equilateral triangular faces, 30 edges, and 12 vertices (see Figure 4-3).

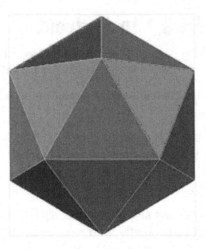

Figure 4-3. Regular icosahedron

The following Cartesian coordinates define the vertices of an icosahedron with edge-length 2, centered at the origin,

(0, ±1, ±φ)

(±1, ±φ, 0)

(±φ, 0, ±1)

where φ = (1+√5)/2, which is the golden ratio (also written as τ). Note that these vertices form five sets of three concentric, mutually orthogonal golden rectangles. In the OpenGL coordinate system, which ranges from [–1, 1] in all axes, the 12 vertices of the icosahedron are defined as the following:

```
// Vertex information
float PtData[][3] = {
{0.5f, 0.0380823f, 0.028521f},
{0.182754f, 0.285237f, 0.370816f},
{0.222318f, -0.2413f, 0.38028f},
{0.263663f, -0.410832f, -0.118163f},
{0.249651f, 0.0109279f, -0.435681f},
{0.199647f, 0.441122f, -0.133476f},
{-0.249651f, -0.0109279f, 0.435681f},
{-0.263663f, 0.410832f, 0.118163f},
{-0.199647f, -0.441122f, 0.133476f},
{-0.182754f, -0.285237f, -0.370816f},
{-0.222318f, 0.2413f, -0.38028f},
{-0.5f, -0.0380823f, -0.028521f},
};
```

The 20 triangular faces (that map to the vertices) are defined as follows:

```
// Face information
unsigned short FaceData[][3] = {
{0,1,2,},
{0,2,3,},
{0,3,4,},
{0,4,5,},
{0,5,1,},
{1,5,7,},
{1,7,6,},
{1,6,2,},
{2,6,8,},
{2,8,3,},
{3,8,9,},
{3,9,4,},
{4,9,10,},
{4,10,5,},
{5,10,7,},
{6,7,11,},
{6,11,8,},
{7,10,11,},
{8,11,9,},
{9,11,10,},
};
```

This information is used by the shaders in your C++ program to render the scene on screen, as you'll see later. But first, let's take a look at the project in more detail.

Tackling the Project

Begin by creating a new Android project to host the code. Start the Eclipse Android project wizard and create a new project, as shown in Figure 4-4.

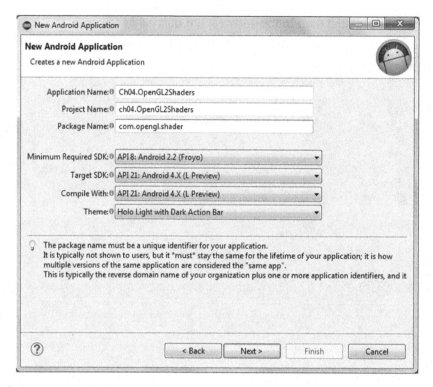

Figure 4-4. Project properties for the icosahedron

Next, perform the following steps:

1. Give the application a name (Ch04.OpenGL2Shaders) and the project a name (ch04.OpenGL2Shaders).

2. Enter a package name (com.opengl.shader in this case).

3. Select a main activity name (ShadersActivity).

4. Select a minimum SDK API number—19 for Android 4.4.2 and 21 for Android 5.0.1 as the target SDK. Click Finish.

Your project should match Figure 4-5.

Figure 4-5. Icosahedron project

Table 4-1 lists the files that compose the project.

Table 4-1. Files for the Icosahedron Project

Language	File Name	Description
XML	AndroidManifest.xml	The file descriptor for the application. It describes the package information, SDK requirements, and the main activity or starting point of the application.
Java	ShadersActivity.java	The entry point of the application. It will be invoked by Android when the application is launched from the device.
Java	ShadersView.java	The GL surface view that contains the OpenGL scene to be rendered.
Java	ViewRenderer.java	The renderer in charge of initializing the scene and drawing the frames.
Java	ConfigChooser.java	The configuration chooser is used to tell Android that you want to use OpenGL ES 3.1.
C++	ico.cpp	The C++ code containing all shader and OpenGL rendering code, plus the icosahedron vertex and face information.
Make	Android.mk	The compilation file for ico.cpp.

> **Tip**   If you get stuck, the source for this project is under ch04.OpenGL2Shaders, available from the publisher.

Now let's look at the files in more detail.

Manifest

Listing 4-4 is the XML file created by the wizard. The most important thing to remember is to use the OpenGL ES 3.1 feature and set the required attribute to true.

Listing 4-4. Android Manifest for the Project

```xml
<?xml version="1.0" encoding="utf-8"?>
<manifest xmlns:android="http://schemas.android.com/apk/res/android"
    package="com.opengl.shader"
    android:versionCode="1"
    android:versionName="1.0" >

<uses-sdk
        android:minSdkVersion="8"
        android:targetSdkVersion="19" />

<uses-feature
        android:glEsVersion="2"
        android:required="true" />

<application
        android:icon="@drawable/ic_launcher"
        android:label="@string/app_name" >
<activity
            android:label="@string/app_name"
            android:name=".ShadersActivity" >
<intent-filter >
<action android:name="android.intent.action.MAIN" />
<category android:name="android.intent.category.LAUNCHER" />
</intent-filter>
</activity>
</application>
</manifest>
```

The next step is the main activity.

Main Activity

Listing 4-5 shows the main program (ShadersActivity) of the icosahedron application. It is simple: when the application starts, the onCreate method is invoked. Within this method, a ShadersView object is created and set as the content view. A set of arguments may be passed to the C++ layer by invoking the setRenderer method with an array of strings.

Listing 4-5. Main Application Activity

```
public class ShadersActivity extends Activity {
  ShadersView view;
  int width;
  int height;

  @Override
  public void onCreate(Bundle savedInstanceState) {
    super.onCreate(savedInstanceState);
      width = getWindowManager().getDefaultDisplay().getWidth();
    height = getWindowManager().getDefaultDisplay().getHeight();

    String[] args = {};

    view = new ShadersView(this);
    view.setRenderer(args, false, 0, 0);

    setContentView(view);
  }
}
```

Now, on to the surface view.

Surface View

The surface view is in charge of creating an OpenGL-capable, hardware-accelerated surface
where objects can be drawn. The process is triggered by the setRenderer method. Because
Android supports a plethora of graphics configuration, resolutions, and hardware specs,
you don't know if the running device is set up to perform OpenGL ES 3.1 calls. Thus you
must create a context factory class ContextFactory, which implements GLSurfaceView.
EGLContextFactory. This class can then be used to tell Android that you want to use an
OpenGL ES 3.1–enabled context by giving the version as an attribute (see Listing 4-6).

```
int[] attrib_list = {EGL_CONTEXT_CLIENT_VERSION, 2, EGL10.EGL_NONE };
EGLContext context = egl.eglCreateContext(display, eglConfig, EGL10.EGL_NO_CONTEXT, attrib_list);
```

Listing 4-6. Surface View Class

```
public class ShadersView extends GLSurfaceView {
  private static final String TAG = "View";

  private String[] mArgs;
  private ViewRenderer mRenderer;

  public ShadersView(Context context) {
    super(context);
  }

  public void setRenderer(String[] args, boolean translucent, int depth,
      int stencil) {
    Log.d(TAG, "Setting startup args & renderer");
```

```
    mArgs = args;

    /*
     * Setup the context factory for rendering. See ContextFactory class
     * definition below
     */
    setEGLContextFactory(new ContextFactory());

    /*
     * We need to choose an EGLConfig that matches the format of our surface
     * exactly. This is going to be done in our custom config chooser. See
     * ConfigChooser class definition below.
     */
    setEGLConfigChooser(translucent ? new ConfigChooser(8, 8, 8, 8, depth,
        stencil) : new ConfigChooser(5, 6, 5, 0, depth, stencil));

    mRenderer = new ViewRenderer();
    setRenderer(mRenderer);
  }

  private static class ContextFactory implements
      GLSurfaceView.EGLContextFactory {
    private static int EGL_CONTEXT_CLIENT_VERSION = 0x3098;

    public EGLContext createContext(EGL10 egl, EGLDisplay display,
        EGLConfig eglConfig) {
      Log.w(TAG, "creating OpenGL ES 3.1 context");

      checkEglError("Before eglCreateContext", egl);

      int[] attrib_list = { EGL_CONTEXT_CLIENT_VERSION, 2, EGL10.EGL_NONE };
      EGLContext context = egl.eglCreateContext(display, eglConfig,
          EGL10.EGL_NO_CONTEXT, attrib_list);

      checkEglError("After eglCreateContext", egl);
      return context;
    }

    public void destroyContext(EGL10 egl, EGLDisplay display,
        EGLContext context) {
      egl.eglDestroyContext(display, context);
    }
  }

  private static void checkEglError(String prompt, EGL10 egl) {
    int error;
    while ((error = egl.eglGetError()) != EGL10.EGL_SUCCESS) {
      Log.e(TAG, String.format("%s: EGL error: 0x%x", prompt, error));
    }
  }
```

```
public void setRotationSpeed(int speed) {
  ViewRenderer.setRotationSpeed(speed);
}

public void setVideoSize(final int width, final int height) {
  queueEvent(new Runnable() {
    public void run() {
      ViewRenderer.initialize(width, height);
    }
  });
}
}
```

ShadersView is also in charge of choosing an EGLConfig that matches the format of the surface exactly. This will be done in the configuration chooser class later. For example, the following fragment tells the surface to use an RGB565 configuration with a depth and stencil size of

```
setEGLConfigChooser( new ConfigChooser(5, 6, 5, 0, depth, stencil) );
```

thereby creating a setting for the surface renderer.

```
mRenderer = new ViewRenderer();
setRenderer(mRenderer);
```

Surface Renderer

The surface renderer (ViewRenderer) contains the following methods, which trigger on different stages of the surface lifecycle, as shown in Listing 4-7:

- onSurfaceCreated: Fires only once when the surface is first created.

- onSurfaceChanged: May fire multiple times whenever a surface change occurs, such as when the device is rotated.

- onDrawFrame: Fires many times by the rendering thread when a frame is drawn.

Listing 4-7. Surface Renderer

```
public class ViewRenderer implements GLSurfaceView.Renderer {

  private static final String TAG = "ViewRenderer";

  // native initializer
  native static void initialize(int width, int height);
  // native draw frame
  native static void drawFrame(int ticks);
  // native set rotation speed
  native static void setRotationSpeed(int speed);
```

```
static {
    System.loadLibrary("icosahedron");
}

@Override
public void onDrawFrame(GL10 arg0) {
    // Log.d(TAG, "onDrawFrame");
    int ticks = (int) System.currentTimeMillis();

    drawFrame(ticks);
}

@Override
public void onSurfaceChanged(GL10 arg0, int w, int h) {
    Log.d(TAG, "onSurfaceChanged w=" + w + " h=" + h);
    initialize(w, h);
}

@Override
public void onSurfaceCreated(GL10 arg0, EGLConfig conf) {
    Log.d(TAG, "onSurfaceCreated " + conf);
}
}
```

ViewRenderer also declares the native C++ methods that will be invoked to initialize the
scene, draw a frame, and set the rotation speed of the object. It also loads the native
C++ library libicosahedron.so, which contains the C++ implementations of these methods:

```
native static void initialize(int width, int height);
native static void drawFrame(int ticks);
native static void setRotationSpeed(int speed);
static {
        System.loadLibrary("icosahedron");
}
```

Next comes the critical GL ES 3.1 configuration chooser.

OpenGL ES 3.1 Configuration Chooser

The configuration chooser is critical to selection of an EGLConfig that supports OpenGL ES 3.1.
ConfigChooser implements the Android interface GLSurfaceView.EGLConfigChooser and
must receive a configuration spec with the attribute EGL10.ELG_RENDERABLE_TYPE containing
the EGL_OPENGL_ES2_BIT flag. With this information, it queries the display for all available
configurations (see Listing 4-8).

```
// Get the number of minimally matching EGL configurations
int[] num_config = new int[1];
egl.eglChooseConfig(display, s_configAttribs2, null, 0, num_config);
```

```
int numConfigs = num_config[0];
// Allocate then read the array of minimally matching EGL configs
EGLConfig[] configs = new EGLConfig[numConfigs];
egl.eglChooseConfig(display, s_configAttribs2, configs, numConfigs, num_config);
```

With this information, it chooses the best configuration that matches the original configuration spec.

Listing 4-8. Configuration Chooser

```
class ConfigChooser implements GLSurfaceView.EGLConfigChooser {
  private static final String TAG = "ConfigChooser";
  private boolean DEBUG = false;

  public ConfigChooser(int r, int g, int b, int a, int depth, int stencil) {
    mRedSize = r;
    mGreenSize = g;
    mBlueSize = b;
    mAlphaSize = a;
    mDepthSize = depth;
    mStencilSize = stencil;
  }

  /*
   * This EGL config specification is used to specify rendering. We use a
   * minimum size of 4 bits for red/green/blue, but perform actual matching
   * in chooseConfig() below.
   */
  private static int EGL_OPENGL_ES2_BIT = 4;
  private static int[] s_configAttribs2 = { EGL10.EGL_RED_SIZE, 4,
      EGL10.EGL_GREEN_SIZE, 4, EGL10.EGL_BLUE_SIZE, 4,
      EGL10.EGL_RENDERABLE_TYPE, EGL_OPENGL_ES2_BIT, EGL10.EGL_NONE };

  public EGLConfig chooseConfig(EGL10 egl, EGLDisplay display) {

    /*
     * Get the number of minimally matching EGL configurations
     */
    int[] num_config = new int[1];
    egl.eglChooseConfig(display, s_configAttribs2, null, 0, num_config);

    int numConfigs = num_config[0];

    if (numConfigs <= 0) {
      throw new IllegalArgumentException("No configs match configSpec");
    }
```

```java
    /*
     * Allocate then read the array of minimally matching EGL configs
     */
    EGLConfig[] configs = new EGLConfig[numConfigs];
    egl.eglChooseConfig(display, s_configAttribs2, configs, numConfigs,
        num_config);

    if (DEBUG) {
      printConfigs(egl, display, configs);
    }
    /*
     * Now return the "best" one
     */
    return chooseConfig(egl, display, configs);
  }

  public EGLConfig chooseConfig(EGL10 egl, EGLDisplay display,
      EGLConfig[] configs) {
    for (EGLConfig config : configs) {
      int d = findConfigAttrib(egl, display, config, EGL10.EGL_DEPTH_SIZE,
          0);
      int s = findConfigAttrib(egl, display, config,
          EGL10.EGL_STENCIL_SIZE, 0);

      // We need at least mDepthSize and mStencilSize bits
      if (d < mDepthSize || s < mStencilSize)
        continue;

      // We want an *exact* match for red/green/blue/alpha
      int r = findConfigAttrib(egl, display, config, EGL10.EGL_RED_SIZE, 0);
      int g = findConfigAttrib(egl, display, config, EGL10.EGL_GREEN_SIZE,
          0);
      int b = findConfigAttrib(egl, display, config, EGL10.EGL_BLUE_SIZE,
          0);
      int a = findConfigAttrib(egl, display, config, EGL10.EGL_ALPHA_SIZE,
          0);

      if (r == mRedSize && g == mGreenSize && b == mBlueSize
&& a == mAlphaSize)
        return config;
    }
    return null;
  }

  private int findConfigAttrib(EGL10 egl, EGLDisplay display,
      EGLConfig config, int attribute, int defaultValue) {

    if (egl.eglGetConfigAttrib(display, config, attribute, mValue)) {
      return mValue[0];
    }
    return defaultValue;
  }
```

```java
    private void printConfigs(EGL10 egl, EGLDisplay display,
        EGLConfig[] configs) {
      int numConfigs = configs.length;
      Log.w(TAG, String.format("%d configurations", numConfigs));
      for (int i = 0; i < numConfigs; i++) {
        Log.w(TAG, String.format("Configuration %d:\n", i));
        printConfig(egl, display, configs[i]);
      }
    }

    private void printConfig(EGL10 egl, EGLDisplay display, EGLConfig config) {
      // code removed for simplicity
      }
    }

    // Subclasses can adjust these values:
    protected int mRedSize;
    protected int mGreenSize;
    protected int mBlueSize;
    protected int mAlphaSize;
    protected int mDepthSize;
    protected int mStencilSize;
    private int[] mValue = new int[1];
}
```

That takes care of the Java side of things; now let's shift gears to the C++ rendering.
Table 4-1 described the native side of the project (contained in the ico.cpp file), which is
the last piece of the puzzle. This file is in charge of the JNI function implementation; it also
contains the source of the shaders, plus scene initialization and rendering. Let's take a look.

Native Icosahedron

The Java native functions declared in ViewRenderer.java are implemented in C++ using the
syntax shown in Listing 4-9.

Listing 4-9. C++ Native Functions for the Project

```cpp
// Java
static {
System.loadLibrary("icosahedron");
}
native static void initialize(int width, int height);
native static void drawFrame(int ticks);
native static void setRotationSpeed(int speed);

// C++
extern "C" {
 JNIEXPORT void JNICALL Java_com_opengl_shader_ViewRenderer_initialize
  (JNIEnv * env, jclass cls, jint w, jint h)
{
      Init(w,h);
}
```

```
JNIEXPORT void JNICALL Java_com_opengl_shader_ViewRenderer_drawFrame
 (JNIEnv * env, jclass cls, jint ticks)
{
     Display(ticks);
}

JNIEXPORT void JNICALL Java_com_opengl_shader_ViewRenderer_setRotationSpeed
 (JNIEnv * env, jclass cls, jint val)
{
     doSetRotationSpeed((double)val);
}
}
```

You have the following three C++ functions:

- Init: To initialize the scene.
- Display: To draw a frame of the scene.
- doSetRotationSpeed: To set the rotation speed.

Before you look at the implementations, you must create the two shader programs, vertex and fragment, which will be used to draw the icosahedron.

Project Shaders

Listing 4-10 declares the two shader programs that will be used to compute the position and color of the vertices and the faces of the icosahedron.

Listing 4-10. Shaders Used in the Icosahedron Project

```
// vertex Shader
attribute vec3 Position;
attribute vec3 Normal;

uniform mat4 Proj;
uniform mat4 Model;
varying vec3 NormVec;
varying vec3 LighVec;

void main(void)
{
vec4 Pos = Model * vec4(Position, 1.0);
gl_Position = Proj * Pos;
NormVec    = (Model * vec4(Normal,0.0)).xyz;
LighVec    = -Pos.xyz;
}

// Fragment Shader
varying highp vec3 NormVec;
varying highp vec3 LighVec;
```

```
void main(void)
{
  lowp vec3 Color = vec3(1.0, 0.0, 0.0);
  mediump vec3 Norm  = normalize(NormVec);
  mediump vec3 Light = normalize(LighVec);
  mediump float Diffuse = dot(Norm, Light);
  gl_FragColor = vec4(Color * (max(Diffuse, 0.0) * 0.6 + 0.4), 1.0);
}
```

Scene Initialization

The scene initialization in Listing 4-11 performs the following steps:

1. It creates two shader programs, vertex, and fragment.

    ```
    Shader[0] = glCreateShader(GL_VERTEX_SHADER);
    Shader[1] = glCreateShader(GL_FRAGMENT_SHADER);
    ```

2. It loads the vertex shader.

    ```
    LoadShader((char *)VertexShader, Shader[0]);
    ```

3. It loads the fragment shader. Note that VertexShader and
    FragmentShaderRed are two strings describing the shaders in
    Listing 3-28 from Chapter 3.

    ```
    LoadShader((char *)FragmentShaderRed, Shader[1]);
    ```

4. It creates the program and attaches the shaders and attributes.

    ```
    Program   = glCreateProgram();
    glAttachShader(Program, Shader[0]);
    glAttachShader(Program, Shader[1]);
    ```

5. It attaches the attributes or variables (Position and Normal) used by
    the master and shader programs to manipulate the vertex and face
    information of the icosahedron.

    ```
    glBindAttribLocation(Program, 0, "Position");
    glBindAttribLocation(Program, 1, "Normal");
    ```

6. It links the program using its program ID, glLinkProgram(Program).

7. It validates the program status by querying the status using the
    GL_VALIDATE_STATUS constant.

    ```
    glValidateProgram(Program);
    glGetProgramiv(Program, GL_VALIDATE_STATUS, &ShaderStatus);
    if (ShaderStatus != GL_TRUE) {
      // handle error
    }
    ```

8. It enables the program plus attributes Position (0) and Normal (1).

```
glUseProgram                (Program);
glEnableVertexAttribArray   (0);
glEnableVertexAttribArray   (1);
```

Listing 4-11. Scene Initialization

```
int Init(int w, int h) {
  width = w;
  height = h;

  LOGD("Init: w=%d h=%d", width, height);

// Vertex shader from listing 3-28
  const char VertexShader[] = "…";

  // Fragment Shader (see listing 3-28)
  const char  FragmentShaderRed[] = "…";

  // Create 2 shader programs
  Shader[0] = glCreateShader(GL_VERTEX_SHADER);
  Shader[1] = glCreateShader(GL_FRAGMENT_SHADER);

  LoadShader((char *) VertexShader, Shader[0]);

  if (id == 2) {
    LoadShader((char *) FragmentShaderBlue, Shader[1]);
  } else {
    LoadShader((char *) FragmentShaderRed, Shader[1]);
  }

  // Create the program and attach the shaders & attributes
  Program = glCreateProgram();

  glAttachShader(Program, Shader[0]);
  glAttachShader(Program, Shader[1]);

  glBindAttribLocation(Program, 0, "Position");
  glBindAttribLocation(Program, 1, "Normal");

  // Link
  glLinkProgram(Program);

  // Validate our work thus far
  int ShaderStatus;
  glGetProgramiv(Program, GL_LINK_STATUS, &ShaderStatus);

  if (ShaderStatus != GL_TRUE) {
    LOGE("Error: Failed to link GLSL program\n");
    int Len = 1024;
    char Error[1024];
```

```
    glGetProgramInfoLog(Program, 1024, &Len, Error);
    LOGE(Error);
    exit(-1);
  }

  glValidateProgram(Program);

  glGetProgramiv(Program, GL_VALIDATE_STATUS, &ShaderStatus);

  if (ShaderStatus != GL_TRUE) {
    LOGE("Error: Failed to validate GLSL program\n");
    exit(-1);
  }

  // Enable the program
  glUseProgram(Program);
  glEnableVertexAttribArray(0);
  glEnableVertexAttribArray(1);

  // Setup the Projection matrix
  Persp(Proj, 70.0f, 0.1f, 200.0f);

  // Retrieve our uniforms
  iProj = glGetUniformLocation(Program, "Proj");
  iModel = glGetUniformLocation(Program, "Model");

  // Basic GL setup
  glClearColor(0.0, 0.0, 0.0, 1.0);
  glEnable ( GL_CULL_FACE);
  glCullFace ( GL_BACK);

  return GL_TRUE;
}
```

Initialization is the first step and it is performed only once. Next, you'll tackle rendering.

Scene Rendering

Scene rendering is performed multiple times when a frame is to be drawn. Listing 4-12 defines the Display C++ function.

Listing 4-12. Scene Rendering

```
void Display(int time) {
  // Clear the screen
  glClear ( GL_COLOR_BUFFER_BIT);

  float Model[4][4];

  memset(Model, 0, sizeof(Model));
```

```
// Set up the Proj so that the object rotates around the Y axis
// We'll also translate it appropriately to Display
Model[0][0] = cosf(Angle);
Model[1][1] = 1.0f;
Model[2][0] = sinf(Angle);
Model[0][2] = -sinf(Angle);
Model[2][2] = cos(Angle);
Model[3][2] = -1.0f;
Model[3][3] = 1.0f;

// Constantly rotate the object as a function of time
int ticks = time;
int thisTicks = ticks - lastTicks; // note delta time
if (thisTicks > 200)
  thisTicks = 200; // throttling
Angle += ((float) thisTicks) * RotationSpeed; // apply animation
lastTicks = ticks; // note for next loop

  // Vertex information
  float PtData[][3] = {
  // see source (removed for simplicity)
  };

  // Face information
  unsigned short FaceData[][3] = {
  // see source (removed for simplicity)
  };

// Draw the icosahedron
glUseProgram(Program);
glUniformMatrix4fv(iProj, 1, false, (const float *) &Proj[0][0]);
glUniformMatrix4fv(iModel, 1, false, (const float *) &Model[0][0]);

glVertexAttribPointer(0, 3, GL_FLOAT, 0, 0, &PtData[0][0]);
glVertexAttribPointer(1, 3, GL_FLOAT, GL_TRUE, 0, &PtData[0][0]);

glDrawElements(GL_TRIANGLES, sizeof(FaceData) / sizeof(unsigned short),
GL_UNSIGNED_SHORT, &FaceData[0][0]);
}
```

The Display C++ function performs the following steps:

1. It clears the screen with glClear (GL_COLOR_BUFFER_BIT);.

2. It creates a model matrix of float Model[4][4] to set up a projection so that the object rotates around the Y axis. It also translates it appropriately to display.

3. It then constantly rotates the object as a function of time.

4. It enables the program with glUseProgram (Program);.

5. It binds the shader attributes Position (iProj) and Normal (iModel)
    to the projection (Proj) and Model matrices.

    ```
    glUniformMatrix4fv       (iProj, 1, false, (const float *)&Proj[0][0]);
    glUniformMatrix4fv       (iModel, 1, false, (const float *)&Model[0][0]);
    ```

6. It sets the icosahedron vertex information with

    ```
    glVertexAttribPointer    (0, 3, GL_FLOAT, 0, 0, &PtData[0][0]);
    glVertexAttribPointer    (1, 3, GL_FLOAT, GL_TRUE, 0, &PtData[0][0]);
    ```

7. Finally, it draws the icosahedron using the GL_TRIANGLES and the face
    information array described at the beginning of the project.

    ```
    glDrawElements (GL_TRIANGLES, sizeof(FaceData) / sizeof(unsigned short),
    GL_UNSIGNED_SHORT, &FaceData[0][0]);
    ```

Setting the Rotation Speed

The rotation speed function in Listing 4-13 is a bonus C++ call that will be used in the next
section to change the rotation speed whenever a finger is swiped in the display. To do so,
it updates a global variable RotationSpeed, which is in turn used by the Display function to
update the angle of the Model matrix used by the shaders. Because RotationSpeed is read
by multiple threads, it is declared as volatile, which tells the compiler to always re-read from
memory when used.

Listing 4-13. Setting the Rotation Speed

```
volatile float RotationSpeed = 0.001f; // Rotation speed of our object
void doSetRotationSpeed(double val)
{
    // we'll make the slowest it goes 0.001, and
    // the fastest 0.01
    double slowest = -0.005;
    double fastest = 0.005;
    double range = fastest - slowest;
    RotationSpeed = (float)(slowest + ((range*val)/100.0f));
}
```

This takes care of the C++ side of things. As a bonus, let's add swipe and pinch zooming
functionality with Android's multi-touch APIs.

Adding Swipe and Multi-Touch Pinch for Zooming

As a bonus, this section describes how to use the Android multi-touch APIs to increase the rotation speed of the icosahedron by the following:

- Increasing the speed whenever finger-swiped to the right or decreasing it when swiping to the left. The rotation switches from left to right whenever a threshold value is reached.

- Zooming the shape in or out whenever pinching inward or outward with two fingers.

Listing 4-14 describes the additions to the ShadersActivity class to perform such tasks.

Listing 4-14. Swipe and Pinch Zooming with Multi-Touch

```
// default rotation speed
int speed = 10;

// pointer 1,2 XY coords
float p1X, p1Y, p2X, p2Y;

// deltas
float DX1, DX2;

// # of fingers
int fingers = 0;

@Override
public boolean onTouchEvent(MotionEvent e) {
  int count = e.getPointerCount();
  int action = e.getAction();
  float X1 = 0f, Y1 = 0f, X2 = 0f, Y2 = 0f;

// finger 1 down
  if (action == MotionEvent.ACTION_DOWN) {
    p1X = e.getX(0);
    p1Y = e.getY(0);
    fingers = 1;
  }

// finger 2 down
  if (action == MotionEvent.ACTION_POINTER_2_DOWN) {
    p2X = e.getX(1);
    p2Y = e.getY(1);
    fingers = 2;
  }

  // pointer 1 up
  if (action == MotionEvent.ACTION_UP) {
    X1 = e.getX(0);
    Y1 = e.getY(0);
    DX1 = X1 - p1X;
```

```java
      X2 = e.getX(1);
      Y2 = e.getY(1);
      DX2 = X2 - p2X;
   }


// 1 or 2 up
   if (action == MotionEvent.ACTION_UP
       || action == MotionEvent.ACTION_POINTER_2_UP) {

     if (fingers == 1) {
       // Swipe
       setRotationSpeed(DX1);
     } else if (fingers == 2) {
       // Pinching
       setPinch(DX1, DX2);
     }
     p1X = p1Y = p2X = p2Y = DX1 = DX2 = 0f;
     fingers = 0;
   }
   return super.onTouchEvent(e);
}


// Pinch: Set Zoom
private void setPinch(float DX1, float DX2) {
   // Pinch inwards: zoom in
   if (DX1 > 0 && DX2 < 0) {
     width *= 0.6;
     height *= 0.8;
     view.setVideoSize(width, height);
   } else {
// Pinch outwards: zoom out
     width *= 1.4;
     height *= 1.2;
     view.setVideoSize(width, height);
   }
}


// Swipe Left/right: Set rotation speed
// 0-50 left, 50-100 right
private void setRotationSpeed(float DX) {
   if (DX < 0) {
     speed -= 20;
   } else {
     speed += 20;
   }
   // clamp 0-100
   if (speed < 0)
     speed = 0;
   if (speed > 100)
     speed = 100;

   view.setRotationSpeed(speed);
}
```

To listen for touch events, the following activity can overload the Android method:

```
public boolean onTouchEvent(MotionEvent e)
```

The MotionEvent type contains all the information you need to access single or multi-touch attributes of the event. Among the most important are the following:

- getPointerCount: Returns the number of pointers (or fingers) on-screen.
- getAction: Returns the action constant being performed, such as:
  - ACTION_DOWN when the first pointer goes down.
  - ACTION_UP when the first pointer goes up.
  - ACTION_MOVE when the first pointer is dragged.

Android supports up to four simultaneous pointers, thus when a second pointer goes down, the action returned will be ACTION_POINTER_2_DOWN, and so forth. When the user swipes a finger, the pointer count will be 1. In that case, you simply save the XY coordinates of the finger and set the number of fingers to 1.

```
// finger 1 down
if (action == MotionEvent.ACTION_DOWN) {
  p1X = e.getX(0);
  p1Y = e.getY(0);
  fingers = 1;
}
```

If pinching, the pointer count will be 2 and the action will be ACTION_POINTER_2_DOWN when the second finger goes down. In such case, you save the down coordinates of the second pointer by calling MotionEvent.getX and MotionEvent.getY with the index of the desired pointer. Also, set the number of fingers to 2.

```
// finger 2 down
if (action == MotionEvent.ACTION_POINTER_2_DOWN) {
  p2X = e.getX(1);
  p2Y = e.getY(1);
  fingers = 2;
}
```

Finally, when the swipe or pinch gesture completes, the MotionEvent.ACTION_UP or MotionEvent.ACTION_POINTER_2_UP actions fire. Here, you calculate the delta coordinates for both fingers in the X and Y coordinates.

```
X1 = e.getX(0);
Y1 = e.getY(0);
DX1 = X1 - p1X;
X2 = e.getX(1);
Y2 = e.getY(1);
DX2 = X2 - p2X;
```

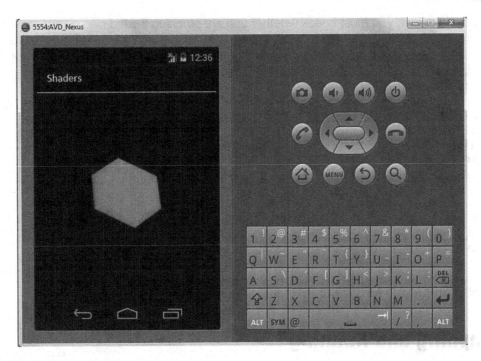

Figure 4-6. Icosahedron in action

Next, you simply check the number of active fingers. A value of 1 indicates a swipe, 2 indicates a pinch. If swiping, you call the setRotationSpeed(DX1) function with the delta coordinates for the first finger in the X axis. If pinching, you call setPinch(DX1, DX2) with the deltas for both fingers in the X coordinate.

When swiping to the left, the delta X value is negative; it is positive when swiping to the right. In either case, you decrease or increase the rotation speed and call the view's setRotationSpeed function, which invokes doSetRotation in C++.

```
if (DX < 0) {
  speed -= 20;
} else {
  speed += 20;
}
// clamp 0-100
if (speed < 0)
  speed = 0;
if (speed > 100)
  speed = 100;
view.setRotationSpeed(speed);
```

For a pinch gesture, you must check whether you are pinching inward or outward. When the deltas are DX1 > 0 && DX2 < 0, you have an inward pinch or zoom in; otherwise, it's a zoom out. In either case, you modify the width and height of the display by an arbitrary factor and invoke the view's setVideoSize(width, height) method. This method invokes the C++ Init(w,h) subroutine.

```
// Pinch inwards: zoom in
if (DX1 > 0 && DX2 < 0) {
  width *= 0.6;
  height *= 0.8;
  view.setVideoSize(width, height);
} else {
  // Pinch outwards: zoom out
  width *= 1.4;
  height *= 1.2;
  view.setVideoSize(width, height);
}
```

Now let's compile and run the project in the device.

Compiling and Running

To compile the native library, start the Cygwin console in Windows, change to the project folder ch04.OpenGL2Shaders, and use the Android compilation script.

```
$ ndk-build
```

The compilation script Android.mk is very simple, as shown in the following fragment. It defines a module called libicosahedron that is bound to the libraries—log (for text logging) and GLESv2 for OpenGL ES 3.1. When compilation completes, the shared library libicosahedron.so will be created in the libs/armeabi folder of your project.

```
LOCAL_PATH:= $(call my-dir)
include $(CLEAR_VARS)
LOCAL_MODULE    := libicosahedron
LOCAL_CFLAGS    := -Werror
LOCAL_SRC_FILES := ico.cpp
LOCAL_LDLIBS    := -llog -lGLESv2
include $(BUILD_SHARED_LIBRARY)
```

The library can now be loaded within Java with the system call of System.loadLibrary("icosahedron ").

You're done! Connect the device to your computer, create a run configuration for the project, and launch it in your device. The result is shown in Figure 4-6. Try swiping a finger to the left or right to change the rotation speed or pinching to zoom in/out—and have some fun with OpenGL 3.0/3.1.

Summary

In this chapter, you learned about the challenges of portability and multiplatform support required to leverage PC code into mobile platforms. The PC code investment can be significant, so it's only logical that organizations want to reuse PC code as much as possible. This translates into savings in time and costs and thus an increased return of investment.

You also learned about the most important features of the new OpenGL ES 3.1 and how they can be used to create a complex shape using vertex and fragment shaders.

At the time of writing this book, OpenGL ES version 3.1 was fully supported by Android SDK version 5.0.1, so it could be easily tested.

In the following chapters, you'll learn how easy it is to bring powerful PC hardware-accelerated game engines to the platform in record time and with minimal development costs. Carry on.

## Chapter 5

3D Shooters for Doom

This chapter looks at another great and very popular PC game: Doom. In 1993, Doom came along shortly after Wolfenstein 3D and put id Software at the lead of the pack in 3D graphics gaming for the PC. In this chapter, you'll learn how to bring the open source Doom engine (PrBoom) to the Android platform.

The chapter starts with fun facts about Doom itself, which will help you understand the breadth of this project. Bringing a PC game to a mobile device with little change to the original code is a difficult task. As you can probably tell from reading the previous chapters, I embrace the Java/C power combo for maximum performance.

Next, you'll dig into the game, which is divided into two big layers: Java and native. This makes sense, because the game is a mix of original C wrapped in Java code. The Java layer contains classes for the main activity, audio, and JNI interface (what I call the native interface class). The native layer has the native method implementations (using JNI) plus changes to the original C code. The latter is required to glue together both layers and requires less than 50 lines of new code (I consider this to be the most difficult to follow, as there are close to 80,000 lines of original C code, but I will explain the new C code as clearly as possible).

Finally, you get to compilation and deployment; then you can play Doom in the emulator! You will learn awesome tips for native library compilation—a subject that is obscure to the average Java developer.

This is a long and complex chapter, and I have tried my best to make it as simple and clean as possible. For the sake of simplicity, I have omitted some of the lengthier code. Even so, there are some big listings throughout this chapter and a lot of things to cover. To make the most of this chapter, you should grab the chapter source code distributed with this book. The project has been built with Eclipse ADT with the Android SDK 5.0.1 for Windows and can be imported into your workspace. The source will help you to understand the layout of the resources as you read through the chapter.

> **Note** All the code included in this chapter was developed, compiled and tested using Eclipse IDE for Java Developers instead of Android Studio 1.0.1 since, when this manuscript was written, NDK and JNI were not supported by Android Studio.

The Sky Is the Limit with the Java/C Power Combo

The goal here is not to explain how the game itself works (that would take a complete book), but to show the kinds of things that can be accomplished by combining the elegant object-oriented features of Java with the raw power of C. Most Java developers dismiss procedural languages like C, failing to see what can be accomplished when this duo coexists harmoniously. The trick is to find the right balance that combines the best of both worlds to solve a complex task with minimal time and effort. Here, you will learn how a task that would take a team of Java developers possibly months to complete can be done in a matter of days by someone who understands that object-oriented and procedural languages are not enemies, but simply pieces of the same puzzle.

Consider Tables 5-1 and 5-2. They show the total number of lines of new Java code plus the number of lines inserted in the existing C code in Doom for Android.

Table 5-1. *Estimated Number of Lines for Java Files of Doom for Android*

File	Description	Lines of Code
DoomClient.java	Main game activity	700
DialogTool.java	Methods to create help dialogs	300
DoomTools.java	Miscellaneous helper subs	450
GameFileDownloader.java	A class to install game files to the SD card	180
WebDownload.java	Web download tool	200
AudioManager.java	Singleton for audio management	200
AudioClip.java	Wrapper for Android MediaPlayer to play sounds	110

Table 5-2. *Estimated Number of Lines Changed from the Original Doom C Code*

File	Description	Lines of Code
jni_doom.c (new)	Implementation of the JNI native methods plus C to Java callbacks	450
i_sound.c	C to Java callbacks to send sound events to Java	3
s_sound.c	C to Java callbacks to send sound events to Java	6
i_video.c	C to Java callbacks to send video events to Java	10

The following is the rundown of the estimated totals:

- ◼ Total number of lines of new Java code = 2,140
- ◼ Total number of lines of original C code = 80,000
- ◼ Total number of lines of new C code = 469

The bottom line? A single developer has managed to reuse about 80,000 lines of C code, thus bringing a PC game to Android with a few thousand lines of new code in a couple of days. Imagine the potential savings in development cost and time. Now compare this to a team of three developers trying to port the 80,000 lines of raw C to pure Java. It would probably take them months of head-pounding work with no financial gain (as the code is open sourced); this simply makes no sense. I hope that at this point you understand why this chapter is my personal favorite and a must-read for the aspiring Android game developer. So get the source code for the chapter—and let's get started.

Bringing Doom to a Mobile Device

I was excited about the challenge of bringing the great game of Doom to the mobile platform. But I had my doubts that this could even be achieved once I looked at the complexity and the amount of original C code. Listing 5-1 shows a portion of the total number of lines of C code of the popular Doom engine, PrBoom (dated 2008 and available from `http://prboom.sourceforge.net/`).

I knew I had two choices for this project:

- Port the C code line by line to Java. I even started porting a few files to Java. Believe me when I say that this is not a good idea. The amount of time that it would take to do this makes the project unfeasible, especially considering that the hard work must be done *pro bono*.

- Find a way to pack the game as a dynamic shared object (DSO) and call it from Java using JNI. This option seems to be simpler and quicker, but it requires expert knowledge of C and JNI, as well as changes to the original game to glue together both languages.

Given these two options, the latter is the best approach to the problem, so I decided to build a DSO and glue it to Java with JNI.

Listing 5-1. Portion of Code for the PrBoom Doom Engine (Approximately 80,000 Lines in Total)

```
$ wc -l *.c
   1585 am_map.c
    554 d_client.c
   3093 d_deh.c
    140 d_items.c
   1744 d_main.c
    759 d_server.c
     48 doomdef.c
    108 doomstat.c
     85 dstrings.c
    668 f_finale.c
    202 f_wipe.c
   2979 g_game.c
   2717 gl_main.c
    957 gl_texture.c
    767 hu_lib.c
   1593 hu_stuff.c
    866 mmus2mid.c
    467 p_ceilng.c
```

```
// ...
    450 r_fps.c
    649 r_main.c
    788 r_patch.c
    468 r_plane.c
    854 r_segs.c
     56 r_sky.c
   1077 r_things.c
    714 s_sound.c
    245 sounds.c
    374 st_lib.c
   1160 st_stuff.c
    128 tables.c
   1037 v_video.c
     38 version.c
    166 w_memcache.c
    335 w_mmap.c
    476 w_wad.c
   1968 wi_stuff.c
    123 z_bmalloc.c
    705 z_zone.c
  73176 total

$ wc -l *.h
    111 am_map.h
    209 config.h
   1118 d_deh.h
    707 d_englsh.h
    125 d_event.h
     59 d_items.h
     82 d_main.h
    214 d_net.h
    234 d_player.h
     94 d_think.h
     59 d_ticcmd.h
    204 doomdata.h
// ...
     64 r_bsp.h
    109 r_data.h
    428 r_defs.h
     45 r_demo.h
    163 r_draw.h
    174 r_filter.h
    100 s_sound.h
    305 sounds.h
    209 st_lib.h
    102 st_stuff.h
     93 tables.h
    207 v_video.h
     40 version.h
    146 w_wad.h
     64 wi_stuff.h
```

```
   52 z_bmalloc.h
  131 z_zone.h
13460 total
```

As I've noted, I chose to use the PrBoom Doom engine. Even though the game was created by id Software and released under the GNU license in 1993 (see http://en.wikipedia.org/wiki/Doom_(video_game)), there are many Doom engines out there. I did try a few engines before settling on PrBoom.

The first engine I tried was the original code from id Software—after all, it is the original creator. But I had a lot of trouble with id Software's Linux implementation of the game due to two main issues:

- *Color palette*: The Linux flavor supports an 8-bit color palette, which looks pretty bad on 32-bit machines. This code was written for old machines (it has not been updated for a long time). There should be a more modern implementation out there.

- *Sine and cosine tables*: These are used for ray casting. I had many compiler idiosyncrasies (using the CodeSourcery GCC 4.3.*x* compiler) where these tables, which have hard-coded values, were not filled in correctly, making sprites go through walls or move in the wrong way and creating many other display problems.

PrBoom is a modern Doom engine. It is highly portable, although it is much bigger than the original game. I found it to be the best choice due to the plethora of platforms it has been ported to and the powerful support available for it from the developer community.

Game Architecture for Doom

When the user starts the game, the main activity, org.doom.DoomClient, will start (see Figure 5-1). This activity is bound to the other pieces in the following manner:

- The main activity is bound to the device UI through an XML layout (doom.xml). This layout defines an image buffer used to display the graphics and a set of controller buttons for navigation (see the "Game Layout" section for details).

- The Doom engine is written in C and compiled as a DSO (libdoom_jni.so). All communication with the DSO goes through the JNI layer (or native interface class Natives.java). Events are cascaded back to the main activity, which dispatches them to their respective handler. Game files are read from the SD card by the DSO, which handles all game aspects except sound.

- Sound requests are delegated by the native library to the native interface class to the main activity and finally to the sound classes, which plays them using the Android MediaPlayer.

- Video buffers (pixels) are cascaded by the native library to the native interface class to the main activity, which renders them into the ImageView of the layout XML.

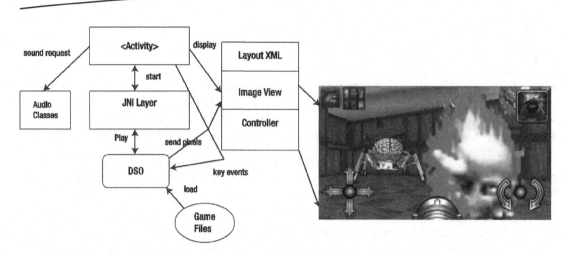

Figure 5-1. Doom for Android architecture

This process continues in an endless loop where key and touch events are dispatched back to the DSO, which updates the game accordingly.

The game is composed of the following Java packages:

- org.doom: This is the main game package and it contains the main activity DoomClient.java. This class controls the application life cycle and the key and touch events, dispatches sound and music requests to the audio classes, and dispatches user events to the DSO through the native interface class.

- doom.audio: This package contains the audio classes AudioManager and AudioClip.

  - AudioManager: This class is in charge of playing sounds and background music using AudioClip. It also caches sounds for better performance.

  - AudioClip.java: This class is capable of playing, stopping, and looping a sound using the Android MediaPlayer. Sound files use the WAVE format.

- doom.jni: This JNI package contains the native interface class Natives.java. This class is a two-way pipe for all access with the DSO. This includes native Java methods and C to Java callbacks.

- doom.util: This package contains the following utility classes:

  - DialogTool.java: This class contains miscellaneous dialogs to start the game and install shareware game files, message boxes, and other items.

  - DoomTools.java: This class contains basic game constants and commonly used subroutines.

- GameFileDownloader.java: This class is capable of downloading shareware game files from the Internet into the SD card.

- LibraryLoader.java: This class loads the DSO, which is required before the native methods can be invoked.

- WebDownload.java: This is a web download tool used by the GameFileDownloader class.

Again, before you look at these components in more detail, make sure you have the chapter code at hand; most of the listings have been stripped down for simplicity.

Java Main Activity

The main activity class is invoked when the user starts the game and controls the life cycle of the application. In Doom, this life cycle is handled by the following:

- *Creation handler*: This handler is implemented by onCreate and it is called when the activity is first created. It sets the UI layout XML (doom.xml) and initializes the game.

- *Menu handlers*: Here you have onCreateOptionsMenu and onOptionsItemSelected. The first method creates the game menu and the latter processes the menu when the user selects an option.

- *Key and touch handlers*: These methods receive key and touch events and dispatch them to the right JNI component.

- *Native callback handlers*: These methods receive video and sound updates from the native interface and dispatch them.

- *Controller toolbar*: The controller toolbar is a set of image buttons displayed at the bottom of the screen for navigation. It is helpful for devices that do not have a keyboard.

Creation Handler

The creation handler is defined by onCreate (see Listing 5-2). For Doom, this method performs the following steps:

1. Sets the display to full screen and hides the title.

2. Sets the content view layout to R.layout.doom, which maps to doom.xml.

3. Gets a reference to the video buffer (R.id.doom_iv), which will be used to display the pixels sent by the DSO.

4. Sets the navigation controls.

Listing 5-2. Main Activity Life Cycle

```
public void onCreate(Bundle savedInstanceState) {
    super.onCreate(savedInstanceState);

    // Full screen
    getWindow().setFlags(WindowManager.LayoutParams.FLAG_FULLSCREEN,
            WindowManager.LayoutParams.FLAG_FULLSCREEN);

    // No title
    requestWindowFeature(Window.FEATURE_NO_TITLE);

    setContentView(R.layout.doom);

    mView = (ImageView)findViewById(R.id.doom_iv);

    if (mGameStarted) {
        setGameUI();
        setupPanControls();
        return;
    }

    // Pan controls
    setupPanControls();

}
```

onCreate() is the first function called when the game starts, and it is called only once while the application is in memory. Next, let's look at the game layout loaded by this function.

Game Layout

GUIs in Android are defined by XML layouts, where visual components are placed in a variety of layout schemes. Doom's layout (doom.xml) is a relative layout, which has widgets placed relative to each other (meaning they can overlap depending on the widget size). The master layout contains an image view and two table layouts.

In Android, an image view encapsulates an array of pixels representing an image. The great thing about image views is that they have efficient automatic resize capabilities. This allows the game to be resized on the fly!

The two table layouts are for the navigation controls. The first table layout defines a three-row table that contains image buttons for up, down, left, and right navigation. The second table layout is a one-row table that contains buttons for the level map, object pick up, and strafing left and right.

Listing 5-3 shows Doom's relative layout XML. The most important attributes are explained in Table 5-3.

Listing 5-3. Doom Game UI Layout doom.xml

```xml
<?xml version="1.0" encoding="utf-8"?>
<RelativeLayout
    xmlns:android="http://schemas.android.com/apk/res/android"
    android:layout_width="fill_parent"
    android:layout_height="fill_parent"
    >

    <!-- GAME IMAGE -->
    <ImageView android:id="@+id/doom_iv"
        android:layout_width="fill_parent"
        android:layout_height="fill_parent"
        android:adjustViewBounds="true"
        android:visibility="visible"
        android:background="@drawable/doom"
        android:focusableInTouchMode="true"
        android:focusable="true"/>

    <!-- Nav Controls -->
    <TableLayout android:id="@+id/pan_ctls"
            android:layout_width="wrap_content"
            android:layout_height="wrap_content"
            android:layout_alignParentBottom="true"
            android:layout_alignParentLeft="true"
            android:visibility="gone"
            android:focusable="false"
            android:focusableInTouchMode="false">

        <TableRow>
        <ImageButton android:id="@+id/btn_upleft"
            android:layout_width="wrap_content"
            android:layout_height="wrap_content"
            android:background="#00000000"
            android:layout_margin="0px"
            android:src="@drawable/blank"
            />
        <ImageButton android:id="@+id/btn_up"
            android:layout_width="wrap_content"
            android:layout_height="wrap_content"
            android:src="@drawable/up"
            android:background="#00000000"
            android:layout_margin="0px"
            />
        <ImageButton android:id="@+id/btn_upright"
            android:layout_width="wrap_content"
            android:layout_height="wrap_content"
            android:src="@drawable/blank"
            android:background="#00000000"
            android:layout_margin="0px"
            />
        </TableRow>
    </TableLayout>
```

```
    <!-- Other controls: Map, Open, strafe -->
     <!--  This XML has been removed for simplicity -->
     <!-- See the file doom.xml for details -->
</RelativeLayout>
```

Table 5-3. *Main Attributes of doom.xml*

Attribute	Meaning
android:id="@+id/doom_iv"	Defines the ID of the widget, which can be used for programmatic access. The format must be @+id/NAME.
android:layout_width="fill_parent"	Defines the width of the widget. The values can be fill_parent or wrap_content.
android:focusableInTouchMode="true"	Specifies that the widget should be focusable and receive touch events from the main activity.
android:focusable="true"	Specifies that the widget should be focusable and receive key events from the main activity.
android:src="@drawable/up"	Defines the bitmap source of the widget (applies to image view only). The format is @drawable/NAME where NAME is the bitmap filename saved under the res/drawable folder of the project.
android:layout_alignParentBottom="true"	Tells the relative layout to align the widget to the bottom of the parent, possibly overlapping other widgets.
android:layout_alignParentLeft="true"	Tells the relative layout to align the widget to the left of the parent, possibly overlapping other widgets.
android:visibility="gone"	Sets the visibility of the widget. Possible values are visible (default value) or gone (indicates the widget occupies no space).

Once the GUI is all set, the next step is to provide a menu and handlers for the application.

Menu and Selection Handlers

The application menu can be easily defined by overriding the following methods:

- onCreateOptionsMenu(Menu menu): Override this method to add items to the menu. To do this, use menu.add(groupId, itemId, order, Menu Label), where groupId is the ID of the group for this item. This can be used to define groups of items for batch state changes. itemId is the unique item ID. order is the order for the item.

- onOptionsItemSelected(MenuItem item): Override this method to process menu selections. The item selected can be obtained with item.getItemId().

The following menus are defined for Doom (see Listing 5-4):

- *Start*: To run the native game loop.

- *Install Game*: To download and install game files.

- *Navigation*: To switch the navigation controls between the keyboard and touch screen.

- *Exit*: To quit the application.

Listing 5-4. Game Menu and Selection

```
public boolean onCreateOptionsMenu(Menu menu) {
    super.onCreateOptionsMenu(menu);
    menu.add(0, 0, 0, "Start").setIcon(R.drawable.icon);
    menu.add(0, 2, 2, "Install Game").setIcon(R.drawable.install);
    menu.add(0, 3, 3, "Navigation").setIcon(R.drawable.nav);
    menu.add(0, 6, 6, "Exit").setIcon(R.drawable.exit);
    return true;
}

/**
 * Menu selection
 */
public boolean onOptionsItemSelected(MenuItem item) {
    super.onOptionsItemSelected(item);
    switch (item.getItemId()) {
    case 0:
        if ( mGameStarted) {
            MessageBox("Game already in progress.");
            return true;
        }
        mMultiPlayer = false;
        showLauncherDialog(this, mMultiPlayer);

        return true;
    case 2:
        if ( mGameStarted) {
            MessageBox("Can't install while game in progress.");
            return true;
        }

        // SD card required
        if ( ! DoomTools.checkSDCard(this) ) return true;

        // Download Game file
        DialogTool.showDownloadDialog(this);
        return true;
```

```
    case 3:
        DialogTool.showNavMethodDialog(this);
        return true;

    case 6:
        // Exit
        DoomTools.hardExit(0);
        return true;

    }
    return false;
}
```

Key and Touch Event Handlers

Key and touch handlers can be overridden to process key and touch events. Doom handles key and touch events as follows (see Listing 5-5):

- The Android keyCode is first translated to an ASCII key symbol by calling int sym = DoomTools.keyCodeToKeySym(keyCode).

- The ASCII symbol is then sent to the DSO through the native interface class Natives.keyEvent(EVENT_TYPE, SYMBOL) where the event type must be either Natives.EV_KEYUP or Natives.EV_KEYDOWN. Note that any errors in the native side (such as a missing symbol or invalid signature) will throw an UnsatisfiedLinkError.

Listing 5-5. Key and Touch Handlers

```
public boolean onKeyUp(int keyCode, KeyEvent event) {
    //
    if (keyCode == KeyEvent.KEYCODE_MENU) {
        return false;
    }

    int sym = DoomTools.keyCodeToKeySym(keyCode);

    try {
        Natives.keyEvent(Natives.EV_KEYUP, sym);

    } catch (UnsatisfiedLinkError e) {
        // Should not happen
        Log.e(TAG, e.toString());
    }
    return false;
}
```

```
public boolean onKeyDown(int keyCode, KeyEvent event) {
    // Ignore menu key
    if (keyCode == KeyEvent.KEYCODE_MENU) {
        return false;
    }

    int sym = DoomTools.keyCodeToKeySym(keyCode);

    try {
        Natives.keyEvent(Natives.EV_KEYDOWN, sym);
    }
    catch (UnsatisfiedLinkError e) {
        // Should not happen
        Log.e(TAG, e.toString());
    }
    return false;
}
public boolean onTouchEvent(MotionEvent event)
{

    try {
        if ( event.getAction() == MotionEvent.ACTION_DOWN) {
            // Fire on tap R-CTL
            Natives.keyEvent(Natives.EV_KEYDOWN, DoomTools.KEY_RCTL);
        }
        else if ( event.getAction() == MotionEvent.ACTION_UP) {
            Natives.keyEvent(Natives.EV_KEYUP, DoomTools.KEY_RCTL);
        }
        else if ( event.getAction() == MotionEvent.ACTION_MOVE) {
            // Motion event
        }
        return true;
    }
    catch (UnsatisfiedLinkError e) {
        // Should not happen!
        Log.e(TAG, e.toString());
        return false;
    }
}
```

For touch events, Android provides three actions: ACTION_DOWN, ACTION_UP, and ACTION_MOVE, when the user is pressing, releasing, and dragging fingers in the device screen, respectively. When a finger press or release occurs, Doom sends a right control (KEY_RCTL) to the native layer, which will result in the weapon being fired.

Native Callback Handlers

The native callback handlers are implemented by the main activity (DoomClient.java) via the Natives.EventListener interface. This allows the activity to listen for native callbacks. The handlers are divided in the following categories:

- *Graphics initialization*: This handler receives information when the native graphics have been initialized. It receives the width and height of the video buffer.

- *Image update*: This handler receives video buffer updates and fires multiple times per second.

- *Message update*: This handler receives string messages from the native rendering engine.

- *Fatal errors*: This handler will fire whenever an unrecoverable error occurs.

- *Sound and music requests*: A series of handlers to handle audio.

All these categories were very much improved with Android SDK 5.0.1 and NDK version r10d.

Graphics Initialization Handler

The graphics initialization handler is critical and must be the first to fire before the game can start. It receives the width and height of the video buffer, which are used to create the Android bitmap that renders the video on the device (see Listing 5–6). To create a 32-bit ARGB bitmap in Android, you use the following call:

```
Bitmap.createBitmap(width, height, Config.ARGB_8888)
```

Config.ARGB_8888 tells the system you want to use a 4-byte (32-bit) ARGB bitmap. You will use this bitmap to set pixels for the video in later sections. Note that this callback fires only once during the lifetime of the game. To set the width and height of the video buffer ImageView, use a call to ImageView.getLayoutParams().

Listing 5-6. Graphics Initialization

```
public void OnInitGraphics(int w, int h) {
    Log.d(TAG, "OnInitGraphics creating Bitmap of " + w + " by " + h);
    mBitmap = Bitmap.createBitmap(w, h, Config.ARGB_8888);
    LayoutParams lp =  mView.getLayoutParams();
    mWidth = w;
    mHeight = h;
    lp.width = w;
    lp.height = h;
}
```

Image Update Handler

The image update handler receives an array of ARGB packed pixels representing a color (see Listing 5-7). It fires multiple times per second, and its job is to replace pixels in the bitmap with the colors in the array by calling the following method:

```
mBitmap.setPixels(pixels, offset, stride, x, y, width, height)
```

The arguments are as follows:

- pixels is the colors to write to the bitmap.

- offset is the index of the first color to read from pixels[].

- stride is the number of colors in pixels[] to skip between rows (normally, this value will be the same as the width of the bitmap).

- x is the x coordinate of the first pixel to write to in the bitmap.

- y is the y coordinate of the first pixel to write to in the bitmap.

- width is the number of colors to copy from pixels[] per row.

- height is the number of rows to write to the bitmap.

Listing 5-7. Image Update Handler

```
public void OnImageUpdate(int[] pixels) {
    mBitmap.setPixels(pixels, 0, mWidth, 0, 0, mWidth, mHeight);
    mHandler.post(new Runnable() {
        public void run() {
            mView.setImageBitmap( mBitmap);
        }
    });
}
```

Note that because this handler fires from a non-UI thread, you cannot set the pixels directly into the ImageView but must use an android.os.Handler to post a Runnable to the message queue, like so:

```
Handler.post(new Runnable() {
    public void run() {
        // Code that updates the UI goes here
    }
});
```

> **Note** A handler allows you to send and process message and runnable objects associated with a thread's message queue. Each handler instance is associated with a single thread and that thread's message queue. When you create a new handler, it is bound to the thread and message queue of the thread that is creating it. Always use a handler when updating UI widgets from a non-UI thread!

Message Updates

The message updates handler receives native messages, which are very helpful for debugging. Listing 5-8 shows this handler, which logs the text to the Android console.

Listing 5-8. Message Update Handler

```
/**
 * Fires on DSO message
 */
public void OnMessage(String text, int level) {
    Log.d(TAG, "**Doom Message: " + text);
}
```

Fatal Error Handler

The fatal error handler deals with unrecoverable errors. This means displaying a message to the user and exiting gracefully. There are many things that can cause unrecoverable errors, such as code bugs, corrupted game files, I/O errors, and network failures.

Listing 5-9 shows how Doom deals with this situation. It uses a message handler to display a message box to the user (remember that this method fires from a non-UI thread, where all UI widget access must go through an OS handler). It then waits for a while so the user can read the message and finally exits gracefully.

Listing 5-9. Fatal Error Handler

```
public void OnFatalError(final String text) {
    mHandler.post(new Runnable() {
        public void run() {
            MessageBox("Fatal Error",
                    text + " - Please report this error.");
        }
    });

    // Wait for the user to read the box
    try {
        Thread.sleep(8000);
    } catch (InterruptedException e) {

    }
    // Must quit here or the LIB will crash
    DoomTools.hardExit(-1);
}
```

Audio Request Handlers

The native Doom engine cannot access the sound device directly. This is due to the nonstandard audio library used by Android (Enhanced Audio System [EAS] by SoniVOX, and in Ice Cream Sandwich, Vorbis). To overcome this serious limitation, audio requests are cascaded back to these handlers, which start sound events at a given volume, start and stop background music events, and set the background music.

Listing 5-10 shows the audio handlers for Doom. Note that all requests are delegated to the doom.audio.AudioManager class, which deals with the Android audio system.

Listing 5-10. Sound and Music Handlers

```
public void OnStartSound(String name, int vol)
{
    if ( mSound && mAudioMgr == null)
        Log.e(TAG, "Bug: Audio Mgr is NULL but sound is enabled!");

    try {
        if ( mSound && mAudioMgr != null)
            mAudioMgr.startSound( name, vol);

    } catch (Exception e) {
        Log.e(TAG, "OnStartSound: " + e.toString());
    }
}

/**
 * Fires on background music
 */
public void OnStartMusic(String name, int loop) {
    if ( mSound && mAudioMgr != null)
        mAudioMgr.startMusic(DoomClient.this, name, loop);
}

/**
 * Stop bg music
 */
public void OnStopMusic(String name) {
    if ( mSound &&  mAudioMgr != null)
        mAudioMgr.stopMusic( name);
}

public void OnSetMusicVolume(int volume) {
    if ( mSound &&  mAudioMgr != null)
        mAudioMgr.setMusicVolume(volume);
}
```

Note   Even though cascading audio in this way makes the game slower, it provides high-quality sound to the game (much improved with the Android SDK version 5.0.1). It also provides a format-independent way of handling audio. Whatever the format of your sound file, Android detects it behind the scenes and calls the appropriate audio driver—as long as your sound file uses a format supported by the platform.

Navigation Controls

Older Android devices feature a trackball, which is cumbersome for mobile games. In fact, most gaming devices, such as PlayStation Portable (PSP) and Game Boy, feature multiple keypad arrows, which are great for navigation. On the plus side, the QWERTY keyboard is helpful for PC games. But the latest Android devices have neither a keyboard nor a trackball. This is where the navigation controls can help. Figure 5-2 shows the navigation controls in action during a game.

Figure 5-2. Navigation controls for Doom

The controls themselves are implemented as image buttons within the game layout (see the "Game Layout" section). The RelativeLayout of the game allows the controls to overlap the video ImageView, as shown in Figure 5-2. To set up events for the buttons, simply load the button widget using its ID and set a touch listener, like so:

```
findViewById(R.id.BUTTON_ID).setOnTouchListener(new View.OnTouchListener(){
    public boolean onTouch(View v, MotionEvent evt) {
        // ACTION_DOWN or ACTION_UP
        int action = evt.getAction();
        // ...
    }
});
```

Depending on the touch event action, ACTION_DOWN or ACTION_UP, you simply send a key event to the native layer with the following code:

```
public static void sendNativeKeyEvent (int type, int sym) {
    try {
        Natives.keyEvent(type, sym);
    } catch (UnsatisfiedLinkError e) {
        Log.e(TAG, e.toString());
    }
}
```

Listing 5-11 shows the setupPanControls() function for the Up, Down, Left, and Right buttons of the Doom controller.

Listing 5-11. Controller Event Setup

```
private void setupPanControls() {
    // Up
    findViewById(R.id.btn_up).setOnTouchListener(
            new View.OnTouchListener(){
        public boolean onTouch(View v, MotionEvent evt) {
            int action = evt.getAction();
            if ( action == MotionEvent.ACTION_DOWN) {
                Natives.sendNativeKeyEvent(Natives.EV_KEYDOWN
                        , DoomTools.KEY_UPARROW);
             }
            else if ( action == MotionEvent.ACTION_UP) {
                Natives.sendNativeKeyEvent(Natives.EV_KEYUP
                        , DoomTools.KEY_UPARROW);
            }
            return true;
        }
    });

    // Down
    findViewById(R.id.btn_down).setOnTouchListener(
            new View.OnTouchListener(){
        public boolean onTouch(View v, MotionEvent evt) {
            int action = evt.getAction();
            if ( action == MotionEvent.ACTION_DOWN) {
                Natives.sendNativeKeyEvent(Natives.EV_KEYDOWN
                        , DoomTools.KEY_DOWNARROW);
            }
            else if ( action == MotionEvent.ACTION_UP) {
                Natives.sendNativeKeyEvent(Natives.EV_KEYUP
                        , DoomTools.KEY_DOWNARROW);
            }
            return true;
        }
    });
```

```
// Right
findViewById(R.id.btn_right).setOnTouchListener(
        new View.OnTouchListener(){
    public boolean onTouch(View v, MotionEvent evt) {
        int action = evt.getAction();
        if ( action == MotionEvent.ACTION_DOWN) {
            Natives.sendNativeKeyEvent(Natives.EV_KEYDOWN
                    , DoomTools.KEY_RIGHTARROW);
        }
        else if ( action == MotionEvent.ACTION_UP) {
            Natives.sendNativeKeyEvent(Natives.EV_KEYUP
                    , DoomTools.KEY_RIGHTARROW);
        }
        return true;
    }
});

// More ...
}
```

Handling Audio Independently of the Format

The audio classes are implemented in the package doom.audio and consist of two files: AudioManager and AudioClip.

AudioManager is a singleton class similar to the AudioManager class presented in the previous chapter. Some of the method signatures are different to accommodate the Doom engine, such as the following:

- preloadSounds(): This method preloads the most common Doom sounds to improve performance. Sounds are encoded in WAVE format.

- startSound(String name, int vol): This method starts the sound given by a name key at volume vol. The key does not include the file extension, and the volume ranges from 0 to 100.

- startMusic (Context ctx, String key, int loop): This method starts a background music file given by key and loops if loop is set to anything other than 0. An Android context is required by the background AudioClip.

- stopMusic (String key): This method stops the background music given by key.

- setMusicVolume (int vol): This method sets the background music volume. vol ranges from 0 to 100.

A great thing about AudioClip is that it provides a format-independent way of playing sound (behind the scenes Android will take care of the dirty work of dealing with the format drivers), plus it will work in all versions of Android, thus giving you the widest range of device support.

Because the audio files (including background music) can occupy more than 5MB, files have been packed in a zip archive and installed at runtime into the SD card. This saves precious disk space in the main file system. The zip archive lives in the assets folder of the Doom project.

> **Tip**   Android features an automated media scanner service that searches for audio files within the file system. This can be really annoying, as your media player will suddenly display a few hundred unwanted Doom sounds and music. You can fix the problem by adding an empty file called .nomedia to the sound folder. This empty file tells the media scanner to bypass this directory.

Native Interface Class

The native interface class is the two-way pipe that sends messages from Java to the Doom engine through native methods, and from the engine to Java using C to Java callbacks (see Listing 5-12). This class consists of three parts: callback listener, native methods, and C to Java callbacks.

Callback Listener

The callback listener is implemented by the interface EventListener. It must be implemented by clients that want to receive C to Java callbacks (in this case, by the main activity DoomClient.java). The C to Java callbacks are as follows:

- OnMessage(String text, int level): This is mostly a debug callback that sends messages to let Java know what is happening on the native side.

- OnInitGraphics(int w, int h): This is the first callback and fires only once after graphics initialization. It tells Java the width and height of the video buffer.

- OnImageUpdate(int[] pixels): This fires many times per second and sends an Android packed video buffer to Java, which uses it to render the game bitmap.

- OnFatalError(String text): This callback fires when there is an unrecoverable error in the engine. The receiver should display the message and terminate.

- OnQuit(int code): This callback fires when the user exits the game. It sends a return code back to the receiver.

- OnStartSound(String name, int vol): This fires when the native engine starts a sound. It delegates to the receiver.

- OnStartMusic(String name, int loop): This fires on background music. It delegates to the receiver.

■ OnStopMusic(String name): This fires on stop music background.
It delegates to the receiver.

■ OnSetMusicVolume(int volume): This fires when the user sets the music
volume. It delegates to the receiver.

Native Methods

The native methods invoke the native Doom engine. The following are the three basic native
methods:

■ static native int DoomMain(String[] argv): This method invokes the
main game loop of the Doom engine.

■ static native int keyEvent(int type, int key): This method sends a
key event to the engine. The event type is either EV_KEYDOWN or EV_KEYUP.
The argument key must be an ASCII symbol, not an Android key code.
This means the key code must be translated before being sent to
the engine.

■ static native int motionEvent(int b, int x, int y): This method
sends a motion event to the engine (such as when the user drags a
finger on the display). The first argument is a mouse button (always zero
in this case) plus the x and y coordinates of the event itself.

■ static native int DoomMain(String[] argv) requires a list of
arguments and blocks execution, so it must be run within a thread. The
following are the most important arguments:

  ■ width defines the width of the video buffer.

  ■ height defines the height of the video buffer.

■ iwad defines the game to be played. The following game files are
supported by the engine:

  ■ doom1.wad: This is the shareware episode of Doom.

  ■ doom.wad: This is the retail episode.

  ■ doom2.wad: This is the second episode in the Doom series.

  ■ plutonia.wad: This is the Plutonia Experiment episode, part of the
  Ultimate Doom series.

  ■ tnt.wad: This is an episode dubbed Evilution, also part of the
  ultimate Doom series.

■ file defines extra game files to be used by the engine.

For example, to play Doom shareware in landscape mode, the list arguments that must be
sent to DoomMain (as a String array) would be doom -width 480 -height 320 -iwad doom1.wad.

C to Java Callbacks

C to Java callbacks are used to delegate engine messages to the listener activity. To do so, the native interface class uses a private listener and a static setter method, like so:

```
private static EventListener listener;
public static void setListener(EventListener l) {
        listener = l;
}
```

Note that there can be only one listener. When the Doom engine sends a message (such as "have some text"), the native interface class simply delegates to the listener, which deals with the event.

```
private static void OnMessage(String text, int level) {
        if (listener != null)
            listener.OnMessage(text, level);
}
```

In this code, the engine is saying "have some text," along with an integer log level. The rest of callbacks are shown in Listing 5-12.

Listing 5-12. Native Interface Class (Natives.java)

```
package doom.jni;

import android.util.Log;

public class Natives {
    public static final String TAG = "Natives";

    private static EventListener listener;

    public static final int EV_KEYDOWN = 0;
    public static final int EV_KEYUP = 1;
    public static final int EV_MOUSE = 2;

    public static interface EventListener {
        void OnMessage(String text, int level);
        void OnInitGraphics(int w, int h);
        void OnImageUpdate(int[] pixels);
        void OnFatalError(String text);
        void OnQuit(int code);
        void OnStartSound(String name, int vol);
        void OnStartMusic(String name, int loop);
        void OnStopMusic(String name);
        void OnSetMusicVolume(int volume);
    }
```

```java
public static void setListener(EventListener l) {
    listener = l;
}
/**
 * Send a key event to the native layer
 *
 * @param type : key up down or mouse
 * @param sym: ASCII symbol
 */
public static void sendNativeKeyEvent(int type, int sym) {
    try {
        Natives.keyEvent(type, sym);
    } catch (UnsatisfiedLinkError e) {
        Log.e(TAG, e.toString());
    }
}


  // Native Main Doom Loop: @param argv: program arguments
public static native int DoomMain(String[] argv);

/**
 * Send a Key Event
 * @param type: event type: UP/DOWN
 * @param key: ASCII symbol
 */
public static native int keyEvent(int type, int key);

/*********************************************************
 * C to Java - Callbacks
 *********************************************************/

/**
 * This fires on messages from the C layer
 */
private static void OnMessage(String text, int level) {
    if (listener != null)
        listener.OnMessage(text, level);
}

private static void OnInitGraphics(int w, int h) {
    if (listener != null)
        listener.OnInitGraphics(w, h);
}

private static void OnImageUpdate(int[] pixels) {
    if (listener != null)
        listener.OnImageUpdate(pixels);

}
```

```java
    private static void OnFatalError(String message) {
        if (listener != null)
            listener.OnFatalError(message);
    }
    private static void OnQuit(int code) {
        if (listener != null)
            listener.OnQuit(code);
    }
    /**
     * Fires when a sound is played in the C layer.
     */
    private static void OnStartSound(byte[] name, int vol) {
        if (listener != null)
            listener.OnStartSound(new String(name), vol);
    }

    /**
     * Start background music callback
     */
    private static void OnStartMusic(String name, int loop) {
        if (listener != null)
            listener.OnStartMusic(name, loop);
    }

    /**
     * Stop background music
     * @param name
     */
    private static void OnStopMusic(String name) {
        if (listener != null)
            listener.OnStopMusic(name);
    }

    /**
     * Set background music volume
     * @param volume Range: (0-255)
     */
    private static void OnSetMusicVolume(int volume) {
        if (listener != null)
            listener.OnSetMusicVolume((int) (volume * 100.0 / 15.0));
    }
}
```

Native Layer

The native layer glues the Java and C code together by defining three types of tasks to be performed:

- *Native method implementations*: These are the C implementations of the native Java methods defined by the native interface class. This code lives in the file jni_doom.c.

- *Original game changes*: The original Doom engine needs to be modified slightly to accommodate the JNI glue. This consists of inserting calls to the C to Java callbacks in the correct files.

- *Removal of invalid dependencies*: Invalid dependencies in the original code must be removed. For example, the original Simple DirectMedia Layer (SDL) dependency used by the PC code must be deleted.

Let's look at these tasks in more detail.

Native Method Implementations

Table 5-4 shows the Java native signatures and their C counterparts in jni_doom.c.

Table 5-4. Java Native Methods and Their Native Counterparts

Java Method	C Method
static native int DoomMain(String[] argv)	JNIEXPORT jint JNICALL Java_doom_jni_Natives_ DoomMain(JNIEnv * env, jclass class, jobjectArray jargv)
static native int keyEvent(int type, int key)	JNIEXPORT jint JNICALL Java_doom_jni_Natives_ keyEvent(JNIEnv * env, jclass cls, jint type, jint key)
static native int motionEvent(int btn, int x, int y)	JNIEXPORT jint JNICALL Java_doom_jni_Natives_ motionEvent(JNIEnv * env, jclass cls, jint btn, jint x, jint y)

Before you can proceed with the implementation, the javah command must be used to generate the required header files and signatures, like so:

```
javah -jni -classpath PATH_TO_PROJECT_FOLDER/bin -d include doom.jni.Natives
```
Note that a class path to the bin folder is required for javah to find the doom.jni.Natives class. The output file doom_jni_Natives.h will be dumped in the include folder by using -d. The header file is then used by jni_doom.c, as shown in this fragment:

```
#include <stdio.h>
#include "include/doom_jni_Natives.h"
#include "include/jni_doom.h"
#include "doomdef.h"
#include "d_event.h"
```

The code uses Doom code, thus the inclusion of doomdef.h and d_event.h. The header jni_doom.h defines prototypes for the C to Java callbacks and miscellaneous constants.

You also need a static reference to the JVM used by the C to Java callbacks, as in the following fragment:

```
// Global  Java VM  reference
static JavaVM *g_VM;
```

For improved performance, static references to the Java native interface class (doom.jni.Natives) are kept in jNativesCls. References to the Java methods to send the video image (jSendImageMethod) and sound file (jStartSoundMethod) are also kept. The reason is that these methods are invoked multiple times, and looking up these names every time can slow things.

```
static jclass jNativesCls;
static jmethodID jSendImageMethod;
static jmethodID jStartSoundMethod;
```

Also, because you may send a pixel buffer (image) multiple times per second, you should keep a reference to the Java array and its size, as in the following fragment:

```
static jintArray jImage;
static int iSize;
extern int doom_main(int argc, char **argv);
```

The line extern int doom_main defines the main engine function and tells the compiler it is defined somewhere else in the library. The header jni_doom.h included up front defines the constants and method signatures required to invoke the C to Java callbacks. For example, the following fragment of the header defines constants for the Java native interface class (doom/jni/Natives) and the method names and signatures for the callbacks OnImageUpdate and OnStartSound (see the "C to Java Callbacks" section for more details):

```
#define CB_CLASS "doom/jni/Natives"
#define CB_CLASS_IU_CB  "OnImageUpdate"
#define CB_CLASS_IU_SIG "([I)V"

#define CB_CLASS_SS_CB  "OnStartSound"
#define CB_CLASS_SS_SIG "([BI)V"
```

Let's take a look at the actual implementations. They are divided into the following three groups:

- *Native game loop*: This invokes the engine loop doom_main.

- *Key and motion events*: These post key and motion events to the engine.

- *C to Java callbacks*: These callbacks are critical for the Java code to receive information from the Doom engine.

Native Game Loop

The native game loop's job is to extract the arguments sent as a jobjectArray into a C char ** array and invoke the main Doom engine function (doom_main). This function performs the following additional steps:

1. Obtains a reference to the JVM using (*env)->GetJavaVM(env, &g_VM). This reference will be used by the C to Java callbacks.

2. Loads the doom.jni.Natives class, also used by the C to Java callbacks.
    jNativesCls = (*env)->FindClass(env, "doom/jni/Natives").

3. Loads the doom.jni.Natives.OnImageUpdate and doom.jni.natives.
    OnStartSound Java methods. This is done for performance reasons,
    as these methods are called many times.

Listing 5-13 shows the native game loop.

Listing 5-13. JNI Call to the Main Game Loop

```
/*
 * Class:     doom_jni_Natives
 * Method:    DoomMain
 * Signature: ([Ljava/lang/String;)V
 */
JNIEXPORT jint JNICALL Java_doom_jni_Natives_DoomMain
  (JNIEnv * env, jclass class, jobjectArray jargv)
{
    // Obtain a global ref to the Java VM
    (*env)->GetJavaVM(env, &g_VM);

    // Extract char ** args from Java array
    jsize clen =  getArrayLen(env, jargv);

    char * args[(int)clen];

    int i;
    jstring jrow;
    for (i = 0; i < clen; i++)
    {
        jrow = (jstring)(*env)->GetObjectArrayElement(env, jargv, i);
        const char *row  = (*env)->GetStringUTFChars(env, jrow, 0);

        args[i] = malloc( strlen(row) + 1);
        strcpy (args[i], row);

        jni_printf("Main argv[%d]=%s", i, args[i]);

        // Free Java string jrow
        (*env)->ReleaseStringUTFChars(env, jrow, row);
    }

    /*
     * Load the Image update class (called many times)
     */
    jNativesCls = (*env)->FindClass(env, CB_CLASS);

    if ( jNativesCls == 0 ) {
        jni_printf("Unable to find class: %s", CB_CLASS);
        return -1;
    }
```

```
// Load doom.util.Natives.OnImageUpdate(char[])
    jSendImageMethod = (*env)->GetStaticMethodID(env, jNativesCls
            , CB_CLASS_IU_CB
            , CB_CLASS_IU_SIG);

    if ( jSendImageMethod == 0 ) {
        jni_printf("Unable to find method OnImageUpdate(): %s"
                , CB_CLASS);
        return -1;
    }

    // Load OnStartSound(String name, int vol)
    jStartSoundMethod = (*env)->GetStaticMethodID(env, jNativesCls
            , CB_CLASS_SS_CB
            , CB_CLASS_SS_SIG);

    if ( jStartSoundMethod == 0 ) {
        jni_printf("Unable to find method OnStartSound signature: %s "
                , CB_CLASS_SS_SIG);
        return -1;
    }

    // Invoke Doom's main sub. This will loop forever
    doom_main (clen, args);

    return 0;
}
```

Key and Motion Events

Key and motion events are posted via the extern symbol D_PostEvent, as shown in Listing 5-14. The event type (event_t) is defined by the engine and consists of the following:

- A type (0 for key down, 1 for key up, and 2 for mouse events).

- An ASCII key stored in event.data1 for key events.

- A mouse button and x and y coordinates for mouse events, stored as event.data1 = MOUSE BUTTON, event.data2 = x, and event.data3 = y. Mouse buttons can be 1 for left, 2 for middle, or 3 for right.

Listing 5-14. Posting Key and Motion Events with JNI

```
/*
 * Class:      doom_util_Natives
 * Method:     keyEvent
 * Signature: (II)V
 */
extern void D_PostEvent (event_t* ev);
```

```
JNIEXPORT jint JNICALL Java_doom_jni_Natives_keyEvent
  (JNIEnv * env, jclass cls, jint type, jint key)
{
    event_t event;
    event.type = (int)type;
    event.data1 = (int)key;
    D_PostEvent(&event);

    return type + key;
}

/*
 * Class:     doom_util_Natives
 * Method:    motionEvent
 * Signature: (II)I
 */
JNIEXPORT jint JNICALL Java_doom_jni_Natives_motionEvent
  (JNIEnv * env, jclass cls, jint x, jint y, jint z)
{
    event_t event;
    event.type = ev_mouse;
    event.data1 = x;
    event.data2 = y;
    event.data3 = z;
    D_PostEvent(&event);
    return 0;
}
```

C to Java Callbacks

Table 5-5 shows the callbacks and the Java methods they invoke. The callbacks can be divided into the following types:

- Graphics initialization (jni_init_graphics)

- Video buffer (jni_send_pixels)

- Sound and music (jni_start_sound, jni_start_music, jni_stop_music, and jni_set_music_volume)

- Fatal errors (jni_fatal_error)

Table 5-5. C to Java Callbacks in jni_doom.c

C Method	Invoked Java Method
void jni_init_graphics(int width, int height)	static void OnInitGraphics(int w, int h)
void jni_send_pixels(int * data)	static void OnImageUpdate(int[] pixels)
void jni_start_sound (const char * name, int vol)	static void OnStartSound(byte[] name, int vol)
void jni_start_music (const char * name, int loop)	static void OnStartMusic(String name, int loop)
void jni_stop_music (const char * name)	static void OnStopMusic(String name)
void jni_set_music_volume (int vol)	static void OnSetMusicVolume(int volume)
void jni_fatal_error(const char * text)	static void OnFatalError(String message)

The callbacks must be inserted in the C code, as explained in the following sections.

Graphics Initialization

Constants for the graphics initialization callback are defined in jni_doom.h, as shown in Listing 5-15. CB_CLASS_IG_CB indicates the Java method name OnInitGraphics. CB_CLASS_IG_SIG "(II)V" defines the signature of two integer parameters and a void return type, as shown in the following fragment:

```
#define CB_CLASS_IG_CB  "OnInitGraphics"
#define CB_CLASS_IG_SIG "(II)V"
```

This callback also performs some critical steps.

1. It attaches to the current thread with (*g_VM)->AttachCurrentThread (g_VM, &env, NULL). This is where the global JVM reference comes into play. Furthermore, the JNI environment (env) will be used to invoke the callback.

2. It allocates space for the Java pixel array (video buffer) used by jni_send_pixels using the width and height of the display: jImage = (*env)-> NewIntArray(env, width * height).

3. It invokes the static void method doom.util.Natives. OnInitGraphics(width, height) using its method ID: (*env)->CallStaticVoidMethod(env, jNativesCls, METHOD_ID, ARGUMENTS) where ARGUMENTS are the width and height of the display. Note that the arguments must match the arguments in the Java method!

Listing 5-15. Graphics Initialization

```
/**
 * Fires when Doom graphics are initialized.
 * params: img width, height
 */
void jni_init_graphics(int width, int height)
{
    JNIEnv *env;

    if ( !g_VM) {
        printf("No JNI VM available.\n");
        return;
    }

    (*g_VM)->AttachCurrentThread (g_VM, (void **) &env, NULL);


    iSize = width * height;

    // Create a new int[] used by jni_send_pixels
    jImage = (*env)-> NewIntArray(env, iSize);

    // Call doom.util.Natives.OnInitGraphics(w, h);
    jmethodID mid = (*env)->GetStaticMethodID(env, jNativesCls
            , CB_CLASS_IG_CB
            , CB_CLASS_IG_SIG);

    if (mid) {
        (*env)->CallStaticVoidMethod(env, jNativesCls
                , mid
                , width, height);
    }
}
```

Video Buffer Callback

The video buffer callback is critical, and it must be lean and mean. It gets called continuously and must not create any objects (see Listing 5-16). Like the previous callback, it attaches to the current thread. It also calls the static void method doom.jni.Natives.OnImageUpdate(int[] pixels). But before calling this method, it must set the pixels into the Java array (jImage):

```
(*env)->SetIntArrayRegion(env, jImage, 0, iSize, (jint *) data)
```

data is an array of integers already formatted as 32-bit ARGB pixels, as required by Android, and iSize is the size of the display calculated in the previous callback.

Listing 5-16. Sending Video Pixels

```
/**
 * Image update Java callback. Gets called many times per sec.
 * It must not look up JNI classes/methods or create any objects; otherwise
 * the local JNI ref table will overflow & the app will crash
 */
void jni_send_pixels(int * data)
{
    JNIEnv *env;
    if ( !g_VM) {
        return;
    }

    (*g_VM)->AttachCurrentThread (g_VM, (void **) &env, NULL);

    // Send img back to Java.
    if (jSendImageMethod) {
        (*env)->SetIntArrayRegion(env, jImage, 0, iSize, (jint *) data);

        // Call Java method
        (*env)->CallStaticVoidMethod(env, jNativesCls
                , jSendImageMethod
                , jImage);
    }

}
```

Sound and Music Callbacks

The sound and music callbacks fire from the engine when a sound or background music must be played. In a perfect world, sound would be handled in the native layer; however, due to the lack of documentation and support for open audio standards in Android, requests are cascaded back to Java for processing.

There are four sound and music callbacks in Doom, with their names and signatures defined in the header jni_doom.h:

```
// doom.jni.Natives.OnStartSound(byte[] name, int volume)
#define CB_CLASS_SS_CB  "OnStartSound"
#define CB_CLASS_SS_SIG  "([BI)V"

// doom.jni.Natives.OnStartMusic (String name , int loop)
#define CB_CLASS_SM_CB  "OnStartMusic"
#define CB_CLASS_SM_SIG  "(Ljava/lang/String;I)V"

// doom.jni.Natives.OnStopMusic (String name )
#define CB_CLASS_STOPM_CB  "OnStopMusic"
#define CB_CLASS_STOPM_SIG  "(Ljava/lang/String;)V"

// doom.jni.Natives.OnSetMusicVolume (int volume)
#define CB_CLASS_SETMV_CB  "OnSetMusicVolume"
#define CB_CLASS_SETMV_SIG  "(I)V"
```

Note the method signature for OnStartSound with ([BI)V, where [B represents an array of bytes (the name of the sound), I represents an integer (volume), and V is the return type of the method (void). Another interesting signature is OnStartMusic with (Ljava/lang/String;I)V where Ljava/lang/String; means the class java.lang.String (enclosed in L;).

Listing 5-17 shows the implementation of these callbacks. They are pretty similar in nature in that they all must attach to the current thread using the global JVM (g_VM). The following are some of the key aspects of the code:

- To create a Java byte array, you can use jbyteArray ARRAY = (*env)-> NewByteArray(env, SIZE) where the words byte/Byte can be replaced with boolean/Boolean, int/Int, object/Object, and other primitive types, depending on your needs.

- To insert data into the array, use (*env)->SetByteArrayRegion(env, ARRAY, START, SIZE, (jbyte *) C_ARRAY) where Byte can be replaced with any Java primitive type.

- To call a static void method, use (*env)->CallStaticVoidMethod(env, CLASS, METHOD_ID, ARG1, ARG2, ...).

- To release resources for an array, use (*env)->DeleteLocalRef(env, ARRAY).

Listing 5-17. Cascading Sound and Music Requests Back to Java

```
/**
 * Fires multiple times when a sound is played
 * @param name Sound name
 * @param volume
 */
void jni_start_sound (const char * name, int vol)
{
    /*
     * Attach to the curr thread; otherwise we get JNI WARNING:
     * threadid=3 using env from threadid=15 which aborts the VM
     */
    JNIEnv *env;

    if ( !g_VM) {
        return;
    }

    (*g_VM)->AttachCurrentThread (g_VM, (void **) &env, NULL);

    if ( jStartSoundMethod == 0 ) {
        jni_printf("BUG: Invalid Doom JNI method OnStartSound %s"
          , CB_CLASS_SS_SIG);
        return ;
    }
```

```
    // Create a new char[] used by jni_send_pixels
    // Used to prevent JNI ref table overflows
    int iSize = strlen(name);
    jbyteArray jSound = (*env)-> NewByteArray(env, iSize);

    (*env)->SetByteArrayRegion(env, jSound, 0, iSize, (jbyte *) name);

    // Call Java method
    (*env)->CallStaticVoidMethod(env, jNativesCls
            , jStartSoundMethod
            , jSound //(*env)->NewStringUTF(env, name)
            , (jint) vol);

    (*env)->DeleteLocalRef(env,jSound);
}

/**
 * Fires when a background song is requested
 */
void jni_start_music (const char * name, int loop)
{
    /*
     * Attach to the curr thread; otherwise we get JNI WARNING:
     * threadid=3 using env from threadid=15 which aborts the VM
     */
    JNIEnv *env;

    if ( !g_VM) {
        return;
    }

    (*g_VM)->AttachCurrentThread (g_VM, (void **) &env, NULL);

    jmethodID mid = (*env)->GetStaticMethodID(env, jNativesCls
        , CB_CLASS_SM_CB
        , CB_CLASS_SM_SIG);

    if (mid) {
        (*env)->CallStaticVoidMethod(env, jNativesCls
                , mid
                , (*env)->NewStringUTF(env, name)
                , (jint) loop );

    }
}
```

```c
/**
 * Fires when a background song is stopped
 */
void jni_stop_music (const char * name)
{
    /*
     * Attach to the curr thread; otherwise we get JNI WARNING:
     * threadid=3 using env from threadid=15 which aborts the VM
     */
    JNIEnv *env;

    if ( !g_VM) {
        return;
    }

    (*g_VM)->AttachCurrentThread (g_VM, (void **) &env, NULL);
    jmethodID mid = (*env)->GetStaticMethodID(env, jNativesCls
        , CB_CLASS_STOPM_CB
        , CB_CLASS_STOPM_SIG);

    if (mid) {
        (*env)->CallStaticVoidMethod(env, jNativesCls
                , mid
                , (*env)->NewStringUTF(env, name)
                );
    }
}

/**
 * Set bg msic vol callback
 */
void jni_set_music_volume (int vol) {
    JNIEnv *env;

    if ( !g_VM) {
        return;
    }

    (*g_VM)->AttachCurrentThread (g_VM, (void **) &env, NULL);

    jmethodID mid = (*env)->GetStaticMethodID(env, jNativesCls
        , CB_CLASS_SETMV_CB
        , CB_CLASS_SETMV_SIG);

    if (mid) {
        (*env)->CallStaticVoidMethod(env, jNativesCls
                , mid
                , (jint) vol
                );
    }
}
```

Fatal Errors

Fatal or unrecoverable errors occur in any type of software. In Doom, these errors are cascaded back to Java where a message is presented to the user and then the application aborts. The following fragment from jni_doom.h shows the callback name and signature for this task:

```
#define CB_CLASS_FATAL_CB  "OnFatalError"
#define CB_CLASS_FATAL_SIG  "(Ljava/lang/String;)V"
```

This callback is simple (see Listing 5-18). It works as follows.

1. It attaches to the current thread, aborting if no JNI environment is available.

2. It looks up the doom.jni.Natives Java class, aborting if not found.

3. It looks up the doom.jni.Natives.OnFatalError(String) using the method name and signature.

4. It calls the static void method.

Listing 5-18. Cascading Fatal Errors

```
/**
 * Called when a fatal error has occurred.
 * The receiver should terminate
 */
void jni_fatal_error(const char * text) {
    JNIEnv *env;

    if ( !g_VM) {
        printf("JNI FATAL: No JNI Environment available. %s\n", text);
        exit(-1);
    }

    (*g_VM)->AttachCurrentThread (g_VM, (void **) &env, NULL);

    if ( !env) {
        printf("JNI FATAL: Unable to attach to thread: %s.\n", text);
        exit(-1);
    }

    if ( !jNativesCls ) {
        jNativesCls = (*env)->FindClass(env, CB_CLASS);

        if ( jNativesCls == 0 ) {
                printf("JNI FATAL: Unable to find class: %s", CB_CLASS);
                exit(-1);
        }
    }
    jmethodID mid = (*env)->GetStaticMethodID(env, jNativesCls
        , CB_CLASS_FATAL_CB
        , CB_CLASS_FATAL_SIG);
```

```
if (mid) {
    (*env)->CallStaticVoidMethod(env, jNativesCls
            , mid
            , (*env)->NewStringUTF(env, text) );
}
else {
    printf("JNI FATAL: Unable to find method: %s, signature: %s\n"
            , CB_CLASS_MSG_CB, CB_CLASS_MSG_SIG );
    exit (-1);
}

}
```

Original Game Changes

In order for the JNI glue to work, changes are required to the original game engine. Some are simple, such as inserting calls to the C to Java callbacks; some are not so simple, such as removing invalid dependencies. Table 5-6 shows the original files and the changes required. Considering that the engine has a total of 90,000 lines of code, these changes are not that bad.

Table 5-6. Changes Required to the Original Engine to Insert the JNI Glue

File	Changes
i_main.c	Rename the main subroutine to doom_main.
i_system.c	In I_Error, insert jni_fatal_error.
i_sound.c	Comment SDL dependencies. In I_StartSound, insert start sound callback jni_start_sound.
s_sound.c	In S_SetMusicVolume, insert volume callback jni_set_music_volume.
i_video.c	Comment SDL dependencies. Insert code to build an Android ARBG pixel array from the video buffer. In I_SetRes, add JNI callback to initialize graphics. In I_FinishUpdate, send pixels to Java with jni_send_pixels.

These changes are explained in more detail in the following sections.

Renaming main

Let's start with the simplest change: renaming the main() subroutine in i_main.c so it can be invoked from the Java native Java_doom_jni_Natives_DoomMain, which will start the game from Java, as shown in the following fragment:

```
// In i_main.c
int main(int argc, char **argv)
int doom_main(int argc, char **argv)
```

```
// In jni_doom.c
extern int doom_main(int argc, char **argv);

JNIEXPORT jint JNICALL Java_doom_jni_Natives_DoomMain

  (JNIEnv * env, jclass class, jobjectArray jargv)

{
  ...
  doom_main (clen, args);
  ...
}
```

Once main is renamed to doom_main, simply add the extern symbol extern int doom_
main(int argc, char **argv) to jni_doom.c and invoke it from the game starter function.

Inserting the Fatal Error Callback

Another simple change is to insert the C to Java callback jni_fatal_error whenever an
unrecoverable error occurs. The changes occur in the I_Error function in the i_system.c file,
as shown in Listing 5-19.

Listing 5-19. Changes Required to i_system.c

```
void I_Error (char *error, ...)
{
    va_list     argptr;
    static char  string[1024];

    // Message first.
    va_start (argptr,error);
    vsprintf (string, error ,argptr);
    va_end (argptr);

    // Shutdown. Here might be other errors.
    if (demorecording)
      G_CheckDemoStatus();

    D_QuitNetGame ();
    I_ShutdownGraphics();

    // Send the error back to JNI layer
    jni_fatal_error(string);

    // Something wrong has happened
    // OLD CODE -> exit(-1);
}
```

Commenting SDL Occurrences

The Doom engine is built on top of SDL, which is an open framework to access system resources such as sound and video hardware. Doom uses SDL to display video and play music. This is a relatively hard problem, as Android has no support for SDL. Thus, any SDL occurrence must be commented or removed and replaced by a JNI equivalent. This happens in two files: i_sound.c and i_video.c.

Changes to i_sound.c are simple and consist of commenting the sdl.h header file and inserting jni_doom.h instead, as shown in the following fragment:

```
#include <sdl.h>
#include "include/jni_doom.h"
```

Furthermore, any function that starts with SDL_ must be commented. Luckily, these functions do not affect the game flow itself, and thus they can be safely commented.

Sound System Changes

Other changes are required to i_sound.c to insert a call to jni_start_sound, as shown in Listing 5-20. The global variable S_sfx[id].name provides the sound name, which will be sent back to Java and loaded from the file system, along with its volume.

Listing 5-20. Changes Required to i_sound.c to Insert the jni_start_sound Callback

```
int I_StartSound(int id, int channel, int vol, int sep, int pitch, int priority)
{
  const unsigned char* data;
  int lump;
  size_t len;

  // ...

  // The entries DSBSPWLK, DSBSPACT, DSSWTCHN
  // and DSSWTCHX are all zero-length sounds
  if (len<=8) return -1;

  /* Find padded length */
  len -= 8;
  // Do the lump caching outside the SDL_LockAudio/SDL_UnlockAudio pair
  // Use locking which makes sure the sound data is in a malloced area and
  // not in a memory mapped one
  data = W_LockLumpNum(lump);

  // JNI changes: Send a sound request to Java
  // id is the sound index, S_sfx[id].name (soundname)
  // vol = volume
  jni_start_sound(S_sfx[id].name , vol);

  // ...

  return channel;
}
```

Changes are also required to s_sound.c to insert a call to jni_set_music_volume (volume) to send the background music volume back to Java (see Listing 5-21). Note that this function is called within the game when the user changes the music volume from the options menu.

Listing 5-21. Changes Required to s_sound.c to Insert the Music JNI Callback

```
void S_SetMusicVolume(int volume)
{
  // Return if music is not enabled
  if (!mus_card || nomusicparm)
    return;

  if (volume < 0 || volume > 15)
    I_Error("S_SetMusicVolume: Attempt to set music volume at %d", volume);

  // JNI Changes: Send a volume request to Java
  // volume = [0..100]
  jni_set_music_volume (volume);

  I_SetMusicVolume(volume);
  snd_MusicVolume = volume;
}
```

Video Buffer Changes

This is where the toughest changes must be done. The i_video.c file is the one that renders the video buffer and uses SDL heavily. All SDL references must be removed and replaced with structures compatible with Android.

Down to the pipe, a video buffer is simply an array of packed colors represented as either bytes indicating the index of a color in a color palette or integers specifying an RGB color. SDL uses a structure called SDL_Surface to encapsulate the video buffer as an array of bytes plus a palette used to map colors to the buffer. Consider the following fragment, which replaces the SDL screen with a similar structure called XImage (actually taken from the X11 structure of the same name):

```
static SDL_Surface *screen;    // OLD CODE
static XImage *     image;     // NEW CODE
```

In Doom, SDL_Surface will be replaced with the equivalent XImage that holds the array of bytes for the video buffer. Note that the video buffer cannot be rendered directly to a display. Instead, it must be cascaded back to Java using the C to Java callbacks, where Android will take care of the actual rendering.

Because XImage doesn't exist, it must be written. This isn't difficult because XImage is simply a C struct holding the width, height, and array of bytes for the video buffer, as shown in Listing 5-22.

Listing 5-22. Video Buffer Image Object from i_video.c

```c
/*********************************************************
 * Class XImage
 *********************************************************/
typedef struct Image XImage;

struct Image
{
  int width;
  int height;
  byte * data;
};

/**
 * Class Color
 */
typedef struct Color XColor;

struct Color
{
  int red;
  int green;
  int blue;
};

// The Image
XImage *            image;

/**
 * XImage Constructor
 */
XImage * XCreateImage(int width, int height)
{
    XImage * this = (XImage*) malloc(sizeof(XImage));

    // set width, height
    this->width = width;
    this->height = height;

    // allocate image buffer
    this->data = (byte *)malloc (width * height);

    return this;
}
/*********************************************************
 * Class XImage
 *********************************************************/
```

In addition to XImage, you need a color palette to map the bytes on XImage to ARGB colors used by Android. For this purpose, you use the struct XColor, which holds the red, green, and blue values of a color. You also need a function to allocate memory for the XImage given its width and height (XCreateImage). This function will allocate space for the image byte buffer. You must modify the palette upload function (I_UploadNewPalette) in i_video.c to use the new XColor structure, as shown in Listing 5-23.

Listing 5-23. Setting the Color Palette in i_video.c

```
// Color palette
static XColor * colours;

static void I_UploadNewPalette(int pal)
{
  // This is used to replace the current 256 color cmap with a new one
  // Used by 256 color PseudoColor modes

  static int cachedgamma;
  static size_t num_pals;

  if (V_GetMode() == VID_MODEGL)
    return;
  if ((colours == NULL) || (cachedgamma != usegamma)) {

    int pplump = W_GetNumForName("PLAYPAL");
    int gtlump = (W_CheckNumForName)("GAMMATBL",ns_prboom);

    register const byte * palette = W_CacheLumpNum(pplump);
    register const byte * const gtable = (const byte *)W_CacheLumpNum(gtlump)
     + 256*(cachedgamma = usegamma);

    register int i;

    num_pals = W_LumpLength(pplump) / (3*256);
    num_pals *= 256;

    if (!colours) {
      // First call - allocate and prepare color array
      colours = malloc(sizeof(*colours)*num_pals);
    }

    // set the colormap entries
    for (i=0 ; (size_t)i<num_pals ; i++) {
      colours[i].red    = gtable[palette[0]];
      colours[i].green  = gtable[palette[1]];
      colours[i].blue   = gtable[palette[2]];
      palette += 3;
    }

    W_UnlockLumpNum(pplump);
    W_UnlockLumpNum(gtlump);
    num_pals/=256;
  }
}
```

In Listing 5-23, the original SDL palette has been replaced by XColor * colours. Note that the Doom engine uses a 768-color palette (256 colors each for red, green, and blue). The palette is read from the game file, along with a gamma table (used to apply a brightness factor to each color). With this information, the palette is filled and kept in memory for later use.

The final change to i_video.c is the function that does the actual rendering, I_FinishUpdate (see Listing 5-24). This function uses the width and height of the screen to create an array of pixels (each one representing an Android-packed ARGB color). It then loops through the array and uses the byte value from the screen buffer to look up the color from the palette.

```
byte b = screens[0].data[i];   // Video buffer byte
XColor color = colours[b];     // Palette color for that byte
```

It then constructs a 32-bit pixel using the RGB values of color.

```
pixels[i] = (0xFF << 24) | (color.red << 16) | (color.green << 8) | color.blue
```

> **Note**   0xFF << 24 represents the alpha (opacity) value of the pixel—fully visible in this case.

Finally, the array is sent back using the callback jni_send_pixels(pixels), where Android will do the rendering.

Listing 5-24. Video Buffer Renderer Function from i_video.c

```
void I_FinishUpdate (void)
{
  if (I_SkipFrame()) return;

  // Screen size
  int size = SCREENWIDTH * SCREENHEIGHT;

  // ARGB pixels
  int pixels[size], i;

  for ( i = 0 ; i < size ; i ++) {
      byte b = screens[0].data[i];

      XColor color = colours[b];

      pixels[i] = (0xFF << 24)
          | (color.red << 16)
          | (color.green << 8)
          | color.blue;
  }
```

```
// Send pixels to Java
jni_send_pixels(pixels);

}
```

At this point, the Doom engine is all set and ready for compilation.

Compiling Doom with the NDK

Since the release of the NDK 1.6 and later, Google has made a lot of nice improvements to support native development. At the time of this writing, the NDK release r10d was used. The most important changes of this new version of the NDK can be found at https://developer.android.com/tools/sdk/ndk/index.html#

All in all, the NDK is a good improvement but still has far to go to catch up with other powerful tools, such as Apple's iPhone Xcode platform. For example, the NDK will recompile the entire library if you change the Makefile, Android.mk (to add a new source file, for example). This is really annoying when you have a big library with lots of source files. Other tools such as GNU make will detect the changes and recompile only the right files in the library. At any rate, for Doom the folder structure for the NDK should look as follows:

- NDK_ROOT/apps/Doom/Application.mk: This file defines the module name to be built.

- NDK_ROOT/apps/Doom/project: This folder contains the actual Android project for the game.

- NDK_ROOT/apps/Doom/project/jni: This folder contains the native code and the Makefile, Android.mk.

The following steps show you how to get Doom to compile with the NDK:

1. Create android-ndk_r1/apps/Doom/Application.mk. This file contains the module (doom) that you are building.

   ```
   APP_PROJECT_PATH := $(call my-dir)/project
   APP_MODULES      := doom
   ```

2. Create the folder NDK_ROOT/apps/Doom/project. Copy the Android project from Android.Doom to this folder. You don't need to copy the native folder (this is the native code).

3. Create the folder android-ndk_r1/apps/Doom/project/jni and copy the native code from ch05.Android.Doom/native/prboom.

4. Create a Makefile called Android.mk in NDK_ROOT/apps/Doom/project/jni. This Makefile should appear as follows:

```
LOCAL_PATH := $(call my-dir)

# clear vars
include $(CLEAR_VARS)

# module name
LOCAL_MODULE := doom
LP := $(LOCAL_PATH)

# doom folder
DOOM := apps/Doom/project/jni

# includes
INC := -I$(DOOM) -I$(DOOM)/include

DOOM_FLAGS := -DNORMALUNIX -DLINUX -DHAVE_CONFIG_H

OPTS := -O3 -ffast-math  -fexpensive-optimizations
LOCAL_CFLAGS := $(DOOM_FLAGS)  $(OPTS) $(INC)

# sources
LOCAL_SRC_FILES          := \
am_map.c    m_cheat.c    p_lights.c p_user.c    sounds.c \
hu_lib.c       md5.c       p_map.c    r_bsp.c    s_sound.c \
d_deh.c    hu_stuff.c   m_menu.c     p_maputl.c r_data.c    st_lib.c \
d_items.c      m_misc.c     p_mobj.c    r_demo.c    st_stuff.c \
d_main.c   info.c          p_plats.c  r_draw.c    tables.c \
doomdef.c      m_random.c   p_pspr.c    r_filter.c version.c \
doomstat.c     p_ceilng.c   p_saveg.c  r_fps.c     v_video.c \
p_checksum.c p_setup.c   r_main.c    wi_stuff.c \
dstrings.c   p_doors.c    p_sight.c   r_patch.c   w_memcache.c \
f_finale.c     p_enemy.c    p_spec.c    r_plane.c   w_mmap.c \
f_wipe.c    lprintf.c    p_floor.c    p_switch.c r_segs.c    w_wad.c \
g_game.c    m_argv.c     p_genlin.c   p_telept.c r_sky.c      z_bmalloc.c \
m_bbox.c       p_inter.c    p_tick.c    r_things.c z_zone.c \
d_client.c   d_server.c \
droid/i_video.c droid/i_network.c droid/i_joy.c \
droid/i_system.c droid/i_main.c droid/i_sound.c \
droid/jni_doom.c

# Build libdoom.so
include $(BUILD_SHARED_LIBRARY)
```

5. Finally, run make APP=Doom from the NDK root folder. The output
    library libdoom.so will be stored in Doom/project/libs/armeabi and
    ready to use. Import the Doom/project into your Eclipse workspace,
    and start the game.

Testing Doom in the Emulator

To test the game in the emulator, create a launch configuration within your Eclipse IDE, as follows:

1. From the main menu, select Run ➤ Run Configurations.

2. Enter a name for the configuration (Doom) and select the project ch05.
   Android.Doom.

3. Set the Launch Action as Launch Default Activity. Figure 5-3 shows
   the completed Run Configurations dialog box for this example.

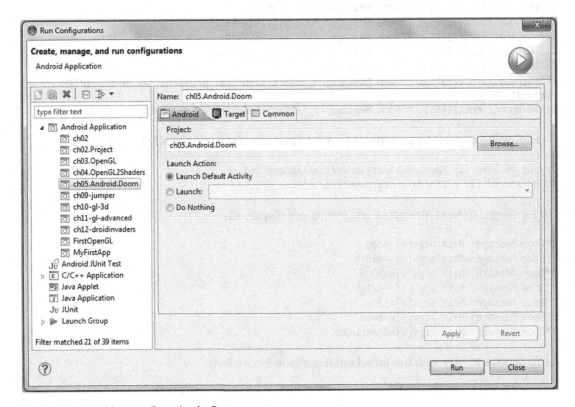

Figure 5-3. Android run configuration for Doom

4. Click Run.

Now let's play some Doom! From the emulator, click Menu ➤ Start and monitor the log view to make sure everything works.

Consider the log fragment in Listing 5-25.

Listing 5-25. Log Fragment from a Doom Run

```
DEBUG/DoomClient(23981): Loading JNI library from doom_jni
DEBUG/LibLoader(23981): Trying to load library doom_jni from LD_PATH: /system/lib
DEBUG/dalvikvm(23981): Trying to load lib /data/data/org.doom/lib/libdoom_jni.so 0x43733de8
DEBUG/dalvikvm(23981): Added shared lib /data/data/org.doom/lib/libdoom_jni.so 0x43733de8
DEBUG/dalvikvm(23981): No JNI_OnLoad found in /data/data/org.doom/lib/libdoom_jni.so&#229x;
  0x43733de8
DEBUG/DoomTools(23981): Sound folder: /sdcard/doom/sound
DEBUG/DoomClient(23981): Starting doom thread with wad doom1.wad sound enabled? true&#229x;
  Orientation:1
DEBUG/DoomClient(23981): **Doom Message: Main argv[0]=doom
DEBUG/DoomClient(23981): **Doom Message: Main argv[1]=-width
DEBUG/DoomClient(23981): **Doom Message: Main argv[2]=480
DEBUG/DoomClient(23981): **Doom Message: Main argv[3]=-height
DEBUG/DoomClient(23981): **Doom Message: Main argv[4]=320
DEBUG/DoomClient(23981): **Doom Message: Main argv[5]=-iwad
DEBUG/DoomClient(23981): **Doom Message: Main argv[6]=doom1.wad
DEBUG/DoomClient(23981): **Doom Message: I_UpdateVideoMode: 480x320 (fullscreen)&#229x;
  default VM=8
DEBUG/DoomClient(23981): **Doom Message: I_SetRes: Creating 480x320 image.
```

The following two lines show that the native library is loaded successfully by the JVM:

```
Trying to load lib /data/data/org.doom/lib/libdoom_jni.so
Added shared lib /data/data/org.doom/lib/libdoom_jni.so
```

So far, so good. Next, the game arguments are displayed.

```
**Doom Message: Main argv[0]=doom
**Doom Message: Main argv[1]=-width
**Doom Message: Main argv[2]=480
**Doom Message: Main argv[3]=-height
**Doom Message: Main argv[4]=320
**Doom Message: Main argv[5]=-iwad
**Doom Message: Main argv[6]=doom1.wad
```

Let's choose to play with the tablet emulator (see Figure 5-4).

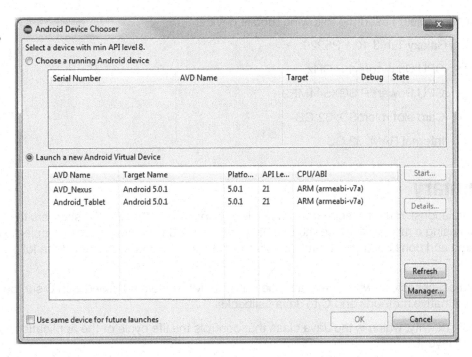

Figure 5-4. Start the tablet emulator

At this point, the game has successfully loaded and is ready for action (see Figure 5-5).

Figure 5-5. Doom running in the Android emulator

To test this project I used the following mobile device:

Samsung Galaxy Tab 3 10.1 P5220:

- CPU Dual-core 1.6 GHz
- GPU PowerVR SGX544MP2
- Card slot microSD: 32 GB
- Internal RAM: 32 GB

Summary

Congratulations! You have seen how easy it is to bring one of the first PC shooters to Android using a mix of Java and the original C engine. You've evaluated the complexity of the game and considered the best way to implement it. This chapter covered the following topics:

The game architecture, where Java activities and UI XML layouts are glued with C subroutines using JNI native methods and C to Java callbacks.

The main activity, which is the Java class that controls the life cycle of the application, along with a UI layout.

User interface handlers, such as menus, keys, and touch event handlers, plus native callback handlers for graphics initialization, video buffer updates, fatal errors, and audio requests

You've also looked at custom touch screen controls for phones that do not have a keyboard. You've seen that the native interface class has callback listeners for clients that wish to receive C to Java callbacks, native methods invoked through JNI to start the game loop and send key and motion event information to the Native library, and C to Java callbacks used to delegate engine messages to the listener activity.

You've looked at the native layer that glues together the Java and C code and provides the native method implementations. Changes to the original code are also required to remove invalid dependencies and insert the C to Java callbacks. Finally, you've seen the Makefile required to compile the Native library and the IDE launch configuration to test the game in the emulator.

Using the Java/C power combo, you have brought one of the great and highly popular PC games, Doom, to the platform. Even though Google is pushing for Java-only development and provides little or no support for native development, Java alone is not the best choice when it comes to advanced mobile gaming. Java-only code works fine for the regular mobile app, but it is not enough for high-performance graphics.

3D Shooters for Quake

This is where things start to get really exciting. I've always been a huge fan of first-person shooters (FPS), and when Android came along, I had to jump at the chance of getting involved in bringing this gem (Quake) to the platform in all its beauty. Almost everybody knows of or has played this astounding game for the PC. It was originally created in 1996 by the great game developer John Carmack for id Software.

Quake is the successor to the Doom game series. At the time of this writing it was possible to play Quake online following this link: `http://www.quakelive.com/#!home`.

The Quake engine of the game was developed by id Software when powering their 1996 video game Quake. It is a 3D real-time rendering and like Doom, it is licensed under the terms of the GNU General Public License (GPL).

In this chapter, you will learn how a minimum investment in development time can translate into maximum return on investment (ROI) for your organization. That is my goal. I am sure you have a lot of invested PC code or engines gathering dust somewhere on your servers. Well, why not reuse that code for your mobile projects? The GPL Quake I Engine brought to Android kept 98% of the original code intact. This chapter demonstrates the power of code reuse.

> **Note** All the code included in this chapter was developed, compiled and tested using Eclipse IDE for Java Developers instead of Android Studio 1.0.1 since, when this manuscript was written, NDK and JNI were not supported by Android Studio.

A Little About the Quake Jargon

The Quake engine, like the Doom engine, uses binary space partitioning (BSP) to optimize the world rendering.

I don't want to explain the inner workings of the Quake engine (an entire book will not be enough for that); instead, I want to demonstrate how to get this engine quickly up and running in Android. But before I do, let's go over the basic lingo used in this 3D engine.

This knowledge will help you understand some of the code if you decide to dig in to the engine source. Here's a rudimentary dictionary:

- *Quake*: A true 3D game that uses a map design system to display a pre-rendered 3D environment to reduce the processing in slow CPUs.

- *Maps*: A 3D environment where the game takes place. Maps are created with a map editor program that uses a number of simple convex 3D geometric objects known as brushes.

- *Brushes*: Brushes are placed and oriented to create an enclosed, empty, volumetric space; they then run through the rendering preprocessor.

- *Pruning*: Maps are preprocessed to reduce polygon count from the original unprocessed count. This step is called *pruning*.

- *Quake sky*: The famous cloudy sky in Quake is, in fact, closed space covered over and enclosed with brushes and then textured with a special skybox texture that always looks the same from any viewing position, giving the illusion of a distant sky.

- *Lightmaps* and *3D light sources*: id Software's innovation that has since become common in many 3D games. A lightmap is a data structure that contains the brightness of surfaces. It is precomputed and normally used with light sources for 3D Surface Model Animation.

- *Map sectioning*: A technique to increase rendering speed by sectioning off large regions of the map that are currently not visible to the player and to render those unseen spaces. With this engine optimization, if the player could not see into a nearby region, the 3D engine could be alerted to not include any of the objects in that space in the rendering calculations, greatly reducing the rendering load on the CPU.

- *Binary space partitioning* (BSP): A technique used to section a map by building a tree from the map. Each leaf represents an area of 3D space. The leaves of this binary tree have polygons of the original map associated with them, which are then used for computing each area's visibility. This process uses large amounts of memory and takes a time complexity of $O(n2)$ (where n is the number of polygons).

- *Run-length encoding* (RLE): A simple form of data compression where sequences of the same data value occur in many consecutive data elements and are stored as a single data value and count, rather than as the original run. This encoding is used to compress sections of the BSP tree and is what allows Quake's sophisticated graphics to run so quickly on low-end hardware.

- *Overdraw*: The process of rendering a new pixel that hides a previously rendered point, meaning the previous work was wasted. To minimize overdraw, the environment was displayed first, from front to back.

- *Z-buffering*: A technique used to decide which elements of a rendered scene are visible and which are hidden by using a two-dimensional array (x-y) with one element for each screen pixel of an object that is rendered. If another object of the scene must be rendered in the same pixel, the graphics card compares the two depths and chooses the one closer to the observer. The chosen depth is then saved to the z-buffer, replacing the old one.

- *Surface cache*: A cache that contains new pre-lighted textures combined with the base and lightmap textures. It is used to speed up the rendering of walls and their lightmap textures.

The Power of Code Reuse: Quake in Less Than 500 Lines of New Code

If I were a full-time PC game developer and I was told that I could have Quake (with the full OpenGL renderer) running in Android with less than 500 lines of new code, while keeping most of the original game intact, I'd probably say, "Are you crazy?" Once you start digging into the source of the OpenGL renderer of the engine, you'd realize how hard it is to bring this engine to a mobile device. Let's examine why.

OpenGL Is Not the Same as OpenGL ES

As mentioned, Quake is an engine written for the PC in 1996; nevertheless even a PC of the '90s is arguably more powerful than some of today's phones. The problem is that the renderer in Quake uses OpenGL, which is a superset of OpenGL ES (used in phones/tablets).

The current version of OpenGL ES 3.1 specification was publicly released in March 2014. We covered many of the details of OpenGL ES 3.1 in Chapter 4. Here is a list of some new functionality included in OpenGL ES 3.1:

- Independent vertex

- Shading language improvements

- Independent fragment shaders

- Optional extensions

- Compute shaders

- Indirect draw commands

Let's take a look at some of the differences between OpenGL and OpenGL ES.

Immediate Mode Drawing

Immediate mode drawing is perhaps the biggest caveat for the Android version of Quake. Immediate mode is a technique used for specifying geometry; for example, consider the following snippet to render an arbitrary polygon and corresponding texture:

```
// Bind some texture
glBegin (GL_POLYGON);
glTexCoord2f (...);
glVertex3fv (...);
...
glEnd ();
```

This code is typical of a desktop application; however, it is not valid in Android (which implements OpenGL ES). This is because OpenGL ES does not support immediate mode (glBegin/glEnd) for simple geometry. Porting this code would require line-by-line changes, which can consume significant resources (especially for a game such as Quake, which has approximately 100,000 lines of C source).

In OpenGL ES, geometry must be specified using vertex arrays, so the preceding code becomes something like the following:

```
const GLbyte Vertices []= { ...};
const GLbyte TexCoords []= { ...};
...
glEnableClientState (GL_VERTEX_ARRAY);
glEnableClientState (GL_TEXTCOORD_ARRAY);

glVertexPointer (..., GL_BYTE , 0, Vertices);
glTexCoordPointer (..., GL_BYTE , 0, TexCoords);
glDrawArrays (GL_TRIANGLES, 0, ...);
```

This code achieves a similar result as the previous one by using arrays of vertices and coordinates to describe the polygon, and then drawing using triangles. Now, the renderer of Quake is full (and I mean full) of immediate mode calls. Believe me when I say that translating immediate mode into array pointers is not an option. As a matter of fact, there is a project called GLES Quake (http://grammerjack.blogspot.com/2009/10/gles-quake-port-of-quake-to-android.html) that did just that. The guy even took the time to convert all the C files into C++. Oh my, I feel sorry for the poor soul who did this work. It must have been painful.

Floating Point Issues

You must also consider floating-point issues. OpenGL ES defines functions that use fixed-point values, as many devices do not have a floating-point unit (FPU). Fixed-point math is a technique to encode floating-point numbers using only integers. OpenGL ES uses 16 bits to represent the integer part and another 16 bits to represent the fractional part. The following is an example of using a fixed-point translation function:

```
glTranslatex (10 << 16, 0, 0, 2 << 16); // glTranslatef (10.0f, 0.0f, 0.0f, 2.0f);
```

Other Issues

The following are other differences between OpenGL and OpenGL ES:

- OpenGL ES does not render polygons as wireframe or points (only solids).

- There is no GLU (OpenGL Utility Library) in OpenGL ES. It is possible, however, to find implementations of GLU functions on the Internet.

- The GL_QUADS, GL_QUAD_STRIP, and GL_POLYGON primitives are not supported.

- The attribute stack used to save OpenGL state is not supported. This essentially means that calls such as glPushAttrib and glPopAttrib are not supported, including their associated constants GL_COLOR_BUFFER_BIT, GL_CURRENT_BIT, GL_ENABLE_BIT, GL_HINT_BIT, etc.

- Quake uses OpenGL standard extensions not supported by ES; for example GL_ARB_multitexture, which is an Architecture Review Board (hence ARB) standard introduced in OpenGL version 1.2.1 is not available on OpenGL ES.

These are some of the things to watch for when you decide to port your OpenGL game to an embedded device. When thinking about a powerful game engine like Quake (or any other engine, for that matter), there are two basic paths when it comes to graphics rendering: software or hardware (OpenGL). Each has its advantages and disadvantages. Let's take a look at each one and the reason I chose to use hardware acceleration.

Is the Software Renderer a Possible Solution?

It certainly is. You could drop the Quake OpenGL (hardware) renderer and use the software renderer also provided with the source; however, this will make the game painfully slow, playable to around 15–20 frames per second (FPS) in a mid-size device. On the positive side, it will also be simpler to compile. Ultimately, this is not a good solution because you can achieve over 50 FPS if you use a hardware renderer.

NanoGL: The Life Saver

So let's definitely drop the software renderer. But what can you use to fix the big problem of immediate mode? Enter NanoGL (www.ohloh.net/p/nanogl). This is a wonderful, tiny piece of software written by Oli Hinka for the Nokia N97 hardware. It is available under the GNU General Public License. (You'll just have to get past the fact that it was written for Nokia. No matter.) You can get this library up and running for Android in no time. Because it is very well written, you can actually keep about 98% of the original C++ code. The only thing you need to do is some initialization and dynamic loading logic, as shown in Listing 6-1.

> **Tip**   The entire NanoGL project is available from this book's source in the NanoGL folder.

Listing 6-1. NanoGL Initializer for Android: nanogl.cpp

```cpp
// nanogl.cpp: Some code has been removed for simplicity
// GL ES structure with GL function pointers
#include "glesinterface.h"

#define GL_ENTRY(_r, _api, ...) #_api,

// function pointer names. Must match glesinterface.h
static char const * const gl_names[] = {
    #include "gl_entries.in"
    NULL
};

// OpenGL ES lib pointer
static void* glesLib = NULL;

GlESInterface* glEsImpl = NULL;

extern void InitGLStructs();

static void gl_unimplemented() {
  LOGE ("Called unimplemented OpenGL ES API\n");
}

// Create GLES interface
// name : Library name
// lib, lib1: 2 shared libraries to try to load GL symbols from
// defaut_func: Function to call if load symbol fails
static int CreateGlEsInterface( const char * name, void * lib, void * lib1, void *
default_func )
{
  // alloc space
  if ( !glEsImpl )
    glEsImpl = (GlESInterface *) malloc(sizeof(GlESInterface));

  if (!glEsImpl) {
      return 0;
    }

  // load GL API calls
  char const * const * api;
  api = gl_names;

  // nanoGL interface pointer
  void ** ptr = (void **)(glEsImpl);

  while (*api)
  {
    void * f;

    f = dlsym(lib, *api); // try ibGLESxx_CM.so
```

```
  if (f == NULL) {
    LOGW( "<%s> not found in %s. Trying libEGL.so.", *api, name);
    // try lib1
    if ( lib1 ) {
      f = dlsym(lib1, *api); // libEGL.so

      if ( f == NULL ) {
        LOGE ( "<%s> not found in libEGL.so", *api);
        f = default_func;          }
      else {
        LOGD ("<%s> @ 0x%p\n", *api, f);
      }
    }
    else
      f = default_func;
  }
  else {
    LOGD ("<%s> @ 0x%p\n", *api, f);
  }

    *ptr++ = f;
    api++;
  }

  return 1;
}

// Load using the dynamic loader
static int loadDriver(const char * name) {
  glesLib = dlopen(name, RTLD_NOW | RTLD_LOCAL);
  int rc = (glesLib) ? 1 : 0;
  return rc;
}

/**
 * Initialize interface
 */
int nanoGL_Init()
{
  const char * lib1 = "libGLESv1_CM.so";  // Opengl ES lib
  const char * lib2 = "libGLESv2.so";
  const char * lib3 = "libEGL.so";
  const char * driver;

  // load lib1: libGLESv1_CM.so
  LOGI("nanoGL: Init loading driver %s\n", lib1);

  if ( ! loadDriver(lib1) )
  {
    LOGE("Failed to load driver %s. Trying %s\n", lib1, lib2);
```

```
      if ( ! loadDriver(lib2) ) {
        LOGE ("Failed to load  %s.\n", lib2);
        return 0;
      }
      else
        driver = lib2;
   }
   else
     driver = lib1;

   void * eglLib;

    LOGD ("**** Will Load EGL subs from %s ****", lib3);

    eglLib = dlopen(lib3, RTLD_NOW | RTLD_LOCAL);

    if ( ! eglLib ) {
       LOGE ( "Failed to load %s", lib3);
    }

   // Load API gl* for 1.5+  else egl* gl*
   if ( !CreateGlEsInterface(driver, glesLib, eglLib, (void *) gl_unimplemented) == -1)
     {
     // release lib
     LOGE ( "CreateGlEsInterface failed.");

     dlclose(glesLib);
       return 0;
     }

   // Init nanoGL
   InitGLStructs();
   return 1;
}

void nanoGL_Destroy()
{
   LOGD ("nanoGL_Destroy");

   if (glEsImpl) {
        free( glEsImpl);
        glEsImpl = NULL;
     }

   // release lib
   dlclose(glesLib);
}
```

Listing 6-1 has the following two public functions and one private function, which drive the entire process:

- nanoGL_Init(): This function is meant to be called from your code to initialize the NanoGL interface, and it must be called before any OpenGL operations. Its job is to load the OpenGL ES library and create an interface between itself and OpenGL ES by calling CreateGlEsInterface. After this process completes, any OpenGL calls (such as immediate mode drawing) will be filtered through this interface and sent transparently to the OpenGL ES backend.

- nanoGL_Destroy(): This function can be called when you are done with OpenGL and want to release resources. It is usually called when your program terminates.

- CreateGlEsInterface(): This is where all the magic happens. This is a private function that loads the OpenGL interface in a very clever way, as explained in the "Quake for Android Architecture" section.

nanoGL_Init starts by searching for an OpenGL ES library to load.

```
const char * lib1 = "libGLESv1_CM.so";
const char * lib2 = "libGLESv2.so";
const char * driver;

if ( ! loadDriver(lib1) ) {
  // failed to load libGLESv1_CM.so

  if ( ! loadDriver(lib2) ) {
    // failed to load libGLESv2.so. Abort.
    return 0;
  }
  else
    driver = lib2; // use libGLESv2.so
}
else
  driver = lib1;   // use libGLESv1_CM.so
```

nanoGL_Init's search order starts with libGLESv1_CM.so, which is the main OpenGL ES library. If libGLESv1_CM.so cannot be found (this should not happen in any standard Android device), then it attempts to load libGLESv2.so (OpenGL ES version 2). If both fail, it bails out and returns an error. To load the library, NanoGL uses loadDriver, which wraps the UNIX system call.

```
dlopen(name, RTLD_NOW | RTLD_LOCAL)
```

This system call loads a dynamic library from the OS search path and returns a pointer to the loaded library. With this pointer, you can then load symbols (functions) and other data structures from the library using the system call.

```
void * function = dlsym(library, "function_name")
```

This system call loads a function given by function_name from the library and stores it in a pointer that can be used to call the function dynamically (on the fly). Finally, nanoGL_Init calls CreateGlEsInterface to create the OpenGL ES interface.

CreateGlEsInterface loops through two data structures, as shown in Listing 6-2. The first is a set of function pointers defined in the structure GlESInterface. This structure contains a function pointer for every API call in OpenGL ES. The second data structure is a set of API entries defined in gl_entries.in. For every function pointer in GlESInterface there must be an equivalent API entry in gl_entries.in in the same order. The order is absolutely crucial, because if it does not match, then horrible things will happen at runtime.

At the end of the loop, the GlESInterface will point to all the OpenGL ES functions defined in the API. This allows NanoGL to work as a filter for OpenGL. Thus, whenever the Quake engine does a GL API call (glBegin, for example), NanoGL will filter the call through its interface, perform its magic, and send the result to the underlying OpenGL ES backend, effectively solving the immediate mode drawing dilemma.

Listing 6-2. Data Structures Used to Initialize the NanoGL Interface

```
/*
    // gl_entries.in
    GL_ENTRY(int,eglChooseConfig,int dpy, const int *attrib_list,
            int *configs, int config_size, int *num_config)
    GL_ENTRY(int,eglCopyBuffers,int dpy, int surface, void* target)
    GL_ENTRY(int,eglCreateContext,int dpy, int config,
            int share_list, const int *attrib_list)

// GL
    GL_ENTRY(void,glActiveTexture,unsigned int texture)
    GL_ENTRY(void,glAlphaFunc,unsigned int func, float ref)
    GL_ENTRY(void,glAlphaFuncx,unsigned int func, int ref)
    GL_ENTRY(void,glBindTexture,unsigned int target, unsigned int texture)
    // More GL functions here
*/
// glesinterface.h
struct GlESInterface
 {
    // entries must match gl_entries.in
    int (*eglChooseConfig) (int dpy, const int *attrib_list, int *configs
            , int config_size, int *num_config);
    int (*eglCopyBuffers) (int dpy, int surface, void* target);
    int (*eglCreateContext) (int dpy, int config, int share_list, const int *attrib_list);

    void (*glActiveTexture) (unsigned int texture);
    void (*glAlphaFunc) (unsigned int func, float ref);
    void (*glAlphaFuncx) (unsigned int func, int ref);
    void (*glBindTexture) (unsigned int target, unsigned int texture);
    // More functions here
 }
```

You'll compile NanoGL as a static library within the Quake project so that it can be reused by other engines, such as Quake II, in Chapter 7. Now let's take a look at the changes required to get the engine going.

Quake for Android Architecture

NanoGL allows you to reuse about 90% of the renderer with no changes and about 95% of the entire engine. Figure 6-1 shows the architecture of this app. The light boxes represent thin Java wrapper classes. The darker box is the C engine where most of the work will take place.

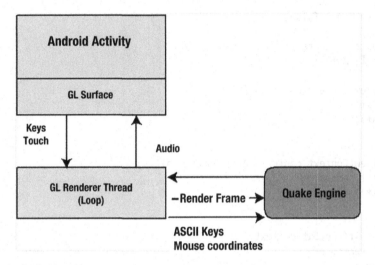

Figure 6-1. *Quake for Android architecture*

In the following sections, you'll learn how to create a nimble Java OpenGL renderer for Quake. Next, you'll see how to handle audio independently of the format and how to provide support for keyboard and multi-touch events. But first, let's see how the rendering works.

Java OpenGL Renderer Architecture

Android provides the built-in classes GLSurfaceView and GLSurfaceView.Renderer, which you can extend for this implementation. These classes are very thin and their only job is to provide a simple interface between the device and the native library. Listing 6-3 shows the implementation.

Tip   The full source for the renderer is available from the book source under ch06.Quake.

Listing 6-3. Implementation of GLSurfaceView and Renderer for Quake

```java
package com.opengl;
// ...
public class QuakeView extends GLSurfaceView implements Natives.EventListener {
  private static final String TAG = "QuakeView";

  {
    // Load native lob
    System.loadLibrary("quake");
  }

  boolean mGameLoaded = false;

  // private Context mContext;
  private String[] mArgs;

  public QuakeView(Context context) {
    super(context);
    init(context);
  }

  public QuakeView(Context context, AttributeSet attrs) {
    super(context, attrs);
    init(context);
  }

  private void init(Context context) {
    // We want events.
    setFocusable(true);
    setFocusableInTouchMode(true);
    requestFocus();

    Log.d(TAG, "QuakeView init");

    // Listen for JNI events
    Natives.setListener(this);
  }

  public void setRenderer(String[] args) {
    mArgs = args;

    Log.d(TAG, "Setting startup args & renderer");

    setRenderer(new QuakeRenderer());
  }

  /**
   * Renderer
   */
```

```java
public class QuakeRenderer implements GLSurfaceView.Renderer {

  @Override
  public void onDrawFrame(GL10 arg0) {
    if (mGameLoaded) {
      Natives.RenderFrame();
    }
  }

  @Override
  public void onSurfaceChanged(GL10 arg0, int width, int height) {
    Log.d(TAG, "onSurfaceChanged w=" + width + " h=" + height);

  }

  @Override
  public void onSurfaceCreated(GL10 arg0, EGLConfig arg1) {
    Log.d(TAG, "onSurfaceCreated");

    if (mArgs != null) {
      mGameLoaded = true;
      Natives.QuakeMain(mArgs);
    }
  }
}

/**
 * Native Callbacks
 */
@Override
public void OnInitVideo(int w, int h) {
  Log.d(TAG, "OnInitVideo. " + w + "x" + h + " Starting native audio.");

  // Native audio
  NativeAudio.start();
}}
```

The class QuakeView from Listing 6-3 extends the built-in class GLSurfaceView, which provides a surface for rendering using OpenGL. QuakeView also includes the following classes:

- QuakeRenderer: An inner class that creates a simple OpenGL renderer, which can be used to call native functions on the C engine. This class provides the following events:

  - onDrawFrame: This event fires whenever the renderer draws a frame and is used to perform OpenGL API calls. It has one argument: GL10, the interface to the OpenGL context. In a pure Java game, this context will be used to perform GL API calls; however, you are rendering everything in the native side so this parameter is not used.

- onSurfaceChanged: This event fires whenever the surface changes, such as when it is first created or when the orientation of the parent changes. It can fire many times throughout the lifetime of the application.

- onSurfaceCreated: This event fires only once when the surface is first created. It receives a GL context (GL10) and the GL configuration (EGLConfig). It is useful to adjust the graphics configuration such as pixel, format, depth buffer, and more.

- Natives: This is a user-defined interface class to all things native. It contains the definitions of the native methods to be called from Java, which are as follows:

  - QuakeMain(String[] argv): This is the main entry point to the engine. It essentially calls the main C function with an array of string arguments.

  - RenderFrame(): This native function renders 1 frame of the game.

  - keyPress(int key): This function sends an ASCII key-pressed event to the engine.

  - keyRelease(int key): This function sends an ASCII key-released event to the engine.

  - mouseLook(int mouseX, int mouseY): This native function is used to send the XY delta coordinates of a touch event used to look around 3D space whenever a finger is dragged on screen.

  - PaintAudio(ByteBuffer buf): This function is used to read a byte buffer from the native audio buffer of the engine. The buffer is then played from Java using the Android MediaTrack API.

- The Natives class also wraps a set of JNI-C callbacks that the engine uses to send information back to the thin Java wrappers (see Listing 6-4). These callbacks are as follows:

  - OnInitVideo(int w, int h): This tells Java that the native video has been initialized. It is used to start the Java audio thread.

  - OnSysError(String message): This method is called by the engine when a fatal system error occurs and the program needs to terminate.

Listing 6-4. Java Class for Native Functions and C Callbacks

```
package quake.jni;

import java.nio.ByteBuffer;
import android.util.Log;

public class Natives {
  public static final String TAG = "Natives";

  private static EventListener listener;
```

```java
public static interface EventListener {
  void OnInitVideo(int w, int h);
}

public static void setListener(EventListener l) {
  listener = l;
}

/**
 * Main Quake Sub
 * @param argv Engine args
 * @return
 */
public static native int QuakeMain(String[] argv);

/**
 * Render 1 frame
 *
 */
public static native int RenderFrame();

/**
 * Key press
 * @param key ascii code
 */
public static native int keyPress(int key);

/**
 * Key release
 */
public static native int keyRelease(int key);

/**
 * Forward movement using mouse coords
 * @param mouseX Delta X
 * @param mousey Delta Y
 */
public static native int mouseMove(int mouseX, int mouseY);

/**
 * Native audio painter. The native code will write audio bytes to the buffer.
 * Mostly PCM 16 stero 22500 (WAV)
 */
public static native int PaintAudio(ByteBuffer buf);

/**********************************************************
 * C - Callbacks
 **********************************************************/
```

```
/**
 * Fires on init graphics
 *
 * @param w  width of the image
 * @param h height
 */
private static void OnInitVideo(int w, int h) {
  if (listener != null)
    listener.OnInitVideo(w, h);
}

/**
 * Fires when the C lib calls SysError()
 * @param message
 */
private static void OnSysError(final String message) {
  Log.e(TAG, "Natives::OnSysError " + message);

  if (listener != null)
    listener.OnSysError(message);

}
}
```

To listen for events from the native engine, QuakeView implements Natives.EventListener
and calls

```
// Listen for JNI events
Natives.setListener(this);
```

An important step is to load the native library using the System class.

```
// Load native lib
System.loadLibrary("quake");
```

This loads the library libquake.so from the project folder libs/armeabi. This library load
takes care of the renderer, but you must also handle audio, keyboard, and touch events.

Handling Audio Independently of the Format

One of the most frustrating things when working with native code in Android is audio
handling. There are few options to work with outside the Java realm, making native
development very tough. In the early days, Google used the obscure Enhanced Audio
System (EAS) API to provide audio. I've never heard about it or seen any game engine use
it. Nevertheless, progress has been made and now new open APIs such as Open Audio
Library, or OpenAL, are supported. OpenAL is used by modern engines, but unfortunately
Quake does not use it.

Luckily, there is a neat feature from JNI to access the memory address from a Java
ByteBuffer within C. This allows the native code to simply write audio bytes to that memory
address, which in turn will be played by the Java code using the Android MediaTrack API.

> **Tip** Using the MediaTrack API provides audio format independence. Whatever the format of your sound file, Android will detect it and call the right driver for it (as long as the format is supported by the platform). Moreover, it works in all versions of Android, thus giving you the widest range of device support.

The process works as follows:

1. Consider a class dubbed NativeAudio that drives the audio playback with a static method start. Within start, you create a Java thread that contains an instance of the Android MediaTrack API.

2. MediaTrack can be used to play audio by declaring an instance of an audio track with a set of user-defined audio parameters. In this case, you want to stream (hence AudioManager.STREAM_MUSIC) at a frequency of 22kHz using two channels (STEREO) with a buffer size of 4 * (22050 / 5).

   ```
   mTrack = new AudioTrack(
       android.media.AudioManager.STREAM_MUSIC,
       22050,
       AudioFormat.CHANNEL_CONFIGURATION_STEREO, // stereo
       AudioFormat.ENCODING_PCM_16BIT,  // 16 bit audio
       4 * (22050 / 5),                 // Buffer size
       AudioTrack.MODE_STREAM);
   ```

3. When the thread starts, it enters a loop continuously reading from the C engine using the native function Natives. PaintAudio(audioBuffer). The process continues until the loop is told to stop using a boolean variable. In that case, the thread terminates and the audio track is disposed, as shown in Listing 6-5.

Listing 6-5. Playing Native Audio Using Android's MediaTrack

```
public class NativeAudio {

  public static void start() {

    mStarted = true;

    new Thread(new Runnable() {
      public void run() {
        // Android Audio API
        AudioTrack mTrack;
```

```
mTrack = new AudioTrack(android.media.AudioManager.STREAM_MUSIC,
    22050,
    AudioFormat.CHANNEL_CONFIGURATION_STEREO, // stereo
    AudioFormat.ENCODING_PCM_16BIT, // 16 bit audio
    4 * (22050 / 5),                // Buffer size
    AudioTrack.MODE_STREAM);

int audioSize = (2048 * 4);
ByteBuffer audioBuffer = ByteBuffer.allocateDirect(audioSize);

byte[] audioData = new byte[audioSize];

Log.d(TAG, "Audio start.");

mTrack.play();

while (!mDone) {
  if (!mPaused) {
    Natives.PaintAudio(audioBuffer);

    audioBuffer.position(0);
    audioBuffer.get(audioData);

    // Write the byte array to the track
    mTrack.write(audioData, 0, audioData.length);
  } else {
    try {
      Thread.sleep(100);
    } catch (Exception e) {
    }
  }
}

    }
  }).start();
  }
}
```

Tip   Quake encodes audio files in 16–bit WAV format at a frequency of 22 kHz.

Finally, whenever you want to start the audio playback, you can simply call `Nativeaudio.start()`. At that point, the Java thread fires and begins reading audio bytes from the C library. This is not an optimal solution (the most efficient one would be to write the audio directly from the native engine), but it works very well with no lag in sound whatsoever. The following are some things to carefully consider:

■ The Java audio buffer must be a direct `ByteBuffer`. This is critical, as the code cannot use short or integer buffers. A direct `ByteBuffer` is required because the Java virtual machine makes a best effort to perform native I/O operations directly upon it. On the other hand, non-direct byte buffers copy the content to (or from) an intermediate buffer before (or after) each invocation of one of the underlying operating system's native I/O operations.

■ The native engine should use a byte array of audio encoded in the same format (in this case 16–bit stereo at 22 kHz), which is copied into the Java byte buffer and then played by the audio track.

■ The `NativeAudio` class requires the companion JNI C function `PaintAudio` to copy the native `ByteBuffer` into the Java byte buffer, as shown in Listing 6-6.

Listing 6-6. Companion PaintAudio JNI Function for NativeAudio

```
// copy len bytes of native audio into stream
extern int paint_audio (void *unused, void * stream, int len);

JNIEXPORT jint JNICALL Java_quake_jni_Natives_PaintAudio
 ( JNIEnv* env, jobject thiz, jobject buf )
{
    void *stream;
    int len;

    stream = (*env)->GetDirectBufferAddress(env,  buf);
    len = (*env)->GetDirectBufferCapacity (env, buf);

    return paint_audio ( NULL, stream, len );
}
```

As you can see from Listing 6-6, `PaintAudio` must be declared as native in the Java class `quake.jni.Natives.java`. Note the calls to `GetDirectBufferAddress`, which fetch and return the starting address of the memory region referenced by the given direct `java.nio.Buffer`. Also note `GetDirectBufferCapacity`, which returns the capacity in bytes of the memory region referenced by the given direct buffer.

Now that you have a reference to the Java byte buffer and its size, you can call the native audio painter to fill it up.

Handling Keyboard Events

You can listen for key presses or releases in Android by simply overriding the methods onKeyDown and onKeyUp in a view or main activity class. The process can be summarized as follows (also see Listing 6-7):

- When a key is pressed or released, the events onKeyDown or onKeyUp fire in the OpenGL view class QuakeView. It is important to note that Quake handles keys in ASCII format, but Android uses a different encoding format, so you must use the delegate class QuakeKeyEvents to translate them.

- The delegate QuakeEvents translates the key into an ASCII code and invokes the native method keyPress or keyRelease, respectively. ASCII code is then sent to the engine for consumption.

- The companion C implementations for keyPress and keyRelease named Java_quake_jni_Natives_keyPress and Java_quake_jni_Natives_ keyRelease push the ASCII key to the engine queue using Key_Event.

The translation of the Android keys to ASCII can be tricky; this is where hardware fragmentation issues come into play. As you can see in Listing 6-7, an array of integers (sKeyCodeToQuakeCode) is used for key translation, where the index of the array represents the Android key and the value is the ASCII code. This array works well in the Motorola Droid 1, but it will not be accurate in other devices, as each vendor builds keyboards with different layouts. Not even among the Motorola Droid versions 1, 2, and 3 are the layouts the same. This means you may have to adjust the array slightly, depending on what device keyboards you need to support. Hardware fragmentation is just a fact of life in open platforms.

Listing 6-7. Keyboard Java/C Handlers

```
// In QuakeView.java

  public boolean onKeyDown(final int keyCode, final KeyEvent event) {
    queueEvent(new Runnable() {
      public void run() {
        QuakeKeyEvents.onKeyDown(keyCode, event);
      }
    });
    return true;
  }

  public boolean onKeyUp(final int keyCode, final KeyEvent event) {

    queueEvent(new Runnable() {
      public void run() {
        QuakeKeyEvents.onKeyUp(keyCode, event);
      }
    });
    return true;
  }
```

```
// In QuakeEvents.java
  public static final int K_TAB = 9;
  public static final int K_ENTER = 13;
  public static final int K_ESCAPE = 27;
  public static final int K_SPACE = 32;

  // more ASCII keys...

  //key maps for motorola droid
  private static final int[] sKeyCodeToQuakeCode = {
        '$', K_ESCAPE, '$', '$',  K_ESCAPE, K_CTRL, '$', '0', // digits 0..7
        '1', '2', '3', '4',  '5', '6', '7', '8', // digits 8..15
        '9', '$', '$', K_UPARROW,  K_DOWNARROW
             , K_LEFTARROW, K_RIGHTARROW, K_ENTER, // digits 16..23
        '$', '$', '$', K_HOME,  '$', 'a', 'b', 'c', // digits 24..31

        'd', 'e', 'f', 'g',  'h', 'i', 'j', 'k',   // 32..39
        'l', 'm', 'n', 'o',  'p', 'q', 'r', 's',   // 40..47
        't', 'u', 'v', 'w',  'x', 'y', 'z', ',',   // 48..55
        '.', K_ALT, K_ALT, K_SHIFT,  K_SHIFT, K_TAB, ' ', '$', // 56..63
        '$', '$', K_ENTER, K_BACKSPACE, '`', '-', '=', '[', // 64..71
        ']', '\\', ';', '\'', '/', K_CTRL,  '#', '$', // 72..79
        K_CTRL, '$', K_ESCAPE, '$',  K_SPACE          // 80..84
  };

  public static boolean onKeyDown(int keyCode, KeyEvent event) {
    try {
      Natives.keyPress(keyCodeToQuakeCode(keyCode));
    } catch (UnsatisfiedLinkError e) {
      Log.d(TAG, e.toString());
    }

    return true;
  }

  public static boolean onKeyUp(int keyCode, KeyEvent event) {
    try {
      Natives.keyRelease(keyCodeToQuakeCode(keyCode));
    } catch (UnsatisfiedLinkError e) {
      Log.d(TAG, e.toString());
    }
  }
}

// In jni_quake.c
// engine key event processor
extern void Key_Event (int key, qboolean down);

JNIEXPORT jint JNICALL Java_quake_jni_Natives_keyPress
  (JNIEnv * env, jclass cls, jint key)
{
  Key_Event((int)key, 1);
  return key;
}
```

```
JNIEXPORT jint JNICALL Java_quake_jni_Natives_keyRelease
  (JNIEnv * env, jclass cls, jint key)
{
  Key_Event((int)key, 0);
  return key;
}
```

Next, you'll tackle touch handling.

Handling Touch Events

Touch events work in a way similar to key events. Listing 6-8 demonstrates how to cascade XY delta touch coordinates to the native engine to control the pitch and yaw of the character in 3D space.

Listing 6-8. Translating XY Touch Coordinates into Pitch and Yaw

```
// in QuakeView.java
  private float moveX = 0f;
  private float moveY = 0f;

  public boolean onTouchEvent(final MotionEvent e) {
    final int action = e.getAction();

    queueEvent(new Runnable() {
      public void run() {
        if (action == MotionEvent.ACTION_DOWN) {
          // QuakeKeyEvents.onKeyDown(KeyEvent.KEYCODE_ENTER, null);
          moveX = e.getX();
          moveY = e.getY();
        }
        else if (action == MotionEvent.ACTION_UP) {
          moveX = moveY = 0;
        }
        else if (action == MotionEvent.ACTION_MOVE) {
          final float dx = e.getX() - moveX;
          final float dy = e.getY() - moveY;

          final float DX = Math.abs(dx);
          final float DY = Math.abs(dy);

          if (DX < 30 && DY < 30) {
            return;
          }
          Natives.mouseMove((int) dx, (int) dy);
        }
      }
    });
    return true;
  }
```

```
// in Natives.java
public static native int mouseMove(int deltaX, int deltaY);

// in jni_quake.c
extern int   mouse_x, mouse_y;
JNIEXPORT jint JNICALL Java_quake_jni_Natives_mouseMove
  (JNIEnv * env, jclass cls, jint mx, jint my)
{
  // for pitch & yaw (look)
  mouse_x = (int)mx;
  mouse_y = (int)my;
/*
  for forward or side movement  use
  mouse_side = (int)mx;
  mouse_fwd = (int)my;
*/
}

// In gl_vidandroid.c (VIDEO DRIVER)
// Set PITCH & YAW
void IN_MouseLook (usercmd_t *cmd)
{
  if (!mouse_avail)
    return;

  if (m_filter.value)
  {
    mouse_x = (mouse_x + old_mouse_x) * 0.5;
    mouse_y = (mouse_y + old_mouse_y) * 0.5;
  }

  old_mouse_x = mouse_x;
  old_mouse_y = mouse_y;

  mouse_x *= sensitivity.value;
  mouse_y *= sensitivity.value;

// Set PITCH and YAW based on mouse XY delta coordinates
  cl.viewangles[YAW] -= m_yaw.value * mouse_x;

  V_StopPitchDrift ();

  cl.viewangles[PITCH] += m_pitch.value * mouse_y;

  if (cl.viewangles[PITCH] > 80)
      cl.viewangles[PITCH] = 80;

  if (cl.viewangles[PITCH] < -70)
      cl.viewangles[PITCH] = -70;

  mouse_x = mouse_y = 0;
}
```

```
// Character move
void IN_Move (usercmd_t *cmd)
{
  // to look
  IN_MouseLook(cmd);
  // to move
  //IN_MouseMove(cmd);
}
```

When the user drags a finger across the screen, the onTouchEvent in the GL view fires. This event receives motion event information such as an action: ACTION_DOWN, ACTION_UP, or ACTION_MOVE, depending on the type of motion. Because the native engine runs in a separate thread, onTouchEvent uses the built-in sub queueEvent to process the action safely into the game thread. When the finger goes down (ACTION_DOWN), the XY coordinates of the press are recorded. When the finger lifts up (ACTION_UP), the XY coordinates are reset to 0. When the finger is dragged (ACTION_MOVE), the delta coordinates (DX, DY) are calculated, and if they exceed a threshold value (30 pixels in this case), they are sent to the engine by consumption using JNI. This requires the native method int mouseMove(int deltaX, int deltaY) in Natives.java and its C counterpart Java_quake_jni_Natives_mouseMove. The C implementation of mouseMove simply records the values of delta XY coordinates to be processed by the video driver.

There is one important function in the video driver that processes movement: IN_Move. Within this function, you use a mouse handler, IN_MouseMove, to control the pitch and yaw of the character in 3D space. More details on this will be explained in the following sections.

Game Startup Activity

This is the final piece of the puzzle, the main entry point to the app: the game activity (see Listing 6-9). Its job is to do the following:

- Create an instance of the view QuakeView.

- Set a renderer with a set of string arguments that will be sent to the engine at startup.

- Set QuakeView as the content that will start the rendering process and begin the game!

Listing 6-9. Main Startup Activity

```
public class QuakeActivity extends Activity {

  QuakeView mQuakeView;

  @Override
  public void onCreate(Bundle savedInstanceState) {
    super.onCreate(savedInstanceState);

    // setContentView(R.layout.main);
    mQuakeView = new QuakeView(this);
```

```
int w = getWindow().getWindowManager().getDefaultDisplay().getWidth();
int h = getWindow().getWindowManager().getDefaultDisplay().getHeight();

// Put the game file pak0.pak files under /sdcard/quake/base!
final String baseDir = "/sdcard/quake";

String args = "quake"
    + ",-width," + String.valueOf(w)
    + ",-height," + String.valueOf(h)
    + ",-basedir," + baseDir
    + ",-game,base"
    + ",+skill,0"
    + ",+crosshair,1"
    + ",+gl_ztrick,0";

mQuakeView.setRenderer(args.split(","));

setContentView(mQuakeView);

}

@Override
public boolean onKeyDown(int keyCode, KeyEvent event) {
  return mQuakeView.keyDown(keyCode, event);
}

@Override
public boolean onKeyUp(int keyCode, KeyEvent event) {
  return mQuakeView.keyUp(keyCode, event);
}
}
```

The array of arguments sent to the engine is critical; if any mistakes are made, the whole thing will fail. Listing 6-9 shows the most important arguments, which include the following:

- -width and -height: These two are important. They tell the engine the size of the video buffer and will differ by device. The easiest way to get their values at runtime is to query the default display.

- -basedir: This is the default base directory that contains all the game files. In this case, you must upload your game files manually to /sdcard/quake. Note that the directory must also be created.

- -skill: Sets the game skill level (0 = easy, 1 = normal, 2 = hard, 3 = nightmare).

- +crosshair: Displays a crosshair wherever you aim your weapon.

- +gl_ztrick: This is required because Quake uses a buffering method that avoids clearing the Z-buffer, but some hardware platforms (like Android) don't like it. It is set to 0 to prevent the status bar and console from flashing every other frame.

This takes care of the thin Java wrappers for Quake. Now you need to modify the C engine slightly to make it work nicely with this Java code.

Changes Required to the Native Quake Engine

Thanks to NanoGL you can keep about 95% of the engine intact. A line count of all the C code (including headers) equals about 75,000 lines of code. Here you realize the amount of work you have saved; thank you again, NanoGL! (There are no words to describe how wonderful this tiny piece of software is). Nevertheless, there are still some cosmetic changes you need to make to the engine to make it play nicely with Android. The following is an overview of what is needed:

- *Video handler*: A video handler is usually required for all platforms where the engine is to be compiled. This is the most difficult and time-consuming change.

- *Movement handlers*: Custom handlers for pitch, yaw, forward, and side movement required to work with their JNI counterparts.

- *Audio handler*: A simple audio handler is needed to configure the native audio buffer and copy its contents to the JNI audio buffer used by the Java MediaTrack API.

- *Game loop*: The main method of the engine needs to be modified slightly to work with the Android renderer thread.

Video Handler Changes

The video handler file is called gl_vidandroid.c and it is located in the project source under ch06.Quake/jni/Quake/android. It is a pretty big file, so I will explain the most important tasks it performs. Every OpenGL video handler must implement a set of standard functions that will be called at certain points on the engine execution, including the following:

- VID_Init: Initializes the video subsystem (see Listing 6-10). It has one argument: an array of bytes representing a 256-size color palette encoded as RGB color elements (1 byte per element, 768 in total). VID_Init performs the following tasks:

  - It loads video user parameters, such as the width and height of the screen (by calling COM_CheckParm).

  - It sets the values for the video data structure, including width, height, and others.

  - It loads the NanoGL wrapper. This must be done before any calls to the OpenGL ES API are performed.

  - It initializes the OpenGL pipeline.

■ It adjusts the brightness. Quake is well known for having a very dark video display. VID_Init uses the user-defined gamma parameter to adjust the brightness of the display at startup.

■ It creates the color palette used by the video renderer.

Listing 6-10 shows an example of video initialization using VID_Init.

Listing 6-10. Video Initialization

```
void VID_Init(unsigned char *palette)
{
// Load user params
  if ((i = COM_CheckParm("-width")) != 0)
    width = atoi(com_argv[i+1]);

  if ((i = COM_CheckParm("-height")) != 0)
    height = atoi(com_argv[i+1]);


// Set video size & others
  vid.width = vid.conwidth = width;
  vid.height = vid.conheight = height;
  ...

// Load NanoGL
  if ( !nanoGL_Init() ){
    Sys_Error("Failed to load NanoGL wrapper.");
  }

// Init GL
  gl_vendor = glGetString (GL_VENDOR);
  Con_Printf ("GL_VENDOR: %s\n", gl_vendor);
  ...

// Adjust Brightness
  Check_Gamma(palette);

// Create palette
  VID_SetPalette(palette);

}
```

Here are some of the functions that are critical.

■ VID_SetPalette: Required to create a palette used to assign colors to textures and other graphical elements in the game. It must be a 256 RGB888 array of bytes.

■ VID_Shutdown: Called whenever the video subsystem is shut down; for instance, when the user quits the game. It performs trivial cleanup tasks.

- GL_BeginRendering: Fires when the rendering starts for each frame of the game. This function needs to know the left and top XY coordinates of the screen, plus the width and height of the video, as shown here:

```
void GL_BeginRendering (int *x, int *y, int *width, int *height)
{
  extern cvar_t gl_clear;

  *x = *y = 0;
  *width = scr_width;
  *height = scr_height;

}
```

Finally, note that GL_EndRendering fires whenever the rendering of a frame of the game completes. A call to glFlush causes all issued GL commands to be executed as quickly as they are accepted by the OpenGL pipeline.

```
void GL_EndRendering (void)
{
  glFlush();
}
```

The brightness of the color palette can be adjusted by altering the values of its RGB pixels. Because Quake uses a 256 RGB888 palette, the brightness can be increased or decreased using the formula:

$$P(i) = \left[\left(P(i)+1/256\right)\right]^{\wedge} gamma * 255 + 0.5; P(i):[0,255]$$

where P(i) represents a pixel in the palette, and gamma is a user parameter read from the command line with a range from 0 to 1. Note that P(i) must be clamped between 0 and 255, as shown in Listing 6-11.

Listing 6-11. Brightness Control

```
static void Check_Gamma (unsigned char *pal)
{
  float f, inf;
  unsigned char palette[768];
  int   i;

  if ((i = COM_CheckParm("-gamma")) == 0) {
    vid_gamma = 0.5; // default to 0.5
  } else
    vid_gamma = Q_atof(com_argv[i+1]);

  for (i=0 ; i<768 ; i++)
  {
    f = pow ( (pal[i]+1)/256.0 , vid_gamma );
    inf = f*255 + 0.5;
```

```
    if (inf < 0)
      inf = 0;
    if (inf > 255)
      inf = 255;
    palette[i] = inf;
  }
  // assign new values
  memcpy (pal, palette, sizeof(palette));
}
```

Handling Pitch and Yaw

In a first-person shooter game like Quake, pitch and yaw are commonly used to aim your weapon. In the PC world, this is usually done using the mouse to control the direction of a crosshair. On a touch device, on the other hand, you don't have such luxury but you can decide which sections of the screen control what. For example, in 3D space, if sweeping on the left half of the screen, you can move your character forwards or sideways. If sweeping on the right half, you can aim. It's all up to you. Listing 6-12 shows how to control aiming by altering the yaw and pitch of the built-in client view angles data structure (cl.viewangles).

Listing 6-12. Aim Control with Yaw and Pitch

```
void IN_LookMove (usercmd_t *cmd)
{
  if (!mouse_avail)
    return;

  if (m_filter.value)
  {
    mouse_x = (mouse_x + old_mouse_x) * 0.5;
    mouse_y = (mouse_y + old_mouse_y) * 0.5;
  }
  old_mouse_x = mouse_x;
  old_mouse_y = mouse_y;

  mouse_x *= sensitivity.value;
  mouse_y *= sensitivity.value;

// set YAW
  cl.viewangles[YAW] -= m_yaw.value * mouse_x;

  V_StopPitchDrift ();

//  PITCH
  cl.viewangles[PITCH] += m_pitch.value * mouse_y;

  if (cl.viewangles[PITCH] > 80)
    cl.viewangles[PITCH] = 80;
  if (cl.viewangles[PITCH] < -70)
    cl.viewangles[PITCH] = -70;
  mouse_x = mouse_y = 0;
}
```

> **Tip** *Yaw* (also known as heading) is the angular movement of the eye in the X axis. *Pitch* is the angular movement of the eye in the Y axis.

Note that yaw and pitch are controlled by the `mouse_x` and `mouse_y` variables. These are delta increments in the XY axis sent through JNI by the `QuakeView` Java class. The center of the screen represents the origin (0,0). Down or left increments are negative, up or right increments are positive. The function `V_StopPitchDrift` stops the drift of the pitch angle back to the origin whenever the movement stops (by lifting the finger). This is typical behavior of Quake in the desktop (if you aim with the mouse, as soon as you move it outside the game view, your aim will drift back to the origin).

Handling Forward and Side Movement

Forward and side movements are handled in a way similar to pitch and yaw. Quake uses built-in data structures: `cmd->sidemove` to control side movements and `cmd->forwardmove` for forward movement (see Listing 6-13). These variables need to be increased or decreased by some increment. In this case, the increments are controlled by the variables `mouse_side` and `mouse_fwd`. These two variables will be updated by JNI whenever you drag a finger on the screen. The companion JNI implementations are described in the previous section, "Handling Touch."

Note that both forward and side movements are multiplied by two Quake default values, `m_side` and `m_forward`. These are used to control the range of movement; also keep in mind that `mouse_side` and `mouse_fwd` are delta values in the XY direction where the origin (0,0) is defined at the point where the finger goes down. The delta values are then calculated by subtracting the XY coordinates of the pointer and then sent through JNI for consumption.

Listing 6-13. Handling Forward and Side Movement

```
// these will be updated by JNI
int mouse_side;
int mouse_fwd;

void IN_FwdSideMove (usercmd_t *cmd)
{
   cmd->sidemove += m_side.value * mouse_side;
   cmd->forwardmove -= m_forward.value * mouse_fwd;
}

void IN_Move (usercmd_t *cmd)
{
  IN_FwdSideMove (cmd);
  IN_LookMove (cmd)
}
```

Audio Handler Changes

To implement your own audio handler code for Android, you must take a look at the sound data structure defined in sound.h (see Listing 6-14). Quake uses a direct memory access (DMA) technique, where the most relevant values are as follows:

- channels: The number of audio channels (1 for mono, 2 for stereo).

- samples: The size of the audio buffer.

- submission_chunk: This has something to do with how Quake mixed the audio buffer internally, but it is not relevant in this case.

- samplepos: This is the position or the current audio byte being played.

- samplebits: This is the audio resolution. Quake uses 16-bit WAV audio.

- speed: This is the audio frequency. It defaults to 22 kHz.

Note that there are also two sound-related variables: shm and sn. The first one is a pointer used to do all the behind-the-scenes work and it must point to sn, which is the real audio data structure. This is done on audio initialization, as seen in the "Fixing the Game Loop" section later in this chapter.

Listing 6-14. Quake Audio Data Structure

```
// In sound.h
// Internal Audio data structure
typedef struct
{
  qboolean    gamealive;
  qboolean    soundalive;
  qboolean    splitbuffer;
  int         channels;
  int         samples;            // mono samples in buffer
  int         submission_chunk;   // don't mix less than this #
  int         samplepos;          // in mono samples
  int         samplebits;
  int         speed;
  unsigned char *buffer;
} dma_t;

extern volatile dma_t *shm;
extern volatile dma_t sn;
```

With this information, you can easily implement a custom audio handler for Android. In Listing 6-15, you have the file snd_android.c, which implements the following functions:

- SNDDMA_Init: Required to initialize the audio handler. It defined the audio parameters described in Listing 6-14: audio resolution (16 bit), frequency (22kHz), number of channels (2 for stereo), the size of the samples (audio buffer); it also tells Quake that audio has been initialized successfully.

- SNDDMA_GetDMAPos: Tells Quake the current position in the audio buffer.

- paint_audio: Gets called by the JNI implementation of the Java class NativeAudio.PaintAudio, described in the "Handling Audio" section. The Java audio handler will use a thread and loop around calling NativeAudio.PaintAudio.

- NativeAudio.PaintAudio: Uses its JNI companion to call paint_audio to store audio bytes from the Quake audio buffer into the Java audio buffer, which will then be played using the Android MediaTrack API.

> **Tip**   snd_android.c is located in the book source under ch06.Quake/jni/Quake/android.

Listing 6-15. Quake Audio Handler for Android

```
// in snd_android.c
// This function is called from JNI to fill the audio buffer
// params: stream (Java audio buffer), len: stream size
int paint_audio (void *unused, void * stream, int len)
{
  if (!snd_inited)
    return 0;

  if (shm) {
    // make the quake au buffer point to stream
    shm->buffer = (unsigned char *)stream;
    shm->samplepos += len / (shm->samplebits / 4);

    // write sound bytes to stream
    S_PaintChannels (shm->samplepos);
    return len;
  }
  return 0;
}

// Audio Initializer
qboolean SNDDMA_Init(void)
{
  /* Most of the wav files are 16 bits, 22050 Hz, mono */
  /* Fill the audio DMA information block */
  shm = &sn;

  shm->samplebits = 16;

  // malloc max : 7 MB  => -12 MB !!
  shm->speed = 22050;
  shm->channels = 2;

  LOGD("SNDDMA_Init Speed %d channels %d", shm->speed, shm->channels);
```

```
shm->samples = 2048 * shm->channels;
shm->samplepos = 0;
shm->submission_chunk = 1;
shm->buffer = NULL;

snd_inited = 1;

return true;
}

// Get
int SNDDMA_GetDMAPos(void)
{
  return shm->samplepos;
}
```

Fixing the Game Loop

Thus far, you have custom video, movement, and audio handlers for Quake. The final piece is to modify the main Quake loop slightly to work nicely with Android. This is necessary because of the way GLSurfaceView.Renderer works. When Android creates a GLSurfaceView, you must set a renderer by implementing GLSurfaceView.Renderer. When this renderer kicks in, the following sequence of events will occur:

- OpenGL initialization occurs, including creating a GL context with drawing information such as pixel format, depth, stencil, buffers, and others.

- GLSurfaceView.Renderer.onSurfaceCreated is called when the surface is created. This is where you must fire the Quake main function to start the game. Note that you must also send the plethora of arguments that Quake will expect from the command line.

- GLSurfaceView.Renderer.onSurfaceChanged is called whenever the surface changes due to some event, such as when the phone goes to sleep, wakes up, or receives a call, and so on.

- GLSurfaceView.Renderer.onDrawFrame fires for every interaction of the renderer thread. This is where you must perform all the OpenGL operations. When this method completes, the OpenGL buffers will be swapped and the frame will be rendered on-screen.

Take a look at Quake's main function in Listing 6-16. It loops forever, rendering a frame at the end of each loop interaction. If you start main from onSurfaceCreated, then the Android thread will hang forever on the while loop. Therefore, you must comment this loop (as shown in Listing 6-17) to let onSurfaceCreated complete normally.

Tip sys_android.c can be found in ch06.Quake/jni/Quake/android in the book source.

Listing 6-16. Changes to Quake's Main Game Loop

```c
// in sys_android.c Quake main function
int main (int c, char **v)
{
  double    time, oldtime, newtime;

  // Quake initialization...

// We don't need this loop in Android
#ifdef HAVE_RENDER_LOOP
    oldtime = Sys_FloatTime () - 0.1;

    while (1)
    {
        newtime = Sys_FloatTime ();
        time = newtime - oldtime;

        if (cls.state == ca_dedicated)
        {   // play vcrfiles at max speed
            if (time < sys_ticrate.value ) // Vladimir && (vcrFile == -1 || recording) )
            {
                usleep(1);
                continue;       // not time to run a server only tic yet
            }
            time = sys_ticrate.value;
        }

        if (time > sys_ticrate.value*2)
            oldtime = newtime;
        else
            oldtime += time;

        Host_Frame (time);

// graphic debugging aids
        if (sys_linerefresh.value)
            Sys_LineRefresh ();

    }
#endif
}
```

But you also need to implement onDrawFrame, which must perform all OpenGL operations before swapping buffers. To do this, you simply take the code you commented out from Quake's main function and put in its own function, called RenderFrame. This function essentially renders a single frame of the game and will be called by the Java class Natives.RenderFrame, described in the "Java OpenGL Renderer Architecture" section earlier in this chapter.

Listing 6-17. Rendering a Single Frame in Quake

```c
// sys_android.c: This will be invoked from JNI on each renderer frame
// This code is taken from the main while loop
void RenderFrame()
{
  double time, newtime;
  static double oldtime;

  // Init this var
  if (oldtime == 0.0 )
    oldtime = Sys_FloatTime () - 0.1;

// find time spent rendering last frame
  newtime = Sys_FloatTime ();
  time = newtime - oldtime;

  if (cls.state == ca_dedicated)
  {
    if (time < sys_ticrate.value )
    {
      usleep(1);
      return; // not time to run a server only tic yet
    }
    time = sys_ticrate.value;
  }

  if (time > sys_ticrate.value*2)
    oldtime = newtime;
  else
    oldtime += time;

  Host_Frame (time);

// graphic debugging aids
  if (sys_linerefresh.value)
    Sys_LineRefresh ();
}
```

The JNI-C companion that implements Natives.RenderFrame and calls RenderFrame is declared in the file jni_quake.c (under the ch06.Quake/jni/Quake/android in the book source).

```c
extern void RenderFrame();

JNIEXPORT jint JNICALL Java_quake_jni_Natives_RenderFrame
  (JNIEnv * env, jclass cls)
{
  RenderFrame();
}
```

You have created the basic Android architecture for the Quake engine, plus you've performed the required changes to the native engine. You now have all the pieces to get Quake up and running in your Android device. Let's look at how this happens.

Running on a Device

Before running on a device, the very first thing you need to do is compile the native library. To do this, you must create the compilation scripts: Application.mk and Android.mk.

Application.mk is tiny. It contains the name of the modules you want to build and the path to Android.mk, which is the real compilation script. In this case, you want to compile two modules: NanoGL as a static library (so it can be reused in Chapter 7) and the Quake engine. NanoGL compiles into libNanoGL.a, and Quake compiles into libquake.so and includes libNanGL.a.

```
APP_BUILD_SCRIPT := $(call my-dir)/Quake/Android.mk
APP_MODULES      := NanoGL quake
```

Android.mk is where all the meat lives. The first thing it does is compile the NanoGL static library, as follows:

```
LOCAL_MODULE := NanoGL
DIR:= $(LOCAL_MODULE)
LOCAL_C_INCLUDES := jni/Quake/NanoGL/GL
LOCAL_SRC_FILES := $(DIR)/eglwrap.cpp  $(DIR)/nanogl.cpp $(DIR)/nanoWrap.cpp
include $(BUILD_STATIC_LIBRARY)
```

- LOCAL_MODULE: Specifies the module to compile.

- LOCAL_C_INCLUDES: Specifies a list of directories where to look for header files.

- LOCAL_SRC_FILES: Specifies the source files to compile.

- BUILD_STATIC_LIBRARY: Calls the Android build system to create libNanoGL.a.

Next, Android.mk compiles the Quake engine, as shown in Listing 6-18.

Listing 6-18. Android.mk Fragment to Compile the Quake Engine

```
LOCAL_MODULE := quake
LOCAL_CFLAGS := -O3 -DANDROID -DGLQUAKE -Wfatal-errors \
  -D_stricmp=strcasecmp -D_strnicmp=strncasecmp -Dstricmp=strcasecmp \
  -Dstrnicmp=strncasecmp

LOCAL_C_INCLUDES := jni/Quake/android jni/Quake/NanoGL
LOCAL_LDLIBS := -ldl -llog
LOCAL_STATIC_LIBRARIES := libNanoGL
```

```
RENDERER_SRC := gl_draw.c gl_mesh.c gl_model.c \
  gl_refrag.c gl_rlight.c gl_rmisc.c \
  gl_screen.c gl_rmain.c gl_rsurf.c \
  gl_warp.c \

SND_SRC := snd_dma.c snd_mem.c  snd_mix.c

ANDROID_SRC :=  android/jni_quake.c \
  android/snd_android.c \
  android/gl_vidandroid.c \
  android/sys_android.c \
LOCAL_SRC_FILES := \
  cl_demo.c \
  cl_input.c \
  cl_main.c \
  ... \
  net_udp.c \
  net_bsd.c \
  cd_null.c \
  crc.c net_vcr.c \
  $(RENDERER_SRC) $(SND_SRC) $(ANDROID_SRC)

include $(BUILD_SHARED_LIBRARY)
```

This time, the name of the module is quake. Note that the name must match the one defined in Application.mk. The following are the compilation options:

- LOCAL_CFLAGS: This variable defines the compiler options for the module. The following flags are used:

    - -O3 tells the compiler to use optimization level 3 (which is heavy and produces fast code).

    - –DANDROID is a flag for conditional compilation within the Android code.

    - –DGLQUAKE is required by the engine to use the OpenGL renderer instead of the default software.

    - -Wfatal-errors aborts compilation when any error occurs.

    - -D_stricmp=strcasecmp and the rest of flags are substitutions of string comparison functions with their standard C counterparts.

Next, the source is divided into the following:

- LOCAL_LDLIBS: Defines shared libraries to link against; in this case, it's the dynamic loader (ldl) and the log system (-llog).

- LOCAL_STATIC_LIBRARIES: This variable is important. Here you tell the compiler to include the static library libNanoGL.a. Without this, compilation will fail.

- RENDERER_SRC: Defines the OpenGL renderer files.

- SND_SRC: Defines the sound subsystem files.

- ANDROID_SRC: Defines the Android-related files, including

    - jni_quake.c: Contains the JNI implementations for all the native methods defined in Natives.java and NativeAudio.java.

    - snd_android.c: Implements the audio driver for Android. It works in conjunction with NativeAudio.java and jni_quake.c.

    - gl_vidandroid.c: Implements the video handler for Android.

    - sys_android.c: Implements changes to the main Quake loop to work along with the Android OpenGL renderer API.

- LOCAL_SRC_FILES: Defines the sources for the engine, including the sources defined in this list.

The following steps show how to compile Quake using Cygwin on a Windows system:

1. Copy the chapter source ch06.Quake into your local machine.

2. Open a Cygwin console and change to the project folder.

    ```
    $ cd   /cygdive/c/temp/ch06.Quake
    ```

3. Compile the native library (see Figure 6-2).

    ```
    $ ndk-build
    ```

```
hardone@NARDONE3 /cygdrive/c/tmp/ch06.Quake
$ ndk-build
[armeabi] Cygwin         : Generating dependency file converter script
[armeabi] Compile++ thumb: NanoGL <= eglwrap.cpp
[armeabi] Compile++ thumb: NanoGL <= nanogl.cpp
[armeabi] Compile++ thumb: NanoGL <= nanoWrap.cpp
[armeabi] StaticLibrary  : libNanoGL.a
[armeabi] Compile thumb  : quake <= cl_demo.c
[armeabi] Compile thumb  : quake <= cl_input.c
[armeabi] Compile thumb  : quake <= cl_main.c
[armeabi] Compile thumb  : quake <= cl_parse.c
[armeabi] Compile thumb  : quake <= cl_tent.c
[armeabi] Compile thumb  : quake <= chase.c
[armeabi] Compile thumb  : quake <= cmd.c
[armeabi] Compile thumb  : quake <= common.c
[armeabi] Compile thumb  : quake <= console.c
[armeabi] Compile thumb  : quake <= cvar.c
[armeabi] Compile thumb  : quake <= host.c
[armeabi] Compile thumb  : quake <= host_cmd.c
[armeabi] Compile thumb  : quake <= keys.c
[armeabi] Compile thumb  : quake <= menu.c
[armeabi] Compile thumb  : quake <= mathlib.c
[armeabi] Compile thumb  : quake <= net_dgrm.c
[armeabi] Compile thumb  : quake <= net_loop.c
[armeabi] Compile thumb  : quake <= net_main.c
[armeabi] Compile thumb  : quake <= pr_cmds.c
[armeabi] Compile thumb  : quake <= pr_edict.c
[armeabi] Compile thumb  : quake <= sbar.c
[armeabi] Compile thumb  : quake <= sv_main.c
[armeabi] Compile thumb  : quake <= sv_phys.c
[armeabi] Compile thumb  : quake <= sv_move.c
[armeabi] Compile thumb  : quake <= sv_user.c
[armeabi] Compile thumb  : quake <= zone.c
[armeabi] Compile thumb  : quake <= view.c
[armeabi] Compile thumb  : quake <= wad.c
[armeabi] Compile thumb  : quake <= world.c
[armeabi] Compile thumb  : quake <= net_udp.c
[armeabi] Compile thumb  : quake <= net_bsd.c
[armeabi] Compile thumb  : quake <= cd_null.c
[armeabi] Compile thumb  : quake <= crc.c
[armeabi] Compile thumb  : quake <= net_vcr.c
[armeabi] Compile thumb  : quake <= gl_draw.c
[armeabi] Compile thumb  : quake <= gl_mesh.c
[armeabi] Compile thumb  : quake <= gl_model.c
[armeabi] Compile thumb  : quake <= gl_refrag.c
[armeabi] Compile thumb  : quake <= gl_rlight.c
[armeabi] Compile thumb  : quake <= gl_rmisc.c
[armeabi] Compile thumb  : quake <= gl_screen.c
[armeabi] Compile thumb  : quake <= gl_rmain.c
[armeabi] Compile thumb  : quake <= gl_rsurf.c
[armeabi] Compile thumb  : quake <= gl_warp.c
[armeabi] Compile thumb  : quake <= snd_dma.c
[armeabi] Compile thumb  : quake <= snd_mem.c
[armeabi] Compile thumb  : quake <= snd_mix.c
[armeabi] Compile thumb  : quake <= jni_quake.c
[armeabi] Compile thumb  : quake <= snd_android.c
[armeabi] Compile thumb  : quake <= gl_vidandroid.c
[armeabi] Compile thumb  : quake <= sys_android.c
[armeabi] SharedLibrary  : libquake.so
[armeabi] Install        : libquake.so => libs/armeabi/libquake.so

hardone@NARDONE3 /cygdrive/c/tmp/ch06.Quake
$
```

Figure 6-2. Compiling the Quake native library

4. Connect your Android device to your laptop or start the emulator.

5. Copy the Quake shareware game file to the sdcard under /sdcard/
    quake/base. From a DOS prompt you can do this by typing

    ```
    C:\>adb shell mkdir -p /sdcard/quake/base
    C:\>adb push /QUAKE_INSTALL/id0/pak0.pak /sdcard/quake/base
    ```

Note The Quake shareware game files are copyrighted by id Software and must be obtained from
the company's website.

6. Create a run configuration for the project. In Eclipse, click the main menu Run ➤ **Run Configuration**. In the Run Configuration wizard, right-click **Android Application** ➤ **New**. Enter a name and select the ch06.Quake project, as shown in Figure 6-3.

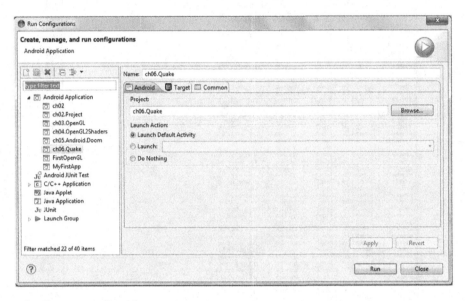

Figure 6-3. Creating a run configuration

7. Click Run and take a look at the Android log to see that everything goes smoothly (see Listing 6-19 and Figure 6-4).

Listing 6-19. Android Log Output for Quake

```
08-10 14:51:02.352: DEBUG/QuakeView(335): onSurfaceCreated
08-10 14:51:02.352: DEBUG/QJNI(335): Quake Main[0]=quake
08-10 14:51:02.352: DEBUG/QJNI(335): Quake Main[1]=-width
08-10 14:51:02.352: DEBUG/QJNI(335): Quake Main[2]=480
08-10 14:51:02.352: DEBUG/QJNI(335): Quake Main[3]=-height
08-10 14:51:02.352: DEBUG/QJNI(335): Quake Main[4]=800
08-10 14:51:02.352: DEBUG/QJNI(335): Quake Main[5]=-basedir
08-10 14:51:02.352: DEBUG/QJNI(335): Quake Main[6]=/sdcard/quake
08-10 14:51:02.363: DEBUG/QJNI(335): Quake Main[7]=-game
08-10 14:51:02.363: DEBUG/QJNI(335): Quake Main[8]=base
08-10 14:51:02.363: DEBUG/QJNI(335): Quake Main[9]=+skill
08-10 14:51:02.363: DEBUG/QJNI(335): Quake Main[10]=0
08-10 14:51:02.363: DEBUG/QJNI(335): Quake Main[11]=+showpause
08-10 14:51:02.363: DEBUG/QJNI(335): Quake Main[12]=0
08-10 14:51:02.363: DEBUG/QJNI(335): Quake Main[13]=+crosshair
08-10 14:51:02.363: DEBUG/QJNI(335): Quake Main[14]=1
08-10 14:51:02.363: DEBUG/QJNI(335): Quake Main[15]=+gl_ztrick
08-10 14:51:02.363: DEBUG/QJNI(335): Quake Main[16]=0
```

```
08-10 14:51:02.363: INFO/QJNI(335): Loading quake/jni/Natives
08-10 14:51:02.682: INFO/SYSLinux(335): Added packfile /sdcard/quake/base/pak0.pak (339 files)
08-10 14:51:02.703: INFO/SYSLinux(335): Playing registered version.
08-10 14:51:02.712: INFO/SYSLinux(335): PackFile: /sdcard/quake/base/pak0.pak : gfx.wad
08-10 14:51:02.824: INFO/SYSLinux(335): Console initialized.
08-10 14:51:02.892: INFO/SYSLinux(335): UDP Initialized
08-10 14:51:02.892: INFO/SYSLinux(335): TCP/IP address 127.0.0.1
08-10 14:51:02.913: INFO/SYSLinux(335): Exe: 10:28:40 Aug 10 2011
08-10 14:51:02.913: INFO/SYSLinux(335): 16.0 megabyte heap
08-10 14:51:02.948: INFO/SYSLinux(335): PackFile: /sdcard/quake/base/pak0.pak :
gfx/palette.lmp
08-10 14:51:02.981: INFO/SYSLinux(335): PackFile: /sdcard/quake/base/pak0.pak :
gfx/colormap.lmp
08-10 14:51:02.983: INFO/SYSLinux(335): Can't register variable in_mouse, allready defined
08-10 14:51:02.983: INFO/SYSLinux(335): Can't register variable m_filter, allready defined
08-10 14:51:02.983: DEBUG/QJNI(335): Initializing Signal Traps.
08-10 14:51:02.983: DEBUG/QJNI(335): Loading nano GL Wrapper
08-10 14:51:02.983: INFO/nanoGL(335): nanoGL: Init loading driver libGLESv1_CM.so
08-10 14:51:02.983: WARN/nanoGL(335): <eglChooseConfig> not found in libGLESv1_CM.so.
Trying libEGL.so.
08-10 14:51:02.993: WARN/nanoGL(335): <eglCopyBuffers> not found in libGLESv1_CM.so.
Trying libEGL.so.
08-10 14:51:02.993: WARN/nanoGL(335): <eglCreateContext> not found in libGLESv1_CM.so.
Trying libEGL.so.
libGLESv1_CM.so. Trying libEGL.so.
08-10 14:51:02.993: WARN/nanoGL(335): <eglDestroySurface> not found in libGLESv1_CM.so.
Trying libEGL.so.
08-10 14:51:03.002: WARN/nanoGL(335): <eglReleaseTexImage> not found in libGLESv1_CM.so.
Trying libEGL.so.
08-10 14:51:03.002: WARN/nanoGL(335): <eglSurfaceAttrib> not found in libGLESv1_CM.so.
Trying libEGL.so.
08-10 14:51:03.002: DEBUG/QuakeView(335): OnInitVideo. 480x480 Starting native audio.
08-10 14:51:03.012: INFO/SYSLinux(335): GL_VENDOR: Android
08-10 14:51:03.012: INFO/SYSLinux(335): GL_RENDERER: Android PixelFlinger 1.4
08-10 14:51:03.012: INFO/SYSLinux(335): GL_VERSION: OpenGL ES-CM 1.0
08-10 14:51:03.062: DEBUG/Audio(335): Audio start.
08-10 14:51:04.722: INFO/SYSLinux(335): Video mode 480x800 initialized.
08-10 14:51:04.793: INFO/SYSLinux(335): PackFile: /sdcard/quake/base/pak0.pak :
gfx/conback.lmp
08-10 14:51:04.993: INFO/SYSLinux(335): Sound Initialization
08-10 14:51:05.602: DEBUG/QSound(335): SNDDMA_Init Speed 22050 channels 2
08-10 14:51:05.602: INFO/SYSLinux(335): Sound sampling rate: 22050
08-10 14:51:06.633: WARN/AudioFlinger(34): write blocked for 726 msecs, 1 delayed writes,
thread 0xc658
08-10 14:51:06.942: INFO/SYSLinux(335): PackFile: /sdcard/quake/base/pak0.pak :
sound/ambience/water1.wav
08-10 14:51:07.033: INFO/SYSLinux(335): PackFile: /sdcard/quake/base/pak0.pak :
sound/ambience/wind2.wav
sound/weapons/ric2.wav
08-10 14:51:07.383: INFO/SYSLinux(335): PackFile: /sdcard/quake/base/pak0.pak :
sound/weapons/ric3.wav
```

```
08-10 14:51:07.428: INFO/SYSLinux(335): PackFile: /sdcard/quake/base/pak0.pak :
sound/weapons/r_exp3.wav
08-10 14:51:07.482: INFO/SYSLinux(335): ========Quake Initialized=========
08-10 14:51:07.494: DEBUG/SYSLinux(335): Linux Quake -- Version 1.300
08-10 14:51:08.253: INFO/SYSLinux(335): 3 demo(s) in loop
```

> **Tip**   If something goes wrong, make sure you have the folder /sdcard/quake/base in your
> device and that it contains the file pa0.pak. This file should be around 19MB in size. The Android
> log will tell you whether there is a failure of any kind.

Figure 6-4. Quake running at an 800×480 pixel resolution

To test this project I used the following tablet device:

- Samsung Galaxy Tab 3 10.1 P5220:
- CPU Dual-core 1.6 GHz
- GPU PowerVR SGX544MP2
- Card slot microSD: 32 GB
- Internal RAM: 32 GB

Summary

In this chapter, you learned how to bring a powerful PC engine like Quake to Android with minimum effort. This chapter delivered the following:

- A slick way to deal with the PC OpenGL caveats, such as immediate mode drawing with almost no code changes to the original source. I showed this by bringing Quake to Android while keeping 98% of the original OpenGL renderer intact and 95% of the entire engine.

- Efficient ways to cascade keyboard and touch events from Java to the C engine for consumption while preserving the original event processors.

- The implementation of these techniques with code samples and chapter source.

Porting a game such as Quake to OpenGL ES would normally take countless hours—probably months—of grueling work by a team of developers. In this chapter, I showed how one person using powerful tools can get this game going with fewer than 500 lines of new code.

7

3D Shooters for Quake II

This chapter builds upon the previous one to deliver the next great and popular PC engine: Quake II. Quake II is the first-person shooter video game developed by id Software and distributed by Activision. What makes this chapter unique is that, thanks to the wonderful reusability of Java and the power of the C language, you can do the following:

- Reuse the thin Java wrappers to the Quake engine from Chapter 6 with no changes whatsoever.
- Keep 99% of the native engine intact with the help of NanoGL.
- Make tiny changes to the C code in the remaining 1% of the native engine in order to make it Android-friendly.

You'll start by learning how to set nimble Java wrappers to get the engine running quickly in Android, including game startup, video rendering, and key and audio events. Next, you'll look at an efficient way of dealing with system errors (the ones that can crash your app). Then, you'll learn about the video handler changes required for the native engine. And finally, you'll tackle building the native code and running it in the emulator, plus learning how to run performance tests on the engine running on multiple devices at different resolutions.

> **Note** All the code included in this chapter was developed, compiled and tested using Eclipse IDE for Java Developers instead of Android Studio 1.0.1 since, when this manuscript was written, NDK and JNI were not supported by Android Studio.

Reviewing the Code

To get an idea of the amount of work you will save, let's take a look at the number of lines of C code for the engine.

```
$ find -name "*.[ch]" | xargs wc -l
   1058 ./client/adivtab.h
    181 ./client/anorms.h
     81 ./client/asm_i386.h
    123 ./client/block16.h
    124 ./client/block8.h
     26 ./client/cdaudio.h
    584 ./client/client.h
    650 ./client/cl_cin.c
   1543 ./client/cl_ents.c
   2298 ./client/cl_fx.c
...
173666 total

$ ref_gl> wc -l *.[ch]
    181 anorms.h
     37 anormtab.h
    416 gl_draw.c
   1590 gl_image.c
    729 gl_light.c
    458 gl_local.h
...
   1756 gl_rmain.c
    248 gl_rmisc.c
   1662 gl_rsurf.c
    662 gl_warp.c
    557 qgl.h
     51 warpsin.h
  10692 total
```

In the first part, you have about 180,000 total lines of code (including header files); this includes almost 11,000 lines of code for the OpenGL renderer. I've estimated less than 2,000 lines of new code to make the engine Android-friendly. Thus, you can squeeze a tremendous amount of work (that would have taken a small team of developers several months to complete) into a project that a single guy can complete over a weekend.

Escaping the Shackles of the Java Heap

The Quake II engine is the perfect proof of concept for graphics rendering on a mobile device. Written around 1998, it has the same hardware requirements as a modern smartphone.

- 600 MHz processor with a powerful GPU

- 80MB RAM

- 40MB of disk (for the shareware version), or 100MB for retail

You can actually still find the original Quake II web site at www.quake2.com/.

Believe or not, Quake II is so portable that some folks took the time to bring the game to pure Java 3D: the name of the project is Jake 2 (www.bytonic.de/html/jake2.html). There is even a port of Quake II by Google that runs on a web browser using WebGL. As a matter of fact, when Android was in its infancy and the NDK didn't even exist, I took a couple of weeks to get Jake 2 to compile on Android's Dalvik VM. It was a lot of hard work just to find out that Java is simply not capable of handling any kind of powerful 3D game engine due to the constraints it imposes on the developer.

When thinking of a project like Jake 2, the key is the amount of RAM required to play the game: 80MB. This is why there will never be a powerful 3D engine written in Java on Android. The Android Java VM only lets programs allocate a maximum of 16MB of RAM—and this cannot be changed. As any Java developer knows, on the PC, the size of the heap (or RAM) can be changed at runtime with a simple command-line argument. This is not possible in Android. I found this out the hard way when playing with Jake 2. All powerful 3D engines must be written in C/C++; there is simply no way around this.

> **Note**   Writing game engines in C/C++ allows the developer to use disk space and RAM in any way he or she chooses, limited only by what the hardware can provide. Java, on the other hand, shackles you to 16MB of RAM.

Taming the Mighty Quake II Engine

To make the Quake II engine work seamlessly in Android, you will reuse most of the Java wrappers from Chapter 6. You'll also have to implement custom video and audio handlers for this particular engine. All in all, most of the work will basically consist of the following:

- About 2,000 lines of new C code (for the video and audio handling).
- The Java code from Chapter 6, with tiny changes to make it fit Quake II.

If you dig around the source of both the Quake I and II engines, you will realize there is a whole lot of common code between them. Nevertheless, Quake II has been greatly modularized (in comparison to Quake I), consisting of basically the following three separate components:

- *The client*: In Linux, this is the game executable, dubbed quake2.
- *The game library*: Quake II was designed to work with a plethora of mission packs, extensible mods, and so forth. By decoupling the game library into a separate component, mod developers can simply create new games by writing a new game library, leaving the other components intact.
- *The renderer*: Quake II supports two renderer types: software and hardware (using Open GL). In Linux, the renderers are called ref_soft. so for software and ref_glx.so (for OpenGL under UNIX/Window). Note that there are multiple OpenGL renderer implementations, each with different names.

This great modularization works wonders on the desktop, where developers simply have to code a new game library and leave the other components intact. In Android (or any mobile platform, for that matter), this can be a pain to develop, as the compiler tools are cumbersome compared to the desktop, plus the way Android loads shared libraries is not the same as in the standard Linux OS. Luckily, Quake II can compile all three components as a stand-alone (hard-linked) library. Thus in Android, to make things even easier, you will compile Quake II as a single, hard-linked library dubbed `libquake2.so`. More details on doing so will be explained in the "Building Quake II with the NDK" section.

Code Reusability

Thanks to the great object-oriented and reusability features of Java, most of the classes from Chapter 6 can be reused without change. There are some tiny changes to the startup class, but besides that, the code is identical. Best of all, this code could be used in any type of native engine, not just Quake I and Quake II. To recap, Table 7-1 lists the Java classes and their tasks.

Table 7-1. Java Classes and Tasks

Package	Class Name	Description
`com.opengl`	`QuakeActivity`	This is the game startup class. It requires tiny changes mostly related to the game startup arguments.
`com.opengl`	`QuakeKeyEvents`	This class translates Android key event codes into ASCII codes understood by the Quake II engine. It will be reused without change.
`com.opengl`	`QuakeView`	This class extends the Android API `GLSurfaceView` to provide a surface for OpenGL rendering. It also contains the API `GLSurfaceView.Renderer` used to implement rendering calls into the native engine. It will be reused without change.
`quake.audio`	`NativeAudio`	This class implements a thread that reads the audio buffer from the native layer and sends it to the device hardware using the Android MediaTrack API. It will be reused without change.
`quake.jni`	`Natives`	This is the most important class. It declares the JNI native methods for communication between the Java and C code, plus it implements a set of callbacks that can be used from the C layer to send messages to the Java layer. This class will be reused without change.

Most of the native access methods reside in the class Natives.java; they are as follows:

- native void QuakeMain(String[] argv): This method calls the Quake II main method. Its job is to convert the Java String arguments (argv) into a C array that can be fed into the engine. It also loads the Natives. java class to fire up callbacks when the native engine needs to send a message back to Java (for example, when a system/fatal error occurs and the application needs to terminate). This method requires no change to work with Quake II.

- native void RenderFrame(): This native method renders a single frame of the game. You must do so to play nice with the Android OpenGL surface renderer, which uses a separate thread to render one frame at a time. This method requires no change to work with Quake II.

- native int keyPress(int key) and keyRelease(int key): These two are used to push ASCII keys into the key processor. Note that the Android key codes will be translated into ASCII by the Java wrappers. These methods need to be updated to work with Quake II.

- native void mouseLook(int mouseX, int mouseY): This method is used to look around the 3D space when the player sweeps a finger across the screen. It receives delta coordinates for yaw (mouseX) and pitch (mouseY). This method requires no change.

- native void mouseMove(int mouseX, int mouseY): This method is used to move the characters forward or sideways in 3D space. It receives delta coordinates in the XY axis. This method requires no change.

- native void PaintAudio(ByteBuffer buf): This method reads a byte buffer of audio from the C engine into a Java buffer and writes it into the device audio hardware using Android's MediaTrack API. This method requires no change.

Game Startup

QuakeMain is the function that kicks things off. It starts the Quake II engine with a given array of arguments. The following fragment shows its declaration and Natives.java and C implementation in jni_quake.c:

Note   The C implementations for all the native Java methods in Natives.java are located in the project source under ch07.QuakeII/jni/quake2-3.21/android/jni_quake.c.

```
// Java
package quake.jni;

public class Natives {
  ...
  public static native int QuakeMain(String[] argv);
  ...
}
```

```
// in jni_quake.c
JNIEXPORT jint JNICALL Java_quake_jni_Natives_QuakeMain
  (JNIEnv * env, jclass cls, jobjectArray jargv)
```

Note that the Java string arguments map into a jobjectArray in C, and they must be converted to the standard char * format. Fortunately, JNI provides the utility functions GetArrayLength, GetObjectArrayElement, GetStringUTFChars, and ReleaseStringUTFChars to do this easily.

1. First, get the size of the Java array using GetArrayLength.

   ```
   jsize clen = (*env)->GetArrayLength(env, jargv);
   ```

2. Next, allocate a C array of the same size.

   ```
   char * args[(int)clen];
   ```

3. Then, loop through the size value, extracting a Java string from the array by calling GetObjectArrayElement, then converting that Java string into a C string using GetStringUTFChars, as shown:

   ```
   int i;
   jstring jrow;
   for (i = 0; i < clen; i++)
   {
       jrow = (jstring)(*env)->GetObjectArrayElement(env, jargv, i);
       const char *row = (*env)->GetStringUTFChars(env, jrow, 0);
   ```

4. Then, simply allocate space for the corresponding C string using the malloc system call.

   ```
   args[i] = malloc( strlen(row) + 1);
   strcpy (args[i], row);
   ```

5. Make sure to release the Java string using ReleaseStringUTFChars when done. Failing to do so will create a memory leak.

   ```
   // free java string jrow
   (*env)->ReleaseStringUTFChars(env, jrow, row);
   }
   ```

6. Finally, invoke Quake II `main` sub with the arguments that you just created.

```
// Invoke Quake's main sub.
main (clen, args);
```

Rendering a Single Frame

Both the Java and C implementations for `RenderFrame` are the same as Chapter 6. In `Natives.java` you declared the native method `RenderFrame()`, which is implemented as shown in the following fragment:

```
extern void RenderFrame();

JNIEXPORT jint JNICALL Java_quake_jni_Natives_RenderFrame
  (JNIEnv * env, jclass cls)
{
    RenderFrame();
}
```

The C keyword `extern` next to `void RenderFrame()` tells the compiler that elsewhere exists a function called `RenderFrame`, which will be invoked within the JNI implementation. `RenderFrame` is a new function and needs to be created.

Listing 7-1 shows the Quake II main function from the project source at `ch07.QuakeII/jni/quake2-3.21/android/sys_linux.c`. You notice that it loops forever (by using a `while (1)` loop).

Listing 7-1. Quake II Main Function

```
int main (int argc, char **argv)
{
  int   time, oldtime, newtime;

  // go back to real user for config loads
  saved_euid = geteuid();
  seteuid(getuid());

  Qcommon_Init(argc, argv);

  nostdout = Cvar_Get("nostdout", "0", 0);
  if (!nostdout->value) {
    printf ("Linux Quake -- Version %0.3f\n", LINUX_VERSION);
  }
  oldtime = Sys_Milliseconds ();

// main render loop
  while (1) {
// find time spent rendering last frame
    do {
      newtime = Sys_Milliseconds ();
```

```
      time = newtime - oldtime;
    } while (time < 1);
    Qcommon_Frame (time);
    oldtime = newtime;
    }
}
```

This infinite loop does not work well with Android because Android's rendering thread already has a loop of its own. Calling an infinite loop within another loop will deadlock the rendering thread and will make your application crash. Therefore, you must comment the infinite loop. You can also see that within the loop, one frame is rendered at a time using Qcommon_Frame(time). This is what you need; you can just extract what is inside this loop and put it in RenderFrame(). Thus, the code in Listing 7-1 becomes the code in Listing 7-2.

Listing 7-2. Modified Quake II Main Function to Render a Single Frame

```
void RenderFrame()
{
  int time, newtime;
  static int oldtime;

  // Init this var
  if (oldtime == 0 )
    oldtime = Sys_Milliseconds ();

  do {
    newtime = Sys_Milliseconds ();
    time = newtime - oldtime;
  } while (time < 1);
  Qcommon_Frame (time);
  oldtime = newtime;
}

int main (int argc, char **argv)
{
// ...
// main render loop?
#ifndef ANDROID
  while (1) {
// find time spent rendering last frame
    do {
      newtime = Sys_Milliseconds ();
      time = newtime - oldtime;
    } while (time < 1);
    Qcommon_Frame (time);
    oldtime = newtime;
    }
#endif
}
```

What you have done is simply extract whatever is inside the while loop and put it in RenderFrame() to render a single frame. Also, notice that you use conditional compilation, like so:

```
#ifndef ANDROID
  while (1) {
  ...
  }
#endif
```

Here #ifndef ANDROID tells the compiler to include the enclosed code only if the flag ANDROID has not been defined at compilation time. This creates portability and allows the same code to work in multiple Linux flavors. Therefore, this tiny change allows the following sequence of events to occur seamlessly:

1. When the application starts, the main activity will start (Java).

2. The activity creates an OpenGL surface and starts a separate rendering thread (Java).

3. When the surface is first created, the QuakeMain native method is invoked only once, which in turn calls the Quake II main function (Java/C), passing game startup arguments.

4. The rendering thread loops continuously, firing the render frame event, which will invoke the native function RenderFrame to draw a single frame of the game.

5. After the single frame rendering completes, Android invokes the OpenGL swap buffers operation to display the graphics on the device; the process will resume back from step 4 until the user decides to terminate the program.

Now that you have the rendering smoothed, let's tackle key events.

Pumping Key Events

Keys are sent from the Java wrappers to the C engine via the native functions of keyPress and keyRelease, which are declared in quake.jni.Natives.java. Both functions have as an argument the ASCII code of the key, which must be translated from the Android key format. The translation is identical to that in Chapter 6 under the "Handling Key Events" section, where you used an array of key mappings between Android codes and ASCII codes. The tricky part is dealing with all the different keyboard layouts of the dozens of keyboard-equipped phones out there. Nevertheless, the C implementations of keyPress and keyRelease need a tiny change to feed the key to the Quake II engine handler, as shown in Listing 7–3.

Listing 7-3. Key Handlers for Quake II Java Wrappers

```
// in jni_quake.c
JNIEXPORT jint JNICALL Java_quake_jni_Natives_keyPress
  (JNIEnv * env, jclass cls, jint key)
{
  Key_Event((int)key, 1);
  return key;
}

JNIEXPORT jint JNICALL Java_quake_jni_Natives_keyRelease
  (JNIEnv * env, jclass cls, jint key)
{
  Key_Event((int)key, 0);
  return key;
}
```

Listing 7–3 shows the parameter key, which must be an ASCII code being fed to the Quake II key handler. I want to stress this because failing to translate the key properly will make all kinds of weird things happen and cause you a lot of headaches.

```
Key_Event((int)key, 1);
```

The first argument of Key_Event is the ASCII code and the second is a Boolean variable where 1 means key pressed and 0 means key released.

Moving in 3D Space

When moving a Quake II character in 3D space, you have four choices: moving forward, moving sideways, and the ability to look around by controlling the yaw (or angular movement in the X coordinate) or pitch (angular movement in the Y coordinate). To do so, there are two native methods in Natives.java:

```
mouseMove(int deltaX, int deltaY)
mouseLook(int deltaX, int deltaY)
```

mouseMove controls forward or sideways movement by feeding XY increments (or deltas) to the Quake II engine. mouseLook does the same thing with yaw and pitch increments. The C companions for mouseMove and mouseLook are identical to Quake I in Chapter 6; however, Quake II requires a movement handler that must be implemented. This handler is called IN_Move and it is shown in Listing 7–4.

Listing 7-4. Moving in 3D Space

```
// jni_quake.c
// forwards/sideways deltas
extern int    mouse_side, mouse_fwd;

// Yaw/pitch deltas
extern int    mx, my;
```

```
JNIEXPORT jint JNICALL Java_quake_jni_Natives_mouseLook
  (JNIEnv * env, jclass cls, jint mousex, jint mousey)
{
  mx = (int)mousex;
  my = (int)mousey;
}

extern int   mouse_side, mouse_fwd;

JNIEXPORT jint JNICALL Java_quake_jni_Natives_mouseMove
  (JNIEnv * env, jclass cls, jint jx, jint jy)
{
  mouse_side = (int)jx;
  mouse_fwd = (int)jy;
}

// vid_so.c
int mouse_side = 0;
int mouse_fwd = 0;
int mx, my; // mouse look

void IN_Move (usercmd_t *cmd)
{
  old_mouse_x = mx;
  old_mouse_y = my;

  mx *= 3; //sensitivity
  my *= 3; //sensitivity

  // Look: yaw/pitch
  in_state.viewangles[YAW] -= m_yaw->value * mx;
  in_state.viewangles[PITCH] += m_pitch->value * my;
  mx = my = 0;

  // Move
  cmd->sidemove += m_side->value * mouse_side;
  cmd->forwardmove -= m_forward->value * mouse_fwd;

}
```

IN_Move is the Quake II input handler for movement. For forward or side movement, IN_Move provides the command structure of usercmd_t *cmd, which can be used to control the character by consuming two delta values in the XY coordinates.

```
cmd->sidemove += m_side->value * DELTA_X;
cmd->forwardmove -= m_forward->value * DELTA_Y;
```

DELTA_X and DELTA_Y are the increments in the XY direction provided by Java when the user drags a finger on screen; m_side and m_forward are two internal constants used to control the sensitivity of the movement; and cmd->sidemove and cmd->forwardmove are the internal variables that contain the actual character position on 3D space. Note that to move forward in the Quake I/II 3D space coordinate system, the increments in the Y axis must be negative. This is the inverse of dragging a finger up the screen, which provides a positive increment.

To control yaw and pitch, on the other hand, you provide another set of increments in XY, but in this case you use the Quake II view angles data structure (in_state.viewangles).

```
in_state.viewangles[YAW] -= m_yaw->value * DELTA_X;
in_state.viewangles[PITCH] += m_pitch->value * DEALTA_Y;
```

By providing an increment in the X coordinate, you can control the yaw or side angular movement, thus making your character look sideways. An increment in the Y coordinate will result in pitch change or up/down angular movement. As before, m_yaw and m_pitch are two internal constants used to control sensitivity, and viewangles[YAW] and viewangles[PITCH] contain the actual angular values.

Tip   It is up to you as a developer to decide how to control the forward/sideways or yaw/pitch Java and C handlers. For example, dragging a finger on the left half of the screen could trigger the side movement handlers and dragging on the right half could trigger the look handlers.

Audio Handling

Android SDK version 5 offers a new audio-capture design with low-latency audio input to:

- quickly capture a thread that never blocks except during a read;
- quickly track capture clients at the native sample rate, channel count, and bit depth;
- offer resampling, up/down channel mix, and up/down bit depth.

Also the multichannel audio stream mixing allows professional audio apps to mix up to eight channels, including 5.1 and 7.1 channels.

Audio handling in Quake II works the same way as in Chapter 6. In the Java class NativeAudio, you declare a native method of PaintAudio that receives a ByteBuffer as its argument.

```
static native PaintAudio( ByteBuffer buf )
```

The Java ByteBuffer represents an array of audio bytes to be played using Android's MediaTrack API. Listing 7–5 shows the C implementation of this function; it simply gets the memory address of the Java buffer using GetDirectBufferAddress plus its size (with GetDirectBufferCapacity), then it calls the external function paint_audio to fill it up. paint_audio is the same as in Quake I and it is defined in snd_android.c; however, the audio initialization is slightly different.

Note   jni_quake.c and snd_android.c can be found on the book source under ch07.QuakeII/jni/quake2-3.21/android.

Listing 7-5. Java/C Audio Handlers

```c
// jni_quake.c
extern int paint_audio (void *unused, void * stream, int len);

JNIEXPORT jint JNICALL Java_quake_jni_Natives_PaintAudio
 ( JNIEnv* env, jobject thiz, jobject buf )
{
  void *stream;
  int len;

  stream = (*env)->GetDirectBufferAddress(env,  buf);
  len = (*env)->GetDirectBufferCapacity (env, buf);

  paint_audio (NULL, stream, len );
  return 0;
}

// snd_android.c
qboolean SNDDMA_Init(void)
{
  // most of the wav files are 16 bits, 22050 Hz, stereo
  dma.samplebits = 16;
  dma.speed = 22050;
  dma.channels = 2;

  LOGD("SNDDMA_Init Speed %d channels %d", dma.speed, dma.channels);

  dmapos = 0;

  // Sample size
  dma.samples = 32768;
  dma.samplepos = 0;
  dma.submission_chunk = 1;

  dmasize = (dma.samples * (dma.samplebits/8));
  dma.buffer = calloc(1, dmasize);

  snd_inited = 1;
  return 1;
}
```

Audio initialization in Listing 7-5 consists of telling Quake II information about its format, such as

- *Resolution*: 16 bit

- *Frequency*: 22 kHz

- *Number of channels*: Two for stereo

- *Buffer size*

For this purpose, Quake II defines the audio data structure dma as

```
// snd_loc.h
typedef struct
{
  int     channels;
  int     samples;          // mono samples in buffer
  int     submission_chunk;   // don't mix less than this #
  int     samplepos;         // in mono samples
  int     samplebits;
  int     speed;
  byte    *buffer;
} dma_t;

extern  dma_t dma;
```

When Quake II starts, it calls SNDDMA_Init to initialize the audio, and the following sequence of events will take place to quickly start the audio playback:

1. When the user starts the game, the Java native method QuakeMain is invoked, which translates the array of Java string arguments into a C array and passes them to the Quake II engine.

2. Quake II starts up, processes the arguments, and at some point calls SNDDMA_Init.

3. Once the audio and video are initialized, the C to Java callback jni_init_video is called to send a message to the Java wrappers that video is ready. At this point, the Java code starts the audio thread declared in NativeAudio.java by invoking NativeAudio.start().

4. Audio playback starts.

The jni_init_video callback is explained in detail in the section on video handling.

What to Do When Fatal Errors Occur

The user needs to be notified when a fatal error such as a crash or missing resource occurs. For this purpose, you can use JNI to invoke a Java method, like so:

```
OnSysError(final String message)
```

This method could pop up a dialog box to notify the user of the error and then terminate the program. Listing 7-6 presents such an implementation.

Listing 7-6. Handling Fatal Errors

```
// sys_linux.c
void Sys_Error (char *error, ...)
{
```

```
va_list     argptr;
char        string[1024];

CL_Shutdown ();
Qcommon_Shutdown ();

va_start (argptr,error);
vsprintf (string,error,argptr);
va_end (argptr);

jni_sys_error(string);
}

// jni_quake.c
void jni_sys_error(const char * text) {
  JNIEnv *env;

  if ( !g_VM) {
    LOGE("jni_fatal No Java VM available. Aborting\n");
    exit (0);
  }

  (*g_VM)->AttachCurrentThread (g_VM, &env, NULL);

  // need a valid environment and class
  if ( !env || !jNativesCls) {
    return;
  }

  jmethodID mid = (*env)->GetStaticMethodID(env, jNativesCls
    , "OnSysError"
    , "(Ljava/lang/String;)V");

  // invoke Your.OnSysError(text)
  if (mid) {
      (*env)->CallStaticVoidMethod(env, jNativesCls
          , mid
          , (*env)->NewStringUTF(env, text) );
  }
}
```

Whenever a fatal error occurs, Quake II calls Sys_Error with a description of the error. The client will be shut down and the arguments will be packed into a string and sent to the C to Java callback of jni_sys_error.

```
va_start (argptr,error);
vsprintf (string,error,argptr);
va_end (argptr);

jni_sys_error(string);
```

jni_sys_error then performs the following steps:

1. Attaches to the current thread by calling `AttachCurrentThread`.

> **Note**   C functions that are not invoked from a JNI function implementation (or main thread) must
> attach to the current thread by calling `(*g_VM)->AttachCurrentThread (g_VM, &env, NULL)`.
> Failing to do so will cause a crash.

2. Loads the static method `OnSysError` from the `quake.jni.Natives`
    Java class with the signature

    `(Ljava/lang/String;)V`

3. `Ljava/lang/String;` simply says there is one argument of type `java.lang.String` (enclosed by the delimiters `L` and `;`). The `V` says that the
    return type is void.

> **Note**   It is critical to get the method name and the signature right when calling
> `GetStaticMethodID`. Otherwise, it won't be able to find the requested Java method.

4. Invokes the method with the string argument. Note that C strings must
    be converted into Java string using `NewStringUTF(env, C_CHAR_ARRAY)`.

Listing 7-7 shows the error handler in action. The JNI function `QuakeMain` starts printing the boot-up arguments and calling the engine main function. Quake II then initializes the audio and video but fails to find a valid game file, so it bails out.

Listing 7-7. Error Log Showing Missing Game Files

```
DEBUG/QuakeActivity(841): Display Size:800,480
DEBUG/QuakeView(841): Setting startup args & renderer
INFO/ActivityManager(72): Displayed com.opengl.q2/com.opengl.QuakeActivity: +2s542ms
DEBUG/QuakeView(841): onSurfaceCreated
DEBUG/Q2JNI(841): Q2Main[0]=quake2
DEBUG/Q2JNI(841): Q2Main[1]=+set
DEBUG/Q2JNI(841): Q2Main[2]=basedir
DEBUG/Q2JNI(841): Q2Main[3]=/sdcard/quake2
DEBUG/Q2JNI(841): Q2Main[4]=+set
DEBUG/Q2JNI(841): Q2Main[5]=skill
DEBUG/Q2JNI(841): Q2Main[6]=0
DEBUG/Q2JNI(841): Q2Main[7]=+set
DEBUG/Q2JNI(841): Q2Main[8]=nocdaudio
DEBUG/Q2JNI(841): Q2Main[9]=1
DEBUG/Q2JNI(841): Q2Main[10]=+set
DEBUG/Q2JNI(841): Q2Main[11]=cd_nocd
DEBUG/Q2JNI(841): Q2Main[12]=1
```

```
DEBUG/Q2JNI(841): Q2Main[13]=+set
DEBUG/Q2JNI(841): Q2Main[14]=s_initsound
DEBUG/Q2JNI(841): Q2Main[15]=1
DEBUG/Q2JNI(841): Q2Main[16]=+set
DEBUG/Q2JNI(841): Q2Main[17]=vid_ref
DEBUG/Q2JNI(841): Q2Main[18]=glx
DEBUG/Q2JNI(841): Q2Main[19]=+set
DEBUG/Q2JNI(841): Q2Main[20]=gl_mode
DEBUG/Q2JNI(841): Q2Main[21]=4
DEBUG/Q2JNI(841): couldn't exec default.cfg
DEBUG/Q2JNI(841): couldn't exec config.cfg
DEBUG/Q2JNI(841): basedir is write protected.
DEBUG/Q2JNI(841): Console initialized.
DEBUG/Q2JNI(841): ------- sound initialization -------
DEBUG/QSound(841): SNDDMA_Init Speed 22050 channels 2
DEBUG/Q2JNI(841): sound sampling rate: 22050
DEBUG/Q2JNI(841): ----------------------------------
DEBUG/Q2JNI(841): ref_gl version: GL 0.01
DEBUG/Q2JNI(841): SDL audio device shut down.
ERROR/Natives(841): Natives::OnSysError Couldn't load pics/colormap.pcx
ERROR/QuakeView(841): Couldn't load pics/colormap.pcx
```

Sys_Error gets invoked, which in turn calls jni_sys_error, which sends the message back to the Java QuakeView class that terminates the program. Of course, you should pop up a message box to the user telling him about the error before terminating the program.

```
ERROR/Natives(841): Natives::OnSysError Couldn't load pics/colormap.pcx
ERROR/QuakeView(841): Couldn't load pics/colormap.pcx
```

OpenGL Immediate-Mode Issues

Before you start digging into the video handlers, I'd like to stress the tremendous amount of work saved in this project by reusing NanoGL to deal with the immediate-mode headaches of OpenGL. As shown at the beginning of this chapter, Quake II's OpenGL renderer is about 11,000 lines of very difficult C code. All this code would have been translated into OpenGL ES and would have taken months of pro bono work by a team of many developers. Now all that work is reduced to a few weekend hours by one dude. Keep this wonderful software tool in mind when you decide to bring other projects to your mobile device, as NanoGL can be reused without change by any mobile program.

Video Handlers

Video handlers are probably the most laborious part of this project. Any Quake II video handler must implement six handler functions. Of the lot, only the following three require actual implementations; the rest are just empty declarations:

- ■ GLimp_Init(void *hinstance, void *hWnd): This function is used to initialize the OpenGL renderer. The arguments hinstance and hWnd are Windows-only variables and do not apply in the Android/Linux world.

- ■ GLimp_SetMode(int *pwidth, int *pheight, int mode, qboolean fullscreen): This function is used to set the video mode of the game, including the width and height of the screen. The argument fullscreen does not apply in this case.

- ■ GLimp_EndFrame (): This function gets called after the rendering of each frame completes. It is meant to tell the OpenGL ES pipeline it is time to draw.

The following video functions are called from various points of the drawing cycle and must be declared but don't apply to this project; thus they will be empty:

- ■ GLimp_Shutdown( ): Called when the OpenGL renderer is shut down. It can fire many times during the life cycle of the game.

- ■ GLimp_BeginFrame(float camera_separation): Called before each frame of the game is drawn.

- ■ GLimp_AppActivate(qboolean active): Called once when the application is activated.

Video Initialization

During video initialization, you load the NanoGL handlers and tell the engine that the renderer is ready to perform OpenGL calls, as shown in Listing 7-8.

Listing 7-8. Video Initialization

```
// gl_glx.c
static qboolean gl_initialized = false;

int GLimp_Init( void *hinstance, void *wndproc )
{
  if ( ! gl_initialized ) {
    //  init NanoGL
    if ( ! nanoGL_Init() ) {
      return false;
    }
    gl_initialized = true;
  }
  return true;
}
```

Because Quake II allows switching screen resolutions and renderers on the fly, GLimp_Init may fire more than once during the game life cycle; thus you must make sure initialization occurs only once.

Setting the Video Mode and Size

The Quake II OpenGL renderer video resolution is calculated from the command line by sending the arguments

```
+ set gl_mode MODE_NUMBER
```

where MODE-NUMBER maps to an array of screen resolutions (see Listing 7-9). For example, gl_mode 3 tells the engine to use a 569×320 video resolution. If the video mode is not specified at startup, the default value is 3.

Listing 7-9. Setting the Video Mode

```
// vid_so.c
typedef struct vidmode_s
{
  const char *description;
  int        width, height;
  int        mode;
} vidmode_t;

vidmode_t vid_modes[] =
{
#ifdef ANDROID
  { "Mode 0: 256x256",   256, 256,   0 },
  { "Mode 1: 320x320",   320, 320,   1 },
  { "Mode 2: 480x320",   480, 320,   2 },
  { "Mode 3: 569x320",   569, 320,   3 },
  { "Mode 4: 800x480",   800, 480,   4 },
#else
  ...
#endif
};

// gl_glx.c
int GLimp_SetMode( int *pwidth, int *pheight, int mode, qboolean fullscreen )
{

  if ( !ri.Vid_GetModeInfo( &width, &height, mode ) )
  {
    ri.Con_Printf( PRINT_ALL, " invalid mode\n" );
    return rserr_invalid_mode;
  }

  ri.Con_Printf( PRINT_ALL, " %d %d\n", width, height );
```

```
  *pwidth = width;
  *pheight = height;

  // let the sound and input subsystems know about the new window
  ri.Vid_NewWindow (width, height);

  return rserr_ok;
}

// vid_so.c
qboolean VID_GetModeInfo( int *width, int *height, int mode )
{
  if ( mode < 0 || mode >= VID_NUM_MODES )
    return false;

  *width  = vid_modes[mode].width;
  *height = vid_modes[mode].height;

  return true;
}

/**
* VID_NewWindow
*/
void VID_NewWindow ( int width, int height)
{
  viddef.width  = width;
  viddef.height = height;

  //tell java  about it
  jni_init_video (width, height);
}
```

For Android, you have defined a set of resolutions that include all possible sizes for the different types of Android devices out there with this code:

```
#ifdef ANDROID
  { "Mode 0: 256x256",   256, 256,   0 },
  { "Mode 1: 320x320",   320, 320,   1 },
  { "Mode 2: 480x320",   480, 320,   2 },
  { "Mode 3: 569x320",   569, 320,   3 },
  { "Mode 4: 800x480",   800, 480,   4 },
...
#endif
```

When the Quake II engine starts up, GLimp_SetMode will be invoked. Here, you must get the screen resolution by calling

```
ri.Vid_GetModeInfo( &width, &height, mode )
```

where width and height are references that will store the size of the screen, and mode is the gl_mode argument sent in the command line. Note that ri.Vid_GetModeInfo is nothing more than a function pointer that references the real Vid_GetModeInfo function declared in vid_so.c.

```
ri.Vid_GetModeInfo = Vid_GetModeInfo
```

This is done because, as mentioned at the beginning of the chapter, Quake II has been greatly modularized. In the default configuration (where the client, game, and renderer are compiled in separate libraries) functions can be called across libraries. This makes the code very complex, but the benefits are well worth it: it's very easy to maintain and enhance. Vid_GetModeInfo simply uses the value of mode to look up the video modes table (vid_modes) and obtain the size of the screen.

```
*width  = vid_modes[mode].width;
*height = vid_modes[mode].height;
```

Once the screen size is received, GLimp_SetMode sends the information back to the parent and tells the other subsystems that a new window has been created.

```
*pwidth = width;
*pheight = height;
// let the sound and input subsystems know about the new window
ri.Vid_NewWindow (width, height);
```

In Android, VID_NewWindow updates the video definition with the screen values and calls the C-to-Java callback jni_init_video.

```
viddef.width  = width;
viddef.height = height;

//tell Java  about it
jni_init_video (width, height);
```

jni_init_video invokes the Java static method OnInitVideo declared in quake.jni.Natives.java with the width and height of the screen.

```
// jni_quake.c
  jmethodID mid = (*env)->GetStaticMethodID(env, jNativesCls
      , "OnInitVideo"
      , "(II)V");

  if (mid) {
      (*env)->CallStaticVoidMethod(env, jNativesCls, mid, width, height);
  }
```

Note that the jni_init_video implementation is the same as Quake I in Chapter 6.

Finally, OnInitVideo calls the listener OnInitVideo (QuakeView in this case), which will start the Java audio thread and start audio playback. Thus, the video initialization call stack can be summarized as follows:

- GLimp_SetMode (width, height, mode) – C
- Vid_GetModeInfo (width, height, mode) – C
- Vid_NewWindow (width, height) – C
- jni_init_video (width, height) – C/JNI
- OnInitVideo (width, height) – Java
- QuakeView (width, height) – Java
- NativeAudio.start() – Java

What to Do When the Rendering Completes

This is the last step in the rendering cycle. GLimp_EndFrame fires after each frame of the game is rendered. Here you issue a qglFlush call, which causes all issued OpenGL commands to be executed as quickly as they are accepted by the actual rendering pipeline.

```
// gl_glx.c
void GLimp_EndFrame (void)
{
  qglFlush();
}
```

Now you are ready to build the engine and start playing Quake II in your mobile device.

Building Quake II with the NDK

The final step is to get the native code compiled into libquake2.so before you can start testing in your device. In the project source (under ch07.QuakeII/jni), you have three files that drive the compilation process: Application.mk, Android.mk, and hardlinkedq2gl. mk. Application.mk defines what modules are to be compiled. In your case, quake2 (as libquake2.so) and NanoGL (from Chapter 6) will be compiled as a static library and embedded within libquake2.so.

```
# Application.mk
APP_BUILD_SCRIPT := $(call my-dir)/Android.mk
APP_MODULES      := quake2 NanoGL
```

Android.mk simply includes the real compilation script hardlinkedq2gl.mk. This is done because of a really annoying Android peculiarity: if you need to update the compilation script Android.mk (if you missed a compiler option, for example), then the compilation process will start all over again from the beginning. This can drive you crazy when you try to compile libraries with dozens and dozens of source files—especially in slow systems.

```
# Android.mk
include $(call my-dir)/hardlinkedq2gl.mk
```

> **Tip**   By including another script within `Android.mk`, the compilation process will resume from the last file whenever updates are performed to the included script.

In `hardlinkedq2gl.mk`, you build NanoGL as a static library first. Note that the source code lives in Chapter 6.

```
# hardlinkedq2gl.mk
LOCAL_PATH := $(call my-dir)

include $(CLEAR_VARS)

DIR:= ../../ch06.Quake/jni/Quake/NanoGL

LOCAL_MODULE     := NanoGL
LOCAL_C_INCLUDES := ../ch06.Quake/jni/Quake/NanoGL/GL
LOCAL_SRC_FILES := $(DIR)/eglwrap.cpp $(DIR)/nanogl.cpp \
        $(DIR)/nanoWrap.cpp

include $(BUILD_STATIC_LIBRARY)
```

Next, you build Quake II as a shared library (`libquake2.so`; see Listing 7-10). Note the following compiler options:

- ■ `-DANDROID`: It tells the compiler to use the custom Android code declared throughout the engine.

- ■ `-DGLQUAKE`: It tells the compiler to build the OpenGL renderer

- ■ `-DLIBQUAKE2`: It tells the compiler to use custom Quake II code.

- ■ `-Dstricmp=strcasecmp`: It replaces all occurrences of `stricmp` with `strcasecmp` for string comparison. Some Linux C-library implementations don't include `stricmp`.

- ■ `-DREF_HARD_LINKED`: This is a critical option. It tells the compiler to pack the renderer and client modules as a single monolithic file. This makes the build/debug/run process much simpler in mobile platforms.

- ■ `-DGAME_HARD_LINKED`: Another critical option. It tells the compiler to include the game module in the pack.

Listing 7-10.   Quake II Android Compilation Script

```
# hardlinkedq2gl.mk
BUILDDIR:=quake2-3.21

include $(CLEAR_VARS)

LOCAL_MODULE := quake2
```

```
COMMON_CFLAGS :=-DANDROID -DGLQUAKE -DLIBQUAKE2 -Dstricmp=strcasecmp

LOCAL_CFLAGS := $(COMMON_CFLAGS) -DREF_HARD_LINKED -DGAME_HARD_LINKED
LOCAL_C_INCLUDES := $(COMMON_C_INCLUDES) ../ch06.Quake/jni/Quake/NanoGL
LOCAL_LDLIBS := -llog -ldl
LOCAL_STATIC_LIBRARIES := libNanoGL

# Q2 client
QUAKE2_OBJS := \
  $(BUILDDIR)/client/cl_cin.c \
  $(BUILDDIR)/client/cl_ents.c \
  $(BUILDDIR)/client/cl_fx.c \
  $(BUILDDIR)/client/cl_input.c \
  $(BUILDDIR)/android/vid_so.c \
  ....
  $(BUILDDIR)/android/sys_linux.c \

# Game
CGAME_SRC := \
  $(BUILDDIR)/game/q_shared.c \
  $(BUILDDIR)/game/g_ai.c \
  $(BUILDDIR)/game/p_client.c \
  ...
  $(BUILDDIR)/game/p_trail.c \
  $(BUILDDIR)/game/p_view.c \
  $(BUILDDIR)/game/p_weapon.c \

# OpenGL renderer
REF_FILES := \
  $(BUILDDIR)/ref_gl/gl_draw.c \
  $(BUILDDIR)/ref_gl/gl_image.c \
  $(BUILDDIR)/ref_gl/gl_light.c \
  $(BUILDDIR)/ref_gl/gl_mesh.c \
  $(BUILDDIR)/ref_gl/gl_model.c \
  $(BUILDDIR)/ref_gl/gl_rmain.c \
  $(BUILDDIR)/ref_gl/gl_rmisc.c \
  $(BUILDDIR)/ref_gl/gl_rsurf.c \
  $(BUILDDIR)/ref_gl/gl_warp.c \
  $(BUILDDIR)/linux/qgl_linux.c \
  $(BUILDDIR)/android/gl_glx.c \

LOCAL_SRC_FILES := $(QUAKE2_OBJS) $(CGAME_SRC) $(REF_FILES)

include $(BUILD_SHARED_LIBRARY)
```

To run the compilation process in Windows using Cygwin, start the Cygwin console, change to the folder containing the chapter source (see Figure 7-1), and invoke the Android build script ndk-build, like so:

```
$ cd /cygdrive/C/tmp/ch07.QuakeII
$ ndk-build
```

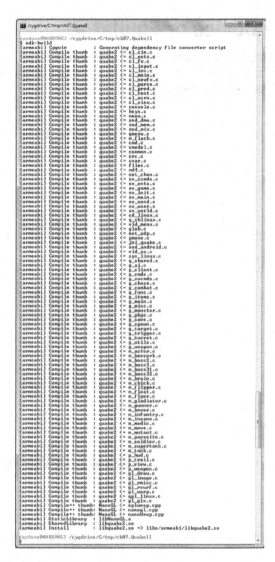

Figure 7-1. Compiling Quake II with the NDK

The native library libquake2.so will be created under the Java project ch07.QuakeII/libs/armeabi/libquake2.so. Thus when the Java app starts, the QuakeView class will invoke:

```
System.load("quake2")
```

which loads the native library and provides access to the JNI methods and the C to Java callbacks used by the Java code. Now let's play some Quake II.

Running on the Device or Emulator

With the native library compiled and ready for use, you can now run the game in the emulator; but first, connect your device/tablet or run an emulator, then create a run configuration in Eclipse, as shown in Figure 7-2.

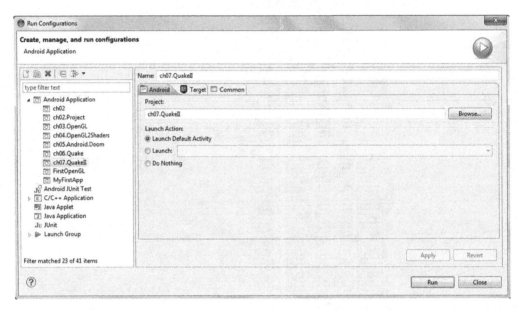

Figure 7-2. Run configuration for Quake II

Before running the game, make sure you put the Quake II game files on your device's SD card under

/sdcard/quake2/baseq2

Run the game and look at the Android log carefully. It should look something like Listing 7-11.

Listing 7-11. Quake II Run Log File

```
DEBUG/QuakeActivity(569): Display Size:800,480
DEBUG/QuakeView(569): Setting startup args & renderer
INFO/ActivityManager(72): Displayed com.opengl.q2/com.opengl.QuakeActivity: +3s469ms
DEBUG/QuakeView(569): onSurfaceCreated
DEBUG/Q2JNI(569): Q2Main[0]=quake2
DEBUG/Q2JNI(569): Q2Main[1]=+set
DEBUG/Q2JNI(569): Q2Main[2]=basedir
DEBUG/Q2JNI(569): Q2Main[3]=/sdcard/quake2
DEBUG/Q2JNI(569): Q2Main[4]=+set
DEBUG/Q2JNI(569): Q2Main[5]=skill
DEBUG/Q2JNI(569): Q2Main[6]=0
DEBUG/Q2JNI(569): Q2Main[7]=+set
DEBUG/Q2JNI(569): Q2Main[8]=nocdaudio
```

```
DEBUG/Q2JNI(569): Q2Main[9]=1
DEBUG/Q2JNI(569): Q2Main[10]=+set
DEBUG/Q2JNI(569): Q2Main[11]=cd_nocd
DEBUG/Q2JNI(569): Q2Main[12]=1
DEBUG/Q2JNI(569): Q2Main[13]=+set
DEBUG/Q2JNI(569): Q2Main[14]=s_initsound
DEBUG/Q2JNI(569): Q2Main[15]=1
DEBUG/Q2JNI(569): Q2Main[16]=+set
DEBUG/Q2JNI(569): Q2Main[17]=vid_ref
DEBUG/Q2JNI(569): Q2Main[18]=glx
DEBUG/Q2JNI(569): Q2Main[19]=+set
DEBUG/Q2JNI(569): Q2Main[20]=gl_mode
DEBUG/Q2JNI(569): Q2Main[21]=4
DEBUG/Q2JNI(569): Added packfile /sdcard/quake2/baseq2/pak0.pak (1106 files)
DEBUG/Q2JNI(569): execing default.cfg
DEBUG/Q2JNI(569): couldn't exec config.cfg
DEBUG/Q2JNI(569): basedir is write protected.
DEBUG/Q2JNI(569): Console initialized.
DEBUG/Q2JNI(569): ------- sound initialization -------
DEBUG/QSound(569): SNDDMA_Init Speed 22050 channels 2
DEBUG/Q2JNI(569): sound sampling rate: 22050
DEBUG/Q2JNI(569): ------------------------------------
DEBUG/Q2JNI(569): ref_gl version: GL 0.01
DEBUG/Q2JNI(569): QGL_Init:
INFO/nanoGL(569): nanoGL: Init loading driver libGLESv1_CM.so
WARN/nanoGL(569): <eglChooseConfig> not found in libGLESv1_CM.so. Trying libEGL.so.
WARN/nanoGL(569): <eglCopyBuffers> not found in libGLESv1_CM.so. Trying libEGL.so.
WARN/nanoGL(569): <eglCreateContext> not found in libGLESv1_CM.so. Trying libEGL.so.
WARN/nanoGL(569): <eglCreatePbufferSurface> not found in libGLESv1_CM.so. Trying libEGL.so.
...
WARN/nanoGL(569): <eglBindTexImage> not found in libGLESv1_CM.so. Trying libEGL.so.
WARN/nanoGL(569): <eglReleaseTexImage> not found in libGLESv1_CM.so. Trying libEGL.so.
WARN/nanoGL(569): <eglSurfaceAttrib> not found in libGLESv1_CM.so. Trying libEGL.so.
DEBUG/Q2JNI(569): Initializing OpenGL display
DEBUG/Q2JNI(569): ...setting fullscreen mode 4:
DEBUG/Q2JNI(569):   800 480
DEBUG/QuakeView(569): OnInitVideo. 800x480 Starting native audio.
DEBUG/Q2JNI(569): GL_VENDOR: Google Inc
DEBUG/Q2JNI(569): GL_RENDERER: Android Pixel Flinger 1.0
DEBUG/Q2JNI(569): GL_VERSION: OpenGL ES-CM 1.0
DEBUG/Q2JNI(569): ...disabling CDS
DEBUG/Q2JNI(569): ...GL_EXT_compiled_vertex_array not found
DEBUG/Q2JNI(569): ...GL_EXT_point_parameters not found
DEBUG/Q2JNI(569): ...GL_EXT_shared_texture_palette not found
DEBUG/Q2JNI(569): ...GL_ARB_multitexture not found
DEBUG/Q2JNI(569): ...GL_SGIS_multitexture not found
DEBUG/Audio(569): Audio start.
DEBUG/Q2JNI(569): ------------------------------------
DEBUG/Q2JNI(569): ------- Server Initialization -------
DEBUG/Q2JNI(569): 0 entities inhibited
DEBUG/Q2JNI(569): 0 teams with 0 entities
DEBUG/Q2JNI(569): ------------------------------------
```

```
DEBUG/Q2JNI(569): ====== Quake2 Initialized ======
DEBUG/QuakeView(569): onSurfaceChanged w=800 h=404
DEBUG/Q2JNI(569): 0.0.0.0:0: client_connect
DEBUG/Q2JNI(569): ----------------------------------
DEBUG/Q2JNI(569): Installation
DEBUG/Q2JNI(569): Map: demo2
DEBUG/Q2JNI(569): pics
DEBUG/Q2JNI(569): maps/demo2.bsp
DEBUG/Q2JNI(569): models/weapons/v_blast/tris.md2
DEBUG/Q2JNI(569): models/objects/gibs/sm_meat/tris.md2
DEBUG/Q2JNI(569): models/objects/gibs/arm/tris.md2
DEBUG/Q2JNI(569): models/objects/debris3/tris.md2
DEBUG/Q2JNI(569): models/objects/barrels/tris.md2
DEBUG/Q2JNI(569): models/monsters/tank/tris.md2
DEBUG/Q2JNI(569): models/weapons/v_shotg/tris.md2
DEBUG/Q2JNI(569): images
```

As soon as the game starts up, you should be able to see the game in action (see Figure 7-3).

Figure 7-3. Quake II running at an 800×480 pixel resolution

If any errors occur, they will be displayed in the Eclipse Android log view. Take a look at the "What to Do When Fatal Errors Occur" section earlier in this chapter for details.

This code was compiled with the SDK version 5 API 21 and tested with the Tablet emulator.

Summary

This is it. You have learned how engines such as Quake I, Quake II, and Doom can be brought to your smartphone in record time by making use of the best that Android can offer, such as

- *Code reusability*: By combining the raw power of C/C++ with the elegant object-oriented features of Java, you can have your games up and running in no time. This is particularly useful if you are building for other platforms, such as iOS, RIM, or Palm.

- *JNI*: The Java Native Interface is what makes all of this possible. It lets you break free of the memory and performance constraints of the Java language, thus reducing development time and costs.

- *Powerful APIs for game development*: This includes hardware-accelerated graphics with OpenGL, audio handling independent of the format, keyboard handling, and single/multi-touch capabilities, plus Bluetooth for external controller support.

My goal in this chapter has been to show you that even though Java is the primary development language for Android, hybrid Java/C development is the best way to develop powerful games. I have done this by featuring three powerful engines that can be run in a mobile device: Doom, Quake I, and Quake II.

## Chapter 8

Fun with Bluetooth Controllers

If you are a hardcore gamer, you may hear complaints about how difficult is to play games (such as first-person shooters) with a touch screen interface or a tiny keyboard. Try playing a game like Doom with a touch screen versus a controller. You will get frustrated very quickly with the touch screen. Some games simply require a controller. Google has wisely used the popular and open BlueZ Bluetooth stack in Android, making it easy to access all sorts of wireless devices. This chapter will show you how easy it is to integrate two popular gaming controllers, Wiimote and Zeemote, with your game.

First you'll look at the always popular Wiimote (Wii Remote) and then you'll look at a far less popular Zeemote Joystick controller, a device designed specifically for mobile gaming. Let's get started.

> **Note** All the code included in this chapter was developed, compiled and tested using Eclipse IDE for Java Developers instead of Android Studio 1.0.1 since, when this manuscript was written, NDK and JNI were not supported by Android Studio.

Dissecting the Wiimote

If you wish to provide external controller support in your game, you must include the Wiimote, which at tens of millions of units sold is the most popular controller. Luckily, Nintendo has made it quite easy to integrate the Wiimote into your game thanks to Bluetooth. This section covers the Wiimote in more detail, including the following aspects:

- *Inquiry process*: This is used to gather information about the device.

- *Device connection*: This section describes the Data and Control Pipes used to send messages to the controller.

- *Report types*: These are some of the messages supported by the Wiimote to receive button information, LED status, and other controller tricks.

But first, we need to make the Wiimote accessible by a host via the standard Bluetooth protocol API. To do so the Wiimote must be placed in discoverable mode by pressing the SYNC button on its back under the battery cover or holding down the 1 and 2 buttons continuously (see Figure 8-1).

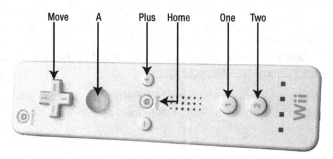

Figure 8-1. When in discoverable mode, the LEDs at the base of the controller will blink

Inquiry Process

To kick things off, the host can perform a Bluetooth device inquiry to find all discoverable nearby Wiimotes. With this information, the host can establish a Bluetooth baseband connection to the Wiimote; no Bluetooth pairing is necessary.

The Wiimote can be queried with the Bluetooth service discovery protocol (SDP) and it will report back the information in Table 8-1.

Table 8-1. *Information Returned by the Wiimote Through SDP*

	Old	New
Name	Nintendo RVL-CNT-01	Nintendo RVL-CNT-01-TR
Vendor ID	0x057e	0x057e
Product ID	0x0306	0x0330
Major Device Class	0x2500	0x0500
Minor Device Class	0x04	0x08

Device Connection

A Bluetooth connection to a Wiimote is done via the HID (human interface device) protocol. This connection involves the use of the Bluetooth L2CAP protocol with two ports (or PSMs, as shown in Figure 8-2) identified as follows:

- *Control Pipe (PSM 11)*: This is used to send control commands to the Wiimote but it only works with the old controllers. **This port is deprecated in the new Wiimotes (RVL-CNT-01-TR) and will no longer work on devices sold after December 2011**. It is strongly recommended that hosts do not use this port to send control commands. This is the reason why most of the Wiimote emulators out there will not work with the new controllers.

- *Data Pipe (PSM 13)*: Nintendo probably got rid of the PSM 11 to make room for the motion plus support in the new controllers. Therefore the Data Pipe (PSM 13) is where all the communication with the controller must take place. It will work with both old and new controllers alike.

Control Pipe PSM11

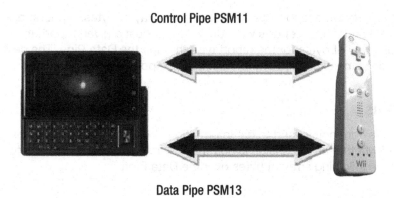

Data Pipe PSM13

Figure 8-2. *Host/Wiimote communications; Control Pipe no longer functions in devices later than December 2011*

When communicating with a Wiimote, a device understands a series of reports. Reports can be of two types: Input or Output. Think of a report as a network port assigned to a particular service. Reports are unidirectional (Input or Output), and the HID descriptor lists the direction and the payload size for each port. Table 8-2 shows some of the reports the Wiimote supports.

Table 8-2. Wiimote Report Types and Sizes (I=Input, O=Output)

I/O	ID(s)	Size	Description
O	0x10	1	Unknown
O	0x11	1	Player LEDs
O	0x12	2	Data reporting mode
O	0x13	1	IR camera enable
O	0x14	1	Speaker enable
O	0x15	1	Status information request
O	0x16	21	Write memory and registers
O	0x17	6	Read memory and registers
O	0x18	21	Speaker data
O	0x19	1	Speaker mute
O	0x1a	1	IR camera enable 2
I	0x20	6	Status information
I	0x21	21	Read memory and registers data
I	0x22	4	Acknowledge output report, return function result
I	0x30-0x3f	2-21	Data reports

Internally, I/O reports are encoded as a hexadecimal array of bytes. Input reports always begin with (0xa1) and output reports with (0xa2). To request a given report, the host must simply send an array of bytes for the report type through the Data Pipe. The next several sections provide some examples of the most useful reports.

Device Status

A status report is commonly used to get information about the core buttons, battery level, LED state, and whether an expansion is currently connected. To request a status report, you need to send the following array of bytes over the Data Pipe:

```
a2 15 00
```

The first byte, 0xa2, indicates the report type (Output), 0x15 is the report name (device status), and 0x00 is the payload.

The response to this report by the Wiimote should be an array of 8 bytes representing

```
a1 20 BB BB LF 00 00 VV
```

- The first byte (0xa1) is the report type (Input in this case).

- Bytes 3 and 4 (BB BB) contain information about the core buttons (see Table 8-3).

- Byte 5 (LF): L is the most significant bit of byte 5, representing the LED state; F is the least significant bit of byte 5, representing a bitmask of flags indicating whether the battery is flat or whether an expansion is currently connected.

- Byte 8 (VV) represents battery level (a value between 0 and 100).

- Bytes 2, 6, and 7 don't contain pertinent information and can be ignored.

Button Status

Information about the core buttons of the Wiimote is encoded as bits in a two-byte bitmask described in Table 8-3.

Table 8-3. Core Buttons of the Wiimote

Bit	Mask	First Byte	Second Byte
0	0x01	D-Pad Left	Two
1	0x02	D-Pad Right	One
2	0x04	D-Pad Down	B
3	0x08	D-Pad Up	A
4	0x10	Plus	Minus
5	0x20	Other uses	Other uses
6	0x40	Other uses	Other uses
7	0x80	Unknown	Home

Player LEDs

These are the four lights in the front face of the Wiimote. During discovery and before initialization, these LEDs blink at a fixed rate. During gameplay with the Wii, one LED is lit to indicate the player number assigned to the Wiimote. This process can be controlled programmatically by sending the following report through the Data Pipe

```
a2 11 LL
```

where 0xa2 indicates an output report, 0x11 the report type (set LED), and LL represents the LED you wish to turn on (see Table 8-4).

Table 8-4. Player LEDs

Bit	Mask	LEDs
4	0x10	1
5	0x20	2
6	0x40	3
7	0x80	4

Other Neat Tricks

You can do a lot of neat stuff with the Wiimote besides receiving button events. For example, to make the Wiimote rumble (after a successful connection perhaps), send:

```
a2 11 01
```

To make it stop, send:

```
a2 11 00
```

Other neat stuff that can be done with the following tools:

- *Sounds*: The Wiimote has a small low-quality electric speaker that can be used for short sound effects during gameplay.

- *Accelerometer*: The accelerometer measures linear acceleration in a free fall frame of reference. If the Wiimote is in free fall, it will report zero acceleration. At rest, it will report an upward acceleration (+Z when horizontal) equal to gravity ($g = 9.8$ m/s^2), but in the opposite direction. This fact can be used to derive tilt movements and more.

- *Camera*: The Wii Remote includes a monochrome camera with built-in image processing. The camera's built-in image processing is capable of tracking up to four moving objects available to the host. Raw pixel data is not available to the host, so the camera cannot be used to take conventional pictures.

Tip   The complete bible about the Wiimote operation modes is available online from the WiiBrew folks at http://wiibrew.org/wiki/Wiimote.

This has been an introduction on how the Wiimote works. Now let's put this knowledge to the test. In the next section you will create an Android app to perform the following tasks:

- Connect or disconnect to the Wiimote and display information about the handshake process.

- Send typical commands such as turning LEDs on or off, or making it rumble.

- Display information when buttons are pressed/released as well as joystick data (if you have a Nunchuk).

Let's continue.

A Wiimote Controller App

This section covers the Wiimote Android app in detail, which is made of three main components:

- *An Android project*: This contains the Java activity and GUI window that can be run to connect and interact with the Wiimote.

- *A native library*: This component uses a modified version of the open source WiiC library (available online at `http://wiic.sourceforge.net/`) to control Wii devices natively. I should mention that the standard WiiC library does not support the latest Wiimote; I have made changes to the original to get it working.

- *A WiiC JNI interface*: This is a small C program that binds WiiC library calls with the Wiimote Java class of your app, thus allowing for WiiC access within your Java code. It is the glue that binds the previous components together.

Let's create an Android project to host your app (the full source is available from the book's companion media).

The Wiimote Android Project

Perform the following steps to create the skeleton for the Wiimote controller app.

1. From the Eclipse main menu, click File ➤ New ➤ Project, then expand the Android tree and select Android Application Project (see Figure 8-3). Click Next.

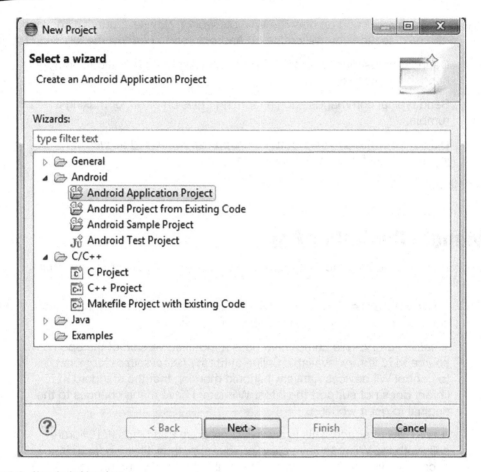

Figure 8-3. New Android project

2. Enter an application name as Ch08.Wiimote.

3. Enter a project name as ch08.Wiimote.

4. Enter a package name as Ch08.Wiimote.

5. Enter an activity name as ProjectActivity.

6. Specify a minimum SDK version 5.0 API 21 in this example. Figure 8-4 shows the completed New Android Project dialog box for this example.

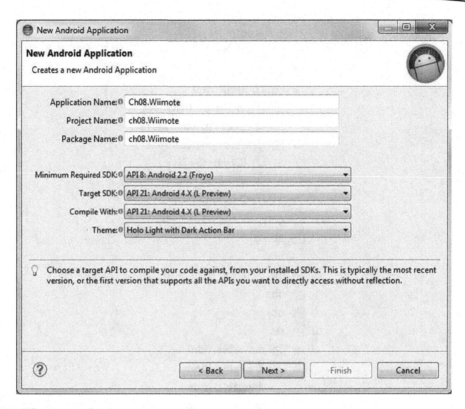

Figure 8-4. Wiimote app wizard

7. Click Next.

8. Create a new activity with the name WiimoteTestActivity and click Finish.

Finally, your project should look like Figure 8-5. Let's take a look at the project Java classes and what they do.

Figure 8-5. Wiimote project class layout

The Java classes of this project are

- `WiiTestActivity`: This is the entry point to your application. It is in charge of loading the GUI XML layout, creating a Wii controller object, and interacting with the Wiimote.

- `IController`: This is an interface designed to wrap the Wiimote calls in a single unity. This will allow you to implement many types of controllers (not just Wiimotes) such as Zeemotes, PS3 Sixaxis, and more. By implementing this simple interface you can easily add support for a variety of Bluetooth controllers. `IController` defines the following methods:

  - `connect( )`: This method starts the connection process to the Bluetooth device.

  - `disconnect( )`: This method disconnects from the controller.

  - `isConnected( )`: This method tells you if there is an active connection.

  - `setListener(IController.IControllerListener listener)`: This method sets an event listener used to notify clients of events occurred in the controller.

- `IController.IControllerListener`: This is an interface within `IController` that can be used to notify clients of controller events such as

  - `onButtonEvent( boolean pressed, int ascii, int scanCode)`: This method fires when a button is pressed in the controller. It gives the state of the button (pressed or released) plus an ASCII and scan code mapping, which can be used to interact with a native game engine.

  - `connected( )`: This event fires on successful connection to the Wiimote.

  - `disconnected(String reason)`: This event fires when the connection has failed. A failure reason is given.

  - `onMessage(String message)`: This is more of a help message to let the host know what is going on behind the scenes.

  - `onJoystickEvent(float angleDeg, float distance)`: This event fires when there is joystick event, such as when the Nunchuck extension is plugged to the Wiimote.

- `Wiimote`: This class is in charge of interacting with the native WiiC library. It loads the native library and provides a set of native methods to interact with the native side. See the native component of the project ("The WiiC Library") for more details.

In the next section, you'll look at Java classes in more detail staring with `WiitestActivity` and working your way down to `Wiimote` (where all the meat resides). But first, let's take a look at the user interface of the application (see Figure 8-6).

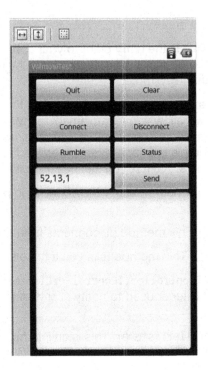

Figure 8-6. Wiimote app user interface

Figure 8-6 shows the XML layout of the app. It has buttons to interact with the Wiimote including Connect, Disconnect, Rumble (to trigger the controller rumble feature), Status (to get the status of the controller), and Send (to post an array of test bytes to the controller), plus a log window that will display messages sent from the device. The XML layout is loaded from the WiiTestActivity, as shown in Listing 8-1.

Listing 8-1. Wiimote Test Main Activity

```java
public class WiiTestActivity extends Activity {

  static final String TAG = "WiiTest";

  IController wii;

  Handler mHandler = new Handler();

  EditText etLog;

  /** Called when the activity is first created. */
  @Override
  public void onCreate(Bundle savedInstanceState) {
    super.onCreate(savedInstanceState);
    // set layout XML
    setContentView(R.layout.main);

    etLog = (EditText) findViewById(R.id.editText2);
```

```
    wii = new Wiimote(this);

    wii.setListener(new IController.IControllerListener() {

        @Override
        public void onButtonEvent(boolean pressed, int ascii, int scanCode) {
            Log.d(TAG, "Event pressed=" + pressed + " ASCII=" + ascii + " sc="
                + scanCode);
            postLog("Event pressed=" + pressed + " ASCII=" + ascii);
        }

        @Override
        public void disconnected(String reason) {
            Log.e(TAG, "Disconnected from wiimote");
            postLog("Disconnected: " + reason);
        }

        @Override
        public void connected() {
            Log.d(TAG, "Connected to wiimote");
            postLog("Connected to wiimote");
        }

        @Override
        public void onMessage(String message) {
            postLog(message);
        }

        @Override
        public void onJoystickEvent(float angleDeg, float distance) {
        }
    });
}
```

Listing 8-1 also shows how to create a Wiimote controller and listen for events by declaring an instance of IController and setting a controller listener, as shown in the next fragment:

```
IController wii;
wii = new Wiimote(this);
wii.setListener(new IController.IControllerListener() {
        public void onButtonEvent(boolean pressed, int ascii, int scanCode) {
        }
        public void disconnected(String reason) {
        }
        public void connected() {
        }

        public void onMessage(String message) {
        }

        public void onJoystickEvent(float angleDeg, float distance) {
        }
});
```

There are four callbacks in the controller listener above.

- onButtonEvent: It fires when a button gets pressed in the controller. Its arguments are a boolean value (pressed) indicating the status of the button—true if pressed, false if released—plus two integers representing ASCII and scan code values for the pressed button.

- connected: It fires when the connection to the controller succeeds.

- onMessage: It fires when there is message sent by the WiiC native library (useful for logging purposes).

- onJoystickEvent: It fires when the joystick is moved on the Nunchuck extension. This event receives the angle in degrees (ranging from 0-360 starting from the top of the XY coordinate system), plus the distance the joystick is moved (ranging from 0 to 1).

Furthermore, when an instance of the Wiimote class gets created in the previous fragment, it triggers the loading of the native WiiC library by invoking

```
static {
  System.loadLibrary("wiimote");
}
```

By implementing the IController interface, the Wiimote class can encapsulate messages between the native side and the Android activity. To do so, Wiimote implements the following set of native methods (which will require C counterparts, as you'll see later):

- native void Initialize( ): This method invokes initialization logic on the native side of the WiiC library.

- native void DiscoverAndConnect( ): This method kick-starts the Bluetooth discovery and connection process of the WiiC library.

- native void DisconnectAll( ): This method disconnect all controllers. WiiC supports up to four simultaneous Wii controllers.

- native void ToggleRumble( ): This method toggles the rumble feature of the device.

- native void SetLed(int led): This method sets the lead (or player) number of the device.

- native void Connect(String address): This is a utility method to connect to a device given its Bluetooth address.

To receive messages from the native side, the Wiimote class implements a simple callback system (this essentially means that the C code will invoke Java methods on Wiimote). This callback system consists of two methods.

- static void OnMessage(int rc, String message): This event fires whenever the WiiC library sends a message to be consumed by the host (to tell you what and where things are happening). RC indicates a return code of either

    - RC_NOERROR: Indicates no error.

    - RC_ERROR_INIT: Indicates an initialization error.

    - RC_ERROR_DISCOVERY: Indicates an error in the Wiimote discovery process.

    - RC_ERROR_DISCOVERY_NOWIIMOTES: Indicates that there are no Wiimotes available.

- static void OnEvent(int code, String message): This event fires whenever there is an event such as

    - Core Button: Core button events occur whenever a button is pressed or released. This may include any buttons pressed on the Nunchuk extension.

    - Nunchuk: This event occurs whenever the Nunchuck extension joystick is moved.

    - Extension Inserted: This event occurs when an extension is inserted. Currently only the Nunchuck is supported by the callback system.

Listing 8-2 shows the implementation of the above methods within the Wiimote class.

Listing 8-2. Callback System for the Wiimote Class

```
/**
 * JNI callback: fires when there is a message
 * @param message
 */
private static void OnMessage(int rc, String message) {
  switch (rc) {
  case RC_NOERROR:
    if (message != null && message.contains("Connected")) {

      Log.d(TAG, "Connection OK");
      connected = true;

      if (mListener != null) {
        mListener.connected();
      }
    } else {
      Log.d(TAG, message);
      if (mListener != null) {
        mListener.onMessage(message);
      }
    }
    break;
```

```
    default:
      Log.e(TAG, "Error code " + rc + ": " + message);
      connected = false;
      if (mListener != null) {
        mListener.disconnected("Error code " + rc + ": " + message);
      }
      break;
  }
}

/**
 * JNI: Fires when there is a controller event:
 * Core button, Nunchuck, Extension Inserted, etc
 * @param code
 * @param message String of the form
 *     EVT_TYPE={BTNPRESS|BTNRELEASE}|BTN={BUTTON}
 */
private static void OnEvent(int code, String message) {
  if (message == null)
    return;

  // parse payload: EVT_TYPE={BTNPRESS|BTNRELEASE}|BTN={BUTTON}
  try {
    Properties payload = new Properties();
    payload.load(new ByteArrayInputStream(message
        .replaceAll("\\|", "\n").getBytes()));

    String type = payload.getProperty("EVT_TYPE");

    if (type.equals("NUNCHUK")) {
      handleNunchuckEvent(payload);
      return;
    } else if (type.equals("EXT_INSERTED")) {
      String name = payload.getProperty("EXT_NAME");
      return;
    }
    handleButtonEvent(payload);
  } catch (Exception e) {
    Log.e(TAG, "Wii:OnEvent: " + e);
  }

}

/**
 * Button event handler
 * @param payload
 */
private static void handleButtonEvent(Properties payload) {
  // button presses
  String type = payload.getProperty("EVT_TYPE");
  String button = payload.getProperty("BTN");
```

```
    Log.d(TAG, "Button Event: " + payload + " Type: " + type + " Btn:"
        + button);
}

/**
 * Nunchuck handler
 * @param payload String of the form
 *     JANGLE=xx.x|JMAGNITUDE=xx
 */
private static void handleNunchuckEvent(Properties payload) {
    try {
        /**
         * The angle \a ang is relative to the positive y-axis into quadrant I and
         * ranges from 0 to 360 degrees. The magnitude is the distance from the
         * center to where the joystick is being held.
         */
        float joyAngle = Float.parseFloat(payload.getProperty("JANGLE"));
        float joyMagnitude = Float.parseFloat(payload
            .getProperty("JMAGNITUDE"));

        if (joyAngle == Float.NaN || joyMagnitude < 0.4) {
            return;
        }

        if (mListener != null) {
            mListener.onJoystickEvent(joyAngle, joyMagnitude);
        }
    } catch (NumberFormatException e) {
        Log.e(TAG, "Nunchuck parse error:" + e);
    }
}
```

In Listing 8-2 you can see the way event data is encoded in the message payload. For example,

- When the A button is pressed on the Wiimote, the OnEvent method fires with the payload.

  ```
  EVT_TYPE=BTNPRESS|BTN=A
  ```

- Similarly, when it is released, you will receive

  ```
  EVT_TYPE=BTNRELEASE|BTN=A
  ```

- When the Nunchuck is inserted, you will receive

  ```
  EVT_TYPE=EXT_INSERTED|EXT_NAME=Nunchuk
  ```

- And finally, when the joystick in the Nunchuk is moved, you will receive

  ```
  EVT_TYPE= NUNCHUK|JANGLE=<Angle in degrees>|JMAGNITUDE=<Stick magnitude [0..1]>
  ```

> **Note**   Buttons in the Nunchuk will trigger core button events in the WiiC library.

Finally, the Wiimote class uses the IController.IControllerListener interface to relay messages back to the listener (see Listing 8-3).

Listing 8-3. Wii Controller Listener Interface

```
public static interface IControllerListener  {
  public void onButtonEvent( boolean pressed, int ascii, int scanCode);
  public void connected( );
  public void disconnected(String reason);
  public void onMessage(String message);
  public void onJoystickEvent(float angleDeg, float distance);
}
```

This is the first component of your application. Now let's take a look at the native side of this app, the WiiC library.

The WiiC Library

There are many libraries out there that provide Wii device connectivity (most of them based on the same source). For instance, you could look at the Softwarebakery Wii libraries at: http://softwarebakery.com/projects/wiidevicelibrary.

I tried them all, and of all those, WiiC appears to work best. The problem with WiiC and the others is that they don't provide support for the new Wiimote (RVL-CNT-01-TR). So I had to painfully figure out what was wrong and try to fix it. Thanks to the folks at WiiBrew I was successful in this endeavor (the details of which I'll provide in the next sections). But first, to make WiiC work with the new Wiimote, the following changes are required in the native side:

- *Handshake fixes*: These are changes to the sockets used to send data between the host and the controller.

- *Check for new device class*: New Wiimotes use a different device class. This is a type of ID used to identify the hardware among a plethora of Bluetooth devices.

- *Other minor changes*: These include report code changes and miscellaneous changes to the Nunchuck handlers.

Fixes to the Handshake

When WiiC connects to the Wiimote it uses two sockets: the Control Pipe in port 11 and the Data Pipe in port 13 (see Figure 8-7). In the old library, the Control Pipe was used to send report requests to the controller.

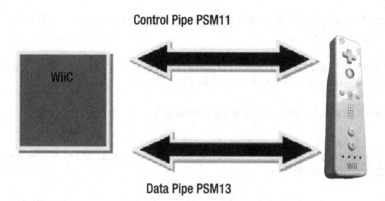

Figure 8-7. Control sockets for WiiC

The new controllers simply ignore any requests sent thru the Control Pipe. All information must now flow thru the Data Pipe (port 13). This will work also with old controllers, which indicates that the Data Pipe was the way to go in the first place. It is unclear why the original developers chose to use the Control Pipe to send requests or why Nintendo chose to have a Control Pipe in the first place.

Luckily, this is a simple change in the WiiC source. Locate the file io_nix.c in the Wiimote project source code for this chapter under Wiimote\jni\WiiCNew\src\wiic within your workspace. There is a method called wiic_io_write (see Listing 8-4).

Listing 8-4. Changes to WiiC to Send Messages Through the Data Pipe

```
int wiic_io_write(struct wiimote_t* wm, byte* buf, int len) {
 // Old way: send bytes thru the Control Pipe
 // return write(wm->ctl_sock, buf, len);
 // Now we send thru the Data Pipe
  return write(wm->data_sock, buf, len);
}
```

wiic_io_write is in charge of writing an array of bytes to the Bluetooth socket of the Wiimote. You simply write the bytes to the data socket (Data Pipe) instead of the control socket (Control Pipe), as seen in Listing 8-4.

Checking for the New Device Class

The device class is the identifier for the Wiimote as a Bluetooth device. The WiiC library checks the device class for the old Wiimotes only. This is the main reason why most emulators out there stopped working after November 2011 when Nintendo released the new controllers. Therefore, WiiC must be patched to read this new device class. The following steps outline how WiiC checks for a Wiimote (the full source is available in the io_nix.c file).

1. It gets a descriptor for the first Bluetooth device by using the BTAPI call of hci_get_route.

```
/* get the id of the first bluetooth device. */
int = device_id = hci_get_route(NULL);
```

2. Then it does a device inquiry by invoking hci_inquiry.

```
/* scan for bluetooth devices for 128 'timeout' seconds */
found_devices = hci_inquiry(device_id, timeout, 128, NULL, &scan_info,
IREQ_CACHE_FLUSH);
```

3. If the number of found devices is greater than zero, then you may have some Wiimote(s) or other Bluetooth devices. To make sure it connects to a valid Wiimote, WiiC must check the device class encoded as a sequence of 3 bytes (see Listing 8-5).

Listing 8-5. WiiC Device Discovery Process

```
int wiic_find(struct wiimote_t** wm, int max_wiimotes, int timeout) {
  // ...
  // Get BT devices

  /* scan for bluetooth devices for 'timeout' seconds */
  found_devices = hci_inquiry(device_id, timeout, 128, NULL, &scan_info, IREQ_CACHE_FLUSH);

  if (found_devices < 0) {
      return 0;
  }

  // got some potential devices. Check device class

  /* display discovered devices */
  for (; (i < found_devices) && (found_wiimotes < max_wiimotes); ++i) {
    if ( ((scan_info[i].dev_class[0] == WM_DEV_CLASS_0) &&
      (scan_info[i].dev_class[1] == WM_DEV_CLASS_1) &&
      (scan_info[i].dev_class[2] == WM_DEV_CLASS_2))
   )
   {
              /* found a wiimote */
              ++found_wiimotes;
    }
  // ...
}
```

In the for loop of Listing 8-5 you must now take into account the device classes for the new Wiimote (declared in wiic_internal.h):

```
// Old Wiimote RVL-CNT-01
#define WM_DEV_CLASS_0                       0x04
#define WM_DEV_CLASS_1                       0x25
#define WM_DEV_CLASS_2                       0x00
```

```
// New Wiimote RVL-CNT-01-TR
#define WM_DEV_CLASS1_0                                     0x08
#define WM_DEV_CLASS1_1                                     0x05
#define WM_DEV_CLASS1_2                                     0x00
```

You now simply change the if statement within the for loop in Listing 8-5 to account for the new device classes; thus Listing 8-5 becomes Listing 8-6.

Listing 8-6. Changes to io_nix.c (wiic_find) to Check for the New Wiimote

```
/* display discovered devices */
for (; (i < found_devices) && (found_wiimotes < max_wiimotes); ++i) {
    if ( ((scan_info[i].dev_class[0] == WM_DEV_CLASS_0) &&
          (scan_info[i].dev_class[1] == WM_DEV_CLASS_1) &&
          (scan_info[i].dev_class[2] == WM_DEV_CLASS_2))
          ||
          // RVL-CNT-01-TR
          ((scan_info[i].dev_class[0] == WM_DEV_CLASS1_0) &&
          (scan_info[i].dev_class[1] == WM_DEV_CLASS1_1) &&
          (scan_info[i].dev_class[2] == WM_DEV_CLASS1_2))
          )
    {
            /* found a wiimote */
            ++found_wiimotes;
    }
}
```

Other Changes

Finally, here are some minor changes to get things working:

- The set report code must be changed from 0x50 to 0xA0 within wiic_internal.h.

  ```
  // OLD #define WM_SET_REPORT    0x50
  #define WM_SET_REPORT        0xA0
  ```

- The report write code (WM_RPT_WRITE) must be changed to a WM_RPT_ACK. This is required because after an input report is received, an acknowledgment (ACK) must be sent back to the Wiimote (again in wiic_internal.h).

  ```
  // OLD #define WM_RPT_WRITE     0x22
  #define WM_RPT_ACK           0x22
  ```

As you can see, the report code remains the same (0x22) but it has been renamed to WM_RPT_ACK; obviously you need an implementation of this ACK event within events.c (see Listing 8-7).

Listing 8-7. Event ACK Implementation

```
static void event_ack(struct wiimote_t *wm, byte *msg)
{
  wiic_pressed_buttons(wm,msg);
  WIIC_DEBUG("Event ACK [%02x %02x %02x %02x]", msg[0], msg[1], msg[2], msg[3]);
  wm->event = WIIC_ACK;
  /* if another request exists send it to the wiimote */
  if (wm->read_req)
    wiic_send_next_pending_read_request(wm);
}

void propagate_event(struct wiimote_t* wm, byte event, byte* msg) {
  // ...
  switch (event) {
    // ...
    case WM_RPT_ACK:
    {
        /* Vladimir ACK */
        event_ack(wm, msg);

        return;
    }
    // ...
}
```

event_ack gets propagated within the main event handler in events.c. Hold on; you're
almost done.

Fixes to the Nunchuk Handler

Finally, if you wish to support a Nunchuck (very useful for first-person shooters), its
handshake logic must be slightly altered. The expansion ID for the Nunchuck in the new
Wiimote has changed, so the code must be changed to reflect this. The following fragment
has been taken from the file wiic_internal.h:

```
#define EXP_ID_CODE_NUNCHUK            0x9A1EFEFE
#define EXP_ID_CODE_NUNCHUK_TR01       0xA4200000
```

It includes an expansion ID for the new Nunchuk (EXP_ID_CODE_NUNCHUK_TR01 with the
value 0xA4200000). Furthermore, the Nunchuck event data sent by the new Wiimote is
now unencrypted. So locate the nunchuk.c file and see how the decryption logic has been
commented out, as shown in the following fragment:

```
int nunchuk_handshake(struct wiimote_t* wm, struct nunchuk_t* nc, byte* data, unsigned short
len) {
  /* decrypt data - old wiimotes only*/
  /*
  for (i = 0; i < len; ++i)
```

```
    data[i] = (data[i] ^ 0x17) + 0x17;
  */
  ...
}
```

If you don't do this, you will get garbage when the buttons on the Nunchuk are pressed or the joystick in moved. Note that this will work for the new Wiimote only. Old Wiimotes still send encrypted data. If you wish to support both (old and new), you need to implement a way to check for the new Wiimote and skip the decryption. This can be done quickly using a global variable that is set whenever the discovery process detects the new Wiimote. Thus the previous fragment becomes

```
/* decrypt data for old wiimotes only*/
if ( !g_isTR ) {
  for (i = 0; i < len; ++i)
    data[i] = (data[i] ^ 0x17) + 0x17;
}
```

This code uses the global variable g_isTR, which is set during discovery if the new Wiimote is detected. To do so, you can use the Bluetooth API call of

```
int hci_read_remote_name(int sock, const bdaddr_t *ba, int len, char *name, int timeout)
```

This API function retrieves the user-friendly name of a device associated with a Bluetooth socket and an address obtained in the inquiry process. For example, the following fragment is included in the file jni_wiic.c and used to check for the new Wiimote:

```
// loop thru devices
for ( i = 0 ; i < size ; i++) {
  ba2str(&scan_info[i].bdaddr, addr);

  // get bt device name
  if ( ! hci_read_remote_name(hci_sock, &scan_info[i].bdaddr, WIIMOTE_CMP_LEN, dev_name,
    5000) ) {
    // check 4 new wiimote TR
    if ( strstr(dev_name, "-TR") != NULL ) {
        g_isTR = 1;
    }
  }
  jni_send_message("Found Device %s/%s ", dev_name, addr);
}
```

This fragment loops through all devices received on inquiry and reads their user-friendly name. If the name contains the string "-TR," a new Wiimote is assumed. The WiiC library is now ready for use with your Android app, but first you must provide a JNI interface so you can talk to WiiC within Java.

WiiC JNI Interface

This is the glue that binds the two previous components together. As mentioned, the native methods described in the Wiimote Java class require their C counterparts (see Table 8-5).

Table 8-5. WiiC JNI Interface Methods

Native Java	JNI Implementation
static void Initialize()	Java_game_engine_controller_Wiimote_Initialize
static void DiscoverAndConnect()	Java_game_engine_controller_Wiimote_DiscoverAndConnect
static void DisconnectAll()	Java_game_engine_controller_Wiimote_DisconnectAll
static void ToggleRumble()	Java_game_engine_controller_Wiimote_ToggleRumble
static void SetLed(int led)	Java_game_engine_controller_Wiimote_SetLed

Plus the interface contains a simple callback system used to send messages and core button or Nunchuk events back to Java. This callback system uses the following C methods:

- void jni_send_message(char *format, ...): It sends a string message back to tell Java what is going on behind the scenes.

- void jni_send_event(int wiimoteNum, char *format, ...): This is a critical method that sends button or Nunchuk events back encoded as a set of key/value pairs. Let's take a closer look, starting with the native methods and then the callbacks.

Native Methods

In the initialization step (see Listing 8-8), you simply load the Java callback class used to send messages back by invoking

```
(*env)->FindClass(env, "game/engine/controller/Wiimote")
```

This creates a local reference to the Java class game.engine.controller.Wiimote. With the local reference you obtain a new global reference (which can be used within other threads). This is very important because as callback functions get called from other threads, you must use the global reference to the callback class. Local references may be removed from memory at any time by the Java virtual machine (JVM), which may result in all sorts of weird behavior, crashes, and headaches.

Listing 8-8. WiiC JNI Interface Initialization

```
JNIEXPORT void JNICALL Java_game_engine_controller_Wiimote_Initialize
  (JNIEnv * env, jclass cls)
{
  // save vm
  (*env)->GetJavaVM(env, &g_VM);
```

```
  // Load callback cclass
  LOGD("Loading callback class %s", CB_CLASS);

  jclass clazz  = (*env)->FindClass(env, CB_CLASS);

// Global ref for other threads
  jCbClass        = (jclass)(*env)->NewGlobalRef(env, clazz);

  if ( jCbClass == 0 ) {
    LOGE("Unable to find cb class: %s", CB_CLASS);
    return;
  }
}
```

After the initialization step is complete, you can proceed to the most important method: DiscoverAndConnect. This is where all the work gets done (see Listing 8-9). The process starts by initializing the Wiimote data structure (which holds information about all controllers) by invoking

```
wiimotes =  wiic_init(MAX_WIIMOTES);
```

The WiiC library supports up to four simultaneous Wiimotes.

Next is the discovery process. To do so, you invoke the WiiC function wiic_find (wiimotes, MAX_WIIMOTES, 10) as shown in the next fragment:

```
static int discover()
{
  // Find, timeout 10 secs
  nmotes = wiic_find(wiimotes, MAX_WIIMOTES, 10);
  if ( !nmotes ) {
    jni_send_error(102, "No wiimotes found.");
    return 0;
  }
 jni_send_message("Found %d wiimote(s)", nmotes);
 return 1;
}
```

Wiic_find takes as arguments the global Wiimote data structure from the previous step, the max number of Wiimotes, and a timeout in seconds. It returns the number of Wiimotes found.

If you get some Wiimotes online, then DiscoverAndConnect (see Listing 8-9) turns on the first LED for the first Wiimote and rumbles for one second. This tells the player he is ready to go.

Listing 8-9. WiiC JNI Connection

```
JNIEXPORT void JNICALL Java_game_engine_controller_Wiimote_DiscoverAndConnect
  (JNIEnv * env, jclass cls)
{
  int i;
  if ( ! wiimotes ) {
    LOGD("Creating wiimotes");
    wiimotes =  wiic_init(MAX_WIIMOTES);
  }
```

```
if ( ! discover() )
  return;

jni_send_message("Connecting to %d wiimote(s)", nmotes);
int connected = wiic_connect(wiimotes, nmotes);

if ( !connected) {
  jni_send_error(110, "Connect: Failed to connect to any wiimote.");
  return ;
}
// LOGD("Connected to %i wiimotes (of %i found).\n", connected, nmotes);
jni_send_message("Connected to %i wiimotes (of %i found).\n", connected, nmotes);

// turn on 1st led
wiic_set_leds(wiimotes[0], WIIMOTE_LED_1);

// rumble for 1 sec
wiic_rumble(wiimotes[0], 1);
usleep(1000000);
wiic_rumble(wiimotes[0], 0);

/*
 * This is the main loop
 */
while (!sig_exit)
{
  process_signals();

  if (wiic_poll(wiimotes, connected)) {
    /*
     * This happens if something happened on any wiimote. So go through each
     * one and check if anything happened.
     */
    for (i = 0; i < MAX_WIIMOTES; ++i) {
      // LOGD("Wii Event %d ", wiimotes[i]->event);
      switch (wiimotes[i]->event) {
        case WIIC_EVENT:
          // a generic event occured
          handle_event(wiimotes[i]);
          break;

        case WIIC_STATUS:
          // a status event occured
          handle_ctrl_status(wiimotes[i]);
          break;

        case WIIC_DISCONNECT:
        case WIIC_UNEXPECTED_DISCONNECT:
          // the wiimote disconnected
          handle_disconnect(wiimotes[i]);
          break;
```

```
        case WIIC_READ_DATA:
          /*
           * Data we requested to read was returned. Take a look at
           * wiimotes[i]->read_req for the data.
           */
          break;

        case WIIC_NUNCHUK_INSERTED:
          /*
           * a nunchuk was inserted This is a good place to set any nunchuk-
           * specific threshold values. By default they are the same as the
           * wiimote.
           */
          printf("Nunchuk inserted.\n");
          jni_send_event(i, "EVT_TYPE=EXT_INSERTED|EXT_NAME=NUNCHUK");
          break;

        case WIIC_CLASSIC_CTRL_INSERTED:
          printf("Classic controller inserted.\n");
          break;

        case WIIC_NUNCHUK_REMOVED:
          // some expansion was removed
          handle_ctrl_status(wiimotes[i]);
          printf("An expansion was removed.\n");
          break;

        default:
          break;
      }
    }
  }
}

LOGD("Connect main loop ended. Cleanup");
wiic_cleanup(wiimotes, MAX_WIIMOTES);
wiimotes = NULL;
nmotes = 0;
sig_exit = 0;
sig_disconnect = 0;
}
```

Once the LED is on and the rumble stops, DiscoverAndConnect enters a blocking loop where it polls continuously for events for all Wiimotes. If an event is received, it is dispatched to an event handler (which will be discussed in the next section). Note that the main loop will block execution of the main thread, thus it is critical that the Wiimote Java class start a new thread within its connect( ) method, as shown in the following fragment taken from Wiimote.java:

```
public void connect() {
  Log.d(TAG, "Starting connection thread");
  new Thread(new Runnable() {
```

```
    public void run() {
        DiscoverAndConnect();
    }
  }).start();
}
```

This fragment starts a thread that invokes the native method `DiscoverAndConnect`. This in turn invokes the C function in Listing 8-9, thus starting the discovery and connection process in the background. To tell the main loop in Listing 8-9 to do something such as rumble, turn on a LED, or quit, a signal is turned on within the JNI interface, as shown in Listing 8-10.

Listing 8-10. JNI Functions to Toggle Rumble, Get Status, Turn On LEDs, or Disconnect Actions

```
JNIEXPORT void JNICALL Java_game_engine_controller_Wiimote_ToggleRumble
  (JNIEnv * env, jclass cls)
{
  sig_toggle_rumble = 1;
}


JNIEXPORT void JNICALL Java_game_engine_controller_Wiimote_Status
  (JNIEnv * env, jclass cls)
{
  sig_get_status = 1;
}


JNIEXPORT void JNICALL Java_game_engine_controller_Wiimote_SetLed
  (JNIEnv * env, jclass cls, jint led)
{
  LOGD("Set LED %2X", led);
  sig_setled = led;
}


JNIEXPORT void JNICALL Java_game_engine_controller_Wiimote_DisconnectAll
  (JNIEnv * env, jclass cls)
{
  if ( nmotes == 0 ) {
    LOGE("No wiimotes to disconnect");
    return;
  }
  sig_disconnect = 1; // Send disconnect
  sig_exit = 1;       // quit main loop
}
```

When any of the JNI functions in Listing 8-10 gets called from Java, a signal is set, which is in turn checked by the main loop of the connection function in Listing 8-9. For example, the user presses the Rumble button in the Android app, so the `rumble()` method in the Wiimote Java class gets called, which then invokes the JNI C function `Java_game_engine_controller_Wiimote_ToggleRumble`. This function enables the rumble signal. Finally, the connect main loop sees this signal is enabled and invokes the corresponding WiiC system call to request a rumble report through the WiiC Data Pipe socket connected to the device.

On the other hand, when the Wiimote sends Input reports back to the host (such as button presses or joystick movement), the main loop of Listing 8-9 dispatches the event to the handler (shown in Listing 8-11).

Listing 8-11. JNI Event Handlers for WiiC

```
static void jni_send_btn_press(int id, const char * btn)
{
  jni_send_event(id, "EVT_TYPE=BTNPRESS|BTN=%s", btn);
}

static void jni_send_btn_release(int id, const char * btn)
{
  jni_send_event(id, "EVT_TYPE=BTNRELEASE|BTN=%s", btn);
}

void handle_event(struct wiimote_t* wm) {
  int id = wm->unid;

  /* if a button is pressed, report it */
  if (IS_PRESSED(wm, WIIMOTE_BUTTON_A))      jni_send_btn_press(id,"A");
  if (IS_PRESSED(wm, WIIMOTE_BUTTON_B))      jni_send_btn_press(id,"B");
  if (IS_PRESSED(wm, WIIMOTE_BUTTON_UP))     jni_send_btn_press(id,"UP");
  if (IS_PRESSED(wm, WIIMOTE_BUTTON_DOWN))   jni_send_btn_press(id,"DOWN");
  if (IS_PRESSED(wm, WIIMOTE_BUTTON_LEFT))   jni_send_btn_press(id,"LEFT");
  if (IS_PRESSED(wm, WIIMOTE_BUTTON_RIGHT))  jni_send_btn_press(id,"RIGHT");
  if (IS_PRESSED(wm, WIIMOTE_BUTTON_MINUS))  jni_send_btn_press(id,"MINUS");
  if (IS_PRESSED(wm, WIIMOTE_BUTTON_PLUS))   jni_send_btn_press(id,"PLUS");
  if (IS_PRESSED(wm, WIIMOTE_BUTTON_ONE))    jni_send_btn_press(id,"ONE");
  if (IS_PRESSED(wm, WIIMOTE_BUTTON_TWO))    jni_send_btn_press(id,"TWO");
  if (IS_PRESSED(wm, WIIMOTE_BUTTON_HOME))   jni_send_btn_press(id,"HOME");

  if (IS_RELEASED(wm, WIIMOTE_BUTTON_A))     jni_send_btn_release(id,"A");
  if (IS_RELEASED(wm, WIIMOTE_BUTTON_B))     jni_send_btn_release(id,"B");
  if (IS_RELEASED(wm, WIIMOTE_BUTTON_UP))    jni_send_btn_release(id,"UP");
  if (IS_RELEASED(wm, WIIMOTE_BUTTON_DOWN))  jni_send_btn_release(id,"DOWN");
  if (IS_RELEASED(wm, WIIMOTE_BUTTON_LEFT))  jni_send_btn_release(id,"LEFT");
  if (IS_RELEASED(wm, WIIMOTE_BUTTON_RIGHT)) jni_send_btn_release(id,"RIGHT");
  if (IS_RELEASED(wm, WIIMOTE_BUTTON_MINUS)) jni_send_btn_release(id,"MINUS");
  if (IS_RELEASED(wm, WIIMOTE_BUTTON_PLUS))  jni_send_btn_release(id,"PLUS");
  if (IS_RELEASED(wm, WIIMOTE_BUTTON_ONE))   jni_send_btn_release(id,"ONE");
  if (IS_RELEASED(wm, WIIMOTE_BUTTON_TWO))   jni_send_btn_release(id,"TWO");
  if (IS_RELEASED(wm, WIIMOTE_BUTTON_HOME))  jni_send_btn_release(id,"HOME");

  /* show events specific to supported expansions */

  if (wm->exp.type == EXP_NUNCHUK) {
    // nunchuk
    struct nunchuk_t* nc = (nunchuk_t*)&wm->exp.nunchuk;
```

```
    // nunchuck buttons
    if ( nc->btns != 0 || nc->btns_released != 0 ) {
      int Z_TR01 = (nc->btns == 3) || (nc->btns_released == 3); /* Old Z=1, New(tr01) Z=(3)ALL */
      if (IS_JUST_PRESSED(nc, NUNCHUK_BUTTON_C) && !Z_TR01) jni_send_btn_press(id,"C");
      if (IS_JUST_PRESSED(nc, NUNCHUK_BUTTON_Z))              jni_send_btn_press(id,"Z");

      if (IS_RELEASED(nc, NUNCHUK_BUTTON_C) && !Z_TR01) jni_send_btn_release(id,"C");
      if (IS_RELEASED(nc, NUNCHUK_BUTTON_Z))              jni_send_btn_release(id,"Z");
    }
    // joystick
    jni_send_event(id,
    "EVT_TYPE=NUNCHUK|ROLL=%.2f|PITCH=%.2f|YAW=%.2f|JANGLE=%.2f|JMAGNITU    DE=%.2f"
    , nc->orient.roll, nc->orient.pitch, nc->orient.yaw, nc->js.ang, nc->js.mag);
  }
}
```

The event handler in Listing 8-11 first checks if the core buttons are pressed or released. If so, it sends the event information thru the JNI callback system back to Java by invoking

```
jni_send_event(id, "EVT_TYPE=BTNPRESS|BTN=%s", btn);
```

For example, when A is pressed, the string "EVT_TYPE=BTNPRESS|BTN=A" will be sent to the OnMessage( ) method of the Wiimote Java class. This class will then parse the event and dispatch the required information to any listeners that implement the IController. IControllerListener interface. In your case, the Android app will log the event in the text box of the app GUI.

The same thing happens when buttons are pressed/released on the Nunchuk. When the joystick is moved, the string sent will be

```
"EVT_TYPE=NUNCHUK|ROLL=%.2f|PITCH=%.2f|YAW=%.2f|JANGLE=%.2f|JMAGNITUDE=%.2f"
```

This string tells the Wiimote class a Nunchuk joystick event has occurred along with information such as roll, pitch, yaw, angle, and magnitude values. Finally, the last pieces of the puzzle are the two methods used by the callback system to send messages back to the Wiimote Java class. Let's take a look.

Callback Methods

Listing 8-12 shows the methods used to send event information back to the Wiimote class. They are critical; without them the Wiimote class won't receive anything when an event occurs in WiiC. These callbacks are the two simple functions: jni_send_message and jni_send_event. Both reuse the function jni_send_str, which is in charge of doing the heavy lifting.

jni_send_str takes three arguments:

1. An integer (return code) that can be used to send a code to the OnMessage Java method or a Wiimote number to the OnEvent method of the Wiimote class.

2. The second argument is the method name to invoke within Wiimote (either OnMessage or OnEvent).

3. The third argument is the string message for OnMessage or the
    encoded event information for OnEvent. In this way the same function
    can be reused for both WiiC callbacks, OnMessage and OnEvent.

Listing 8-12. WiiC Callback Methods to Wiimote.java

```
static void jni_send_str(int rc, const char * methodName, const char * text) {
  JNIEnv *env;

  if ( !g_VM) {
    LOGE("%s\n", text);
    return;
  }

  (*g_VM)->AttachCurrentThread (g_VM,  &env, NULL);

  if ( jCbClass == 0 ) {
    LOGE("No callback class. Abort!");
      return;
  }

  // Call Java method
  jmethodID mSendStr = (*env)->GetStaticMethodID(env, jCbClass
    , methodName
    , "(ILjava/lang/String;)V");

  if (mSendStr) {
      jstring jstr = (*env)->NewStringUTF(env, text);

      (*env)->CallStaticVoidMethod(env, jCbClass
          , mSendStr , rc, jstr );

      (*env)->DeleteLocalRef(env,jstr);
  }
}

/**
 * Send message callback. Invokes jni_send_str
 */
void jni_send_message(char *format, ...)
{
  va_list       argptr;
  static char   string[1024];

  va_start (argptr, format);
  vsprintf (string, format,argptr);
  va_end (argptr);

  jni_send_str(0, "OnMessage", string);
}
```

```
/**
 * Event callback
 */
void jni_send_event(int wiimoteNum, char *format, ...)
{
  va_list        argptr;
  static char    string[1024];

  va_start (argptr, format);
  vsprintf (string, format,argptr);
  va_end (argptr);

  jni_send_str(wiimoteNum, "OnEvent", string);
}
```

You can see from the previous listing the way WiiC interacts with Java by simply sending events encoded as strings by these functions:

- jni_send_message: This function sends a string to the OnMessage method of the Wiimote Java class. This class notifies the listener about the message, which can then display it on screen. For example, to tell Java that an N number of Wiimote(s) are connected, you could use

  ```
  jni_send_message("Connected to %i wiimotes (of %i found).", connected, nmotes);
  ```

- jni_send_event: This function sends event information to the Wiimote class encoded as key/value sets delimited by |. For example, to notify that the A button has been pressed, you use

  ```
  jni_send_event(id, "EVT_TYPE=BTNPRESS|BTN=%s", "A");
  ```

Note that encoding events as strings avoids having to marshal objects between C and Java, which is very difficult and makes the code unnecessarily complex and hard to maintain. As a bonus, code can be reused greatly as both jni_send_message and jni_send_event simply invoke jni_send_str with a different set of arguments. Other things that must be taken into account in the callbacks in Listing 8-12 include

- *Thread safety*: Because both callbacks are invoked outside of the main thread, they must attach to the current thread by calling

  ```
  (*g_VM)->AttachCurrentThread (g_VM,  &env, NULL)
  ```

  This is a basic rule of thumb of JNI development. If you don't do this, a segmentation fault will occur and the app will crash.

- *Variable arguments*: This is one of the most useful features of the C language. The ability to pack dynamic arguments sent to a function into a single variable for consumption. It is really a life saver. For example, a function like void jni_send_message(char *format, ...) can pack its sequence of arguments as shown in the following fragment:

  ```
    va_list        argptr;
    static char    string[1024];
  ```

```
va_start (argptr, format);
vsprintf (string, format,argptr);
va_end (argptr);
```

With these bits in mind, you are now ready to test the Wiimote controller app, but before you do, you must compile the WiiC library using the Android NDK.

Compilation and Test

To compile the WiiC library, open a Cygwin console, change to the folder containing the Wiimote project that you downloaded from the companion source code, in my case cd /cygdrive/C/tmp/ch08.Wiimote, and type:

```
$ ndk-build
```

Figure 8-8 shows the compilation in progress.

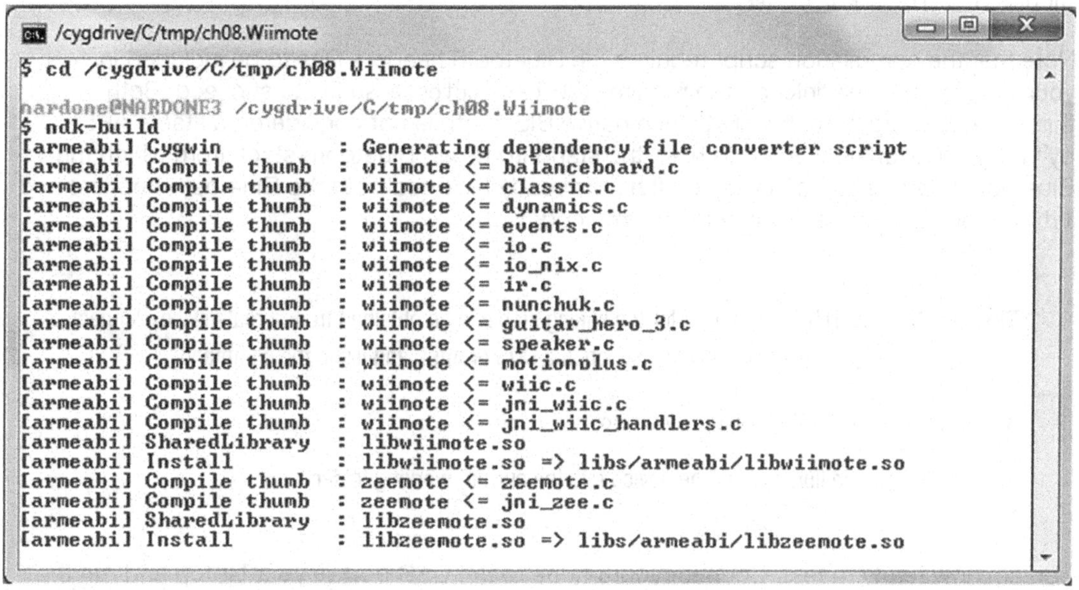

```
/cygdrive/C/tmp/ch08.Wiimote
$ cd /cygdrive/C/tmp/ch08.Wiimote

nardone@NARDONE3 /cygdrive/C/tmp/ch08.Wiimote
$ ndk-build
[armeabi] Cygwin          : Generating dependency file converter script
[armeabi] Compile thumb    : wiimote <= balanceboard.c
[armeabi] Compile thumb    : wiimote <= classic.c
[armeabi] Compile thumb    : wiimote <= dynamics.c
[armeabi] Compile thumb    : wiimote <= events.c
[armeabi] Compile thumb    : wiimote <= io.c
[armeabi] Compile thumb    : wiimote <= io_nix.c
[armeabi] Compile thumb    : wiimote <= ir.c
[armeabi] Compile thumb    : wiimote <= nunchuk.c
[armeabi] Compile thumb    : wiimote <= guitar_hero_3.c
[armeabi] Compile thumb    : wiimote <= speaker.c
[armeabi] Compile thumb    : wiimote <= motionplus.c
[armeabi] Compile thumb    : wiimote <= wiic.c
[armeabi] Compile thumb    : wiimote <= jni_wiic.c
[armeabi] Compile thumb    : wiimote <= jni_wiic_handlers.c
[armeabi] SharedLibrary    : libwiimote.so
[armeabi] Install          : libwiimote.so => libs/armeabi/libwiimote.so
[armeabi] Compile thumb    : zeemote <= zeemote.c
[armeabi] Compile thumb    : zeemote <= jni_zee.c
[armeabi] SharedLibrary    : libzeemote.so
[armeabi] Install          : libzeemote.so => libs/armeabi/libzeemote.so
```

Figure 8-8. WiiC compilation with the Android NDK

> **Note**   You must put the root folder of the NDK in your system path so the ndk-build command can be located. In Windows, edit the Environment Variables within the System Properties of My Computer, and add the NDK root to the system Path variable.

After compilation, the file `libwiimote.so` will be created in the project `libs/armeabi` folder. Listing 8-13 shows the Android make file for WiiC.

Listing 8-13. Android Make File for the WiiC Library

```
LOCAL_MODULE    := wiimote
DIR := WiiCNew/src/wiic
SOURCES :=      $(DIR)/balanceboard.c $(DIR)/classic.c \
 $(DIR)/dynamics.c $(DIR)/events.c \
 $(DIR)/io.c $(DIR)/io_nix.c \
 $(DIR)/ir.c  $(DIR)/nunchuk.c \
 $(DIR)/guitar_hero_3.c $(DIR)/speaker.c \
 $(DIR)/motionplus.c $(DIR)/wiic.c \
 android/jni_wiic.c android/jni_wiic_handlers.c \

LOCAL_C_INCLUDES := $(LOCAL_PATH)/include $(LOCAL_PATH)/$(DIR)
LOCAL_CFLAGS := -DLINUX  -DANDROID
LOCAL_SRC_FILES := $(SOURCES)
LOCAL_LDLIBS := -L$(LOCAL_PATH)/lib -Ljni/lib -llog -lbluetooth
include $(BUILD_SHARED_LIBRARY)
```

Note that the compilation script requires the Bluetooth headers files to be included in your project, plus the linking step requires the `libbluetooth.so` file to succeed. Both things are missing from the NDK since native Bluetooth is not considered a stable API by Google. Fortunately, Android uses the standard BlueZ Bluetooth stack from which the Bluetooth headers can be obtained (I have already included both the Bluetooth headers and `libbluetooth.so` in the companion source code).

Tip `libbluetooth.so` required for the linking step can be obtained from a real device. Connect the device to your PC using the USB cable, open a DOS prompt, and issue the command

```
adb pull /system/lib/libbluetooth.so
```

This will extract the library from the device into the current working folder.

You are now ready to test. Connect your phone to the USB port of your laptop and run the app. From the Eclipse menu, click Run ➤ Run Configurations, type a new name, select the Wiimote project from the book source code, and click Run. Figure 8-9 shows the app in action using the Android emulator.

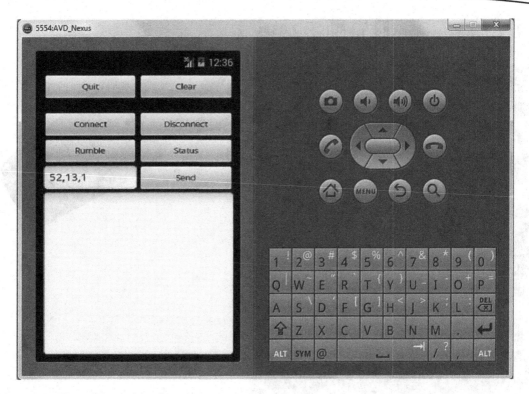

Figure 8-9. Wiimote Test app in action

Note that the app requires access to the Bluetooth and Internet services, as shown in the following fragment of the AndroidManifest.xml descriptor:

```
<uses-permission android:name="android.permission.BLUETOOTH"/>
<uses-permission android:name="android.permission.BLUETOOTH_ADMIN"/>
<uses-permission android:name="android.permission.INTERNET"/>
<uses-permission android:name="android.permission.ACCESS_NETWORK_STATE"/>
```

Make sure you turn on Bluetooth before running, then get your Wiimote, press the SYNC button in the back of the controller, and press Connect. As the connection handshake goes through, messages will be displayed in the log box. When a connection succeeds, press any button in the Wiimote: press/release events will be displayed as well.

There are many types of Bluetooth controllers out there besides a Wiimote. The next section describes another popular controller for mobile devices, the Zeemote.

Zeemote

Zeemote is a Bluetooth joystick controller that is very popular in Nokia phones and others. With the rising in popularity of other smartphones, its creators released an SDK for other platforms such as Android and iPhone. The Zeemote consists of a joystick and four buttons (A, B, C, and D, as shown in Figure 8-10).

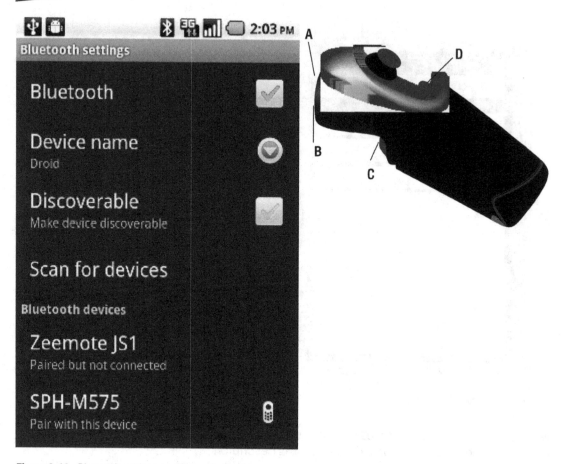

Figure 8-10. Bluetooth settings and Zeemote joystick

Refer to http://www.zeemote.com/ for more info on Zeemote.

Before you can start using a Zeemote, it needs to be paired.

1. *Turn on the Zeemote.* Put two AAA batteries in the controller and press the D button for 3 seconds until the light starts blinking.

2. *Pair the Zeemote with your phone.* To do so, enable Bluetooth as shown in Figure 8-10. Press "Scan for devices." Android should show the controller in the device list. Press Zeemote JS1 and select Pair Device. You don't need to connect; pairing is enough.

> **Tip** Pairing stores the Zeemote message authentication code (MAC) address in your phone. This is sort of a device ID used to communicate between both devices. You need to pair a Bluetooth device only once.

Now you can start writing code that connects to your Zeemote. First, you must download the SDK with the libraries required to enable it in your app. The latest Zeemote SDK is available online at http://devzone.zeemote.com:8088/devzone/account/devInfo. Download them and put under the libs directory of your project.

The required JARs for the Zeemote SDK 1.9.2 are:

- ZControllerLib-android-1.9.2.jar

- ZControllerLib-android-ui-1.9.2.jar

- ZControllerLib-common-1.9.2.jar

- zc-strings-1.9.2.jar

It also includes the native libZControllerLib_Android.so. You will need to include all these files in the app you wish to enable the Zeemote.

Listing 8-14 shows the simple class of Zeemote that connects to a controller and listens for status, button, and joystick events. The steps can be summarized as follows.

1. Create an instance of Controller by calling new Controller(Controller.CONTROLLER_1). This object is used to interface with the device.

2. Listen for controller events by implementing any of the API interfaces:

   - IStatusListener: This interface fires the events batteryUpdate(BatteryEvent), which gives information about power levels; connected(ControllerEvent), which fires when the controller is successfully connected; and disconnected(DisconnectEvent), which fires when a disconnection occurs.

   - IButtonListener: This interface fires the events buttonPressed(ButtonEvent) or buttonPressed(ButtonEvent) whenever any of the four buttons is pressed and released.

   - IJoystickListener: This interface fires the event joystickMoved(JoystickEvent), which gives the scaled XY coordinated of the joystick.

3. Handle the above events accordingly.

Listing 8-14. Class to Connect a Zeemote

```
public class Zeemote implements IStatusListener, IJoystickListener,
    IButtonListener
{
  private static final String TAG = "Zeemote";
  private Controller mZeeController;
  private Context mContext;

  public Zeemote(Context context) {
    mContext = context;
    mZeeController = new Controller(Controller.CONTROLLER_1);
```

```java
    mZeeController.addStatusListener(this);
    mZeeController.addJoystickListener(this);
    mZeeController.addButtonListener(this);
  }

  public void connect() {
    ControllerAndroidUi controllerUi = new ControllerAndroidUi(mContext,
        mZeeController);
    controllerUi.startConnectionProcess();
  }

  /***********************************************
   * ZEEMOTE EVENTS
   ***********************************************/
  public void batteryUpdate(BatteryEvent event) {
    int id = event.getController().getId();
    int max = event.getMaximumLevel();
    int min = event.getMinimumLevel();
    int warn = event.getWarningLevel();
    int cur = event.getCurrentLevel();
    int pctLeft = (int) (((float) (cur - min) / (float) (max - min)) * 100);

    Log.d(TAG, "Battery Update: Controller ID=" + id + " cur=" + cur + ",
        max=" + max + ", min=" + min + ", warn=" + warn + " %left=" + pctLeft);

    /* battery low? */
    if (cur <= warn) {
      // do something
    }
  }

  public void connected(ControllerEvent event) {
    com.zeemote.zc.Configuration config = event.getController()
        .getConfiguration();

    Log.d(TAG, "Connected to controller:");
    Log.d(TAG, "Num Buttons=" + config.getButtonCount());
    Log.d(TAG, "Num Joysticks=" + config.getJoystickCount());

  }

  public void disconnected(DisconnectEvent event) {
    Log.d(TAG, "Disconnected from controller: "
        + (event.isUnexpected() ? "unexpected" : "expected"));

    if (mZeeController != null) {
      Log.d(TAG, "Removing Zee listeners.");

      mZeeController.removeStatusListener(this);
      mZeeController.removeJoystickListener(this);
      mZeeController.removeButtonListener(this);
    }
  }
```

```
/*************************************************
 * ZEEMOTE BUTTON EVENTS
 *************************************************/
public void buttonPressed(ButtonEvent event) {
  int b = event.getButtonID();
  String label = event.getController().getConfiguration().getButtonLabel(b);

}

public void buttonReleased(ButtonEvent event) {
  String buttonName = event.getController().getConfiguration()
      .getButtonLabel(event.getButtonID());
}

/*************************************************
 * ZEEMOTE JOYSTIC EVENT
 *************************************************/
public void joystickMoved(JoystickEvent e) {
  // A joystick moved. Scale the values between -100 and 100
  int x = e.getScaledX(-100, 100);
  int y = e.getScaledY(-100, 100);

  Log.d(TAG, "X=" + x + ",Y=" + y);
  }
}
```

To connect to the Zeemote from your app activity, call the connect method of the Zeemote class, like so:

```
Zeemote zee = new Zeemote(this);
zee.connect();
```

When the connect method fires, the Zeemote connection UI will take over and allow you to connect (if the controller is on and close to the phone). As a bonus, you can check programmatically if Bluetooth is enabled using BluetoothAdapter.getDefaultAdapter(), and if not enabled, use the built-in Android UI to do it (see Listing 8-15).

Listing 8-15. Enabling the Bluetooth Adapter

```
BluetoothAdapter mBluetoothAdapter = BluetoothAdapter.getDefaultAdapter();

if (mBluetoothAdapter == null) {
  // Device does not support Bluetooth
}
// Enable it
if (!mBluetoothAdapter.isEnabled()) {
  Intent enableBtIntent = new Intent(BluetoothAdapter.ACTION_REQUEST_ENABLE);
  ctx.startActivityForResult(enableBtIntent, REQUEST_ENABLE_BT);
}
```

You can now easily integrate the Wiimote and Zeemote into your mobile game.

Finally, a word about using other kinds of popular Bluetooth controllers. I wanted to include in this chapter support for the PlayStation Sixaxis® and the Xbox 360® controllers. Along with the Wiimote, these are the top three game pads out there and chances are that you have one of them. Unfortunately, I was not able to do so.

First of all, the PS Sixaxis does not follow the standard handshake protocol described by the Bluetooth API. Sony has taken some liberties with the handshake even though they use Bluetooth API calls to do it. This makes the BlueZ API in Android incompatible with the Sixaxis. As a matter of fact, it will require changes to the core BlueZ API to support it. This is not likely to happen any time soon.

Then there is the Xbox 360. Microsoft is well known for rejecting open standards in favor of their own APIs. It is sad that one of the most popular gaming platform controllers cannot be used to play games in Android. The Xbox 360 uses its own wireless protocol to access the controller and will not work with Android at all.

To test this project I used the Samsung Galaxy Grand 2 mobile device.

Summary

This chapter has been for the hardcore gamer in you. You learned how easy it is to integrate a wireless controller with your game; in the process you learned about the Bluetooth API, the inner workings of the Wiimote and Zeemote, plus a little about JNI, asynchronous threads, and more. I used the two most popular wireless controllers available today, but there are many more. The next and final chapter explores the future of casual gaming: augmented reality and Android TV. It is a technical introduction to two brand new and buzz-wordy technologies coming soon to your living room. Check it out.

## Chapter 9

A Look into the Future: Augmented reality (AR) and Android TV

This chapter covers augmented reality (AR) and also explores the next big wave coming to your living room: Internet TV (Android TV, to be precise). Here you'll learn about the some of the SDKs and Toolkits to be used for the future AR and Android TV applications.

There is a lot of hype surrounding augmented reality, but what is it and how can you build games around it? Furthermore, what kinds of games are good for it? These are some of the questions I will answer in this chapter. Let's get started.

What Is AR?

"AR" is the term used to describe the software tools used to overlay virtual imagery onto the real world. For example, an app could render a virtual house on top of a kitchen table. On a mobile device, AR uses the video camera and OpenGL to project virtual objects on top of the video, as shown in Figure 9-1.

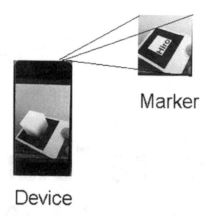

Marker

Device

Figure 9-1. Components of a basic AR app

Three elements are illustrated in Figure 9-1.

- *Marker*: This is a real world object (usually a printed card with some kind of pattern) that is used to render the virtual object. As the marker moves in 3D space so does the virtual object bound to it.

- *Phone or device*: The mobile device with a video camera where all the action takes place.

- *Software*: This may include the computer vision algorithms that calculate the real camera position and orientation relative to the physical marker in real time.

AR is in its infancy in the mobile world, making it virgin ground for a wide range of applications. Some of the applications today include?

- *AR browsers*: Here is where all the hype got started in mobile. An AR browser is a neat application that lets you use your camera to render geo-coded information on top of video in real time. For example, you could be walking along in the city looking for your favorite restaurant. Instead of searching for it on a map, you could start the video feature in your AR browser, and as you move around, the browser would render information about your specific location such as points of interest, hospitals, restaurants, etc. With a simple click, you could select the restaurant, make a reservation, and take a look at the menu.

- *AR gaming*: Here is where things get really interesting. By merging the real world and the game world, augmented reality lets you discover new ways of enjoying casual games.

AR SDKs

Augmented Reality SDKs provide developers the tools and libraries to more easily develop Augmented Reality applications (for instance, to add AR technology to Android, iOS applications, and so on).

Currently you can use many AR SDKs for

- image recognition & tracking
- 3D model rendering
- video overlay
- location based

Here are some of the most used augmented reality SDK:

- Qualcomm Vuforia
- Metaio
- Total Immersion D'Fusion
- Wikitude

AR and Android

At the time of this writing, the state of AR gaming in Android is close to non-existent. Some may say that is not good, but I think it is an opportunity for developers to explore new ground and new potential sources of revenue. Other hardcore mobile gaming platforms such as the PlayStation PS Vita® have taken the first step by offering a simple yet solid set of AR games out of the box. On the other hand, and unfortunately for Android, Google has not been able to monetize their gaming market enough to attract potential investment for this new ground (compared to other gaming markets such as the iOS). Nevertheless, AR gaming will come to Android eventually. It should be mentioned that other kinds of AR apps, such as browsers (Layar and Junaio to name two), have been around Android for a while now.

So who among you will be the first to come up with an AR game idea for Android? The following are some of the challenges that must be met in order to make that wish a reality:

- *An AR library/toolkit*: Because we don't have a PhD in Neural Nets, Artificial Intelligence, or Advanced Computer Graphics, plus a few years to spare to write the required complex recognition algorithms required by AR, we need an existing AR library or toolkit to start with. This library should provide the backbone required to build all kinds of AR apps including games. There are existing open source options out there, so it's just a matter of digging around, but more on that later.

■ *A portability layer*: Assuming that you have selected an AR toolkit, a relative amount of work may be required to port/compile this toolkit for Android. Even though there are some C/C++ toolkits designed to run in multiple platforms (including Linux), it may take some time to get it running in Android. C/C++ is definitely the language of choice for this kind of work.

■ *Video drivers*: Because of the nature of AR, where 3D objects get rendered on top of real time video (usually provided by a webcam or phone camera), a video driver will have to be developed to access the video from the phone or tablet. This may seem simple in a Linux-based OS like Android, but the caveat is that Google doesn't expose low-level video hardware natively (or in Java for that matter). I believe this will be the toughest part: writing a video driver to access the camera on your phone/tablet and bind it to the AR library.

Finding a Suitable AR Library

While scouting the Web for a suitable AR library, I came across the ARToolKit by the Human Interface Technology Laboratory of the University of Washington[1]. It suddenly occurred to me that this would be the perfect toolkit for AR apps in Android. It has the following desirable qualities that make it relatively easy to use in mobile:

■ It is built in portable C/C++.

■ It is multi-platform, supporting SGI IRIX, Linux, Mac OS and Windows out of the box.

■ It has a complete set of samples and utilities.

■ It is open source with GPL license for non-commercial use.

Here are some of the most used Augmented Reality libraries existing for Android:

■ ARToolKit

■ ARLab

■ ARmsk

■ Moodstocks

■ popcode

■ QCAR

■ SATCH

A later section looks at how to bring the ARToolKit to Android, but first, let's take a look at a simple example to understand how the ARToolKit works. Refer to http://artoolkit.sourceforge.net/ for more information.

---

[1]Human Interface Technology Laboratory of the University of Washington www.hitl.washington.edu/home/.

Understanding the ARToolKit (ARTK)

ARToolKit Professional for Android is a special version of ARToolKit that can be used especially when developing Android applications.

ASToolkit info and libraries can be found at:
http://www.artoolworks.com/support/library/ARToolKit_for_Android as well as at
http://artoolkit.sourceforge.net/

Listing 9-1 shows the source code for the simpleTest program bundled with the ARToolKit binaries for Windows. Let's take a closer look.

Listing 9-1. Rendering a Solid Cube on Top of a Pattern

```
char          *patt_name      = "Data/patt.hiro";
int            patt_id;
double         patt_width      = 80.0;
double         patt_center[2]  = {0.0, 0.0};
double         patt_trans[3][4];

static void    init(void);
static void    mainLoop(void);
static void    draw( void );

int main(int argc, char **argv)
{
    init();

    arVideoCapStart();
    argMainLoop( NULL, keyEvent, mainLoop );
    return (0);
}

/* main loop */
static void mainLoop(void)
{
    ARUint8         *dataPtr;
    ARMarkerInfo    *marker_info;
    int              marker_num;
    int              j, k;

    /* grab a video frame */
    if( (dataPtr = (ARUint8 *)arVideoGetImage()) == NULL ) {
        arUtilSleep(2);
        return;
    }
    if( count == 0 ) arUtilTimerReset();
    count++;

    argDrawMode2D();
    argDispImage( dataPtr, 0, 0 );
```

```
    /* detect the markers in the video frame */
    if( arDetectMarker(dataPtr, thresh, &marker_info, &marker_num) < 0 ) {
        cleanup();
        exit(0);
    }

    arVideoCapNext();

    /* check for object visibility */
    k = -1;
    for( j = 0; j < marker_num; j++ ) {
        if( patt_id == marker_info[j].id ) {
            if( k == -1 ) k = j;
            else if( marker_info[k].cf < marker_info[j].cf ) k = j;
        }
    }
    if( k == -1 ) {
        argSwapBuffers();
        return;
    }

    /* get the transformation between the marker and the real camera */
    arGetTransMat(&marker_info[k], patt_center, patt_width, patt_trans);

    draw();

    argSwapBuffers();
}

static void init( void )
{
    ARParam  wparam;

    /* open the video path */
    if( arVideoOpen( vconf ) < 0 ) exit(0);
    /* find the size of the window */
    if( arVideoInqSize(&xsize, &ysize) < 0 ) exit(0);
    printf("Image size (x,y) = (%d,%d)\n", xsize, ysize);

    /* set the initial camera parameters */
    if( arParamLoad(cparam_name, 1, &wparam) < 0 ) {
        printf("Camera parameter load error !!\n");
        exit(0);
    }
    arParamChangeSize( &wparam, xsize, ysize, &cparam );
    arInitCparam( &cparam );
    printf("*** Camera Parameter ***\n");
    arParamDisp( &cparam );
```

```
    if( (patt_id=arLoadPatt(patt_name)) < 0 ) {
        printf("pattern load error !!\n");
        exit(0);
    }

    /* open the graphics window */
    argInit( &cparam, 1.0, 0, 0, 0, 0 );
}

/* cleanup function called when program exits */
static void cleanup(void)
{
    arVideoCapStop();
    arVideoClose();
    argCleanup();
}

static void draw( void )
{
    double gl_para[16];

    argDrawMode3D();
    argDraw3dCamera( 0, 0 );
    glClearDepth( 1.0 );
    glClear(GL_DEPTH_BUFFER_BIT);
    glEnable(GL_DEPTH_TEST);
    glDepthFunc(GL_LEQUAL);

    /* load the camera transformation matrix */
    argConvGlpara(patt_trans, gl_para);
    glMatrixMode(GL_MODELVIEW);
    glLoadMatrixd( gl_para );

    glEnable(GL_LIGHTING);
    glEnable(GL_LIGHT0);
    glMatrixMode(GL_MODELVIEW);
    glTranslatef( 0.0, 0.0, 25.0 );
    /* DRAW A SOLID CUBE */
    glutSolidCube(50.0);

    glDisable( GL_LIGHTING );
    glDisable( GL_DEPTH_TEST );
}
```

The main function in Listing 9-1 is divided in three logical steps: initialization, video capture, and main loop, as shown in this fragment:

```
init();
arVideoCapStart();
argMainLoop( NULL, keyEvent, mainLoop );
```

Let's look at these steps in more detail.

Initialization

This step opens the video device with the AR API call:

```
if( arVideoOpen( vconf ) < 0 ) exit(0);
```

Note that the API requires a video configuration descriptor. This is required for Windows platforms only. In Linux/Android, it can be NULL. If the call fails, you should abort with an error message. Once the video is opened, you can get the size of the display with a call to

```
if( arVideoInqSize(&xsize, &ysize) < 0 ) exit(0);
```

The display size is then stored in xsize and ysize. Next, it loads the default camera parameters and adjusts the size based on the display parameters.

```
/* set the initial camera parameters */
ARParam   wparam;
ARParam   cparam;

if( arParamLoad("Data/camera_para.dat", 1, &wparam) < 0 ) {
  printf("Camera parameter load error !!\n");
exit(0);
}

arParamChangeSize( &wparam, xsize, ysize, &cparam );
arInitCparam( &cparam );

// display camera params
arParamDisp( &cparam );
```

The initial (or default) camera parameters are loaded from the binary file Data/camera_para.dat. Then the camera size is adjusted to match the values returned by xsize and ysize. In Video4Linux, default camera parameters include)

- *The device name*: Usually /dev/video[0-1]. In Android the default video device is /dev/video0.

- *The palette type*: It can be RGB32 or RGBA32 for 32-bit red, blue, and green pixel format.

- *Pixel format*: It should match the palette value used above.

Refer to https://archive.fosdem.org/2014/schedule/event/v4l_intro/ for more information about Video4Linux.

Next, it loads a pattern Data/patt.hiro from disk on which the 3D objects will be rendered.

```
if( ( patt_id = arLoadPatt("Data/patt.hiro")) < 0 ) {
        printf("pattern load error !!\n");
        exit(0);
}
```

The pattern can be referenced by the main rendering loop using its pattern ID. Note that you must print this pattern (see Figure 9-2) before your run the sample. The file is provided as a PDF (pattHiro.pdf) under the patterns folder of the ARToolKit binary distribution. Finally, the graphics windows is opened using the camera parameters with a call to argInit(&cparam, 1.0, 0, 0, 0, 0).

Figure 9-2. *Pattern used by the simpleTest example of the ARToolKit*

Figure 9-3. *A test run of the simpleTest program bundled with the ARToolKit*

Start Video Capture

This step is very simple and it only invokes the API function arVideoCapStart() to tell the ARToolKit to start grabbing video and feed it to the main rendering loop of the program.

Main Rendering Loop

The main rendering loop starts by grabbing a video frame and displaying it on screen, as seen in this fragment:

```
if( (dataPtr = (ARUint8 *)arVideoGetImage()) == NULL ) {
        arUtilSleep(2);
        return;
}
argDrawMode2D();
argDispImage( dataPtr, 0, 0 );
```

The image returned by arVideoGetImage() is an array of bytes representing the pixels encoded in the default pixel format defined by the toolkit. This format is defined at compile time. For Android, it should be either RGB32 or RGBA32. Next, it detects any markers in the video frame obtained from the previous step.

```
if( arDetectMarker(dataPtr, thresh, &marker_info, &marker_num) < 0 ) {
        cleanup();
        exit(0);
}
```

The API call arDetectMarker takes a pointer to the video frame, a threshold value for detection, and returns information about all markers detected plus the number of detected markers. With this information, it checks whether the marker (loaded in in the initialization step and referenced by patt_id) is present. If not, it renders the frame and returns. Otherwise, the rendering process continues.

```
/* check for object visibility */
k = -1;
for( j = 0; j < marker_num; j++ ) {
  if( patt_id == marker_info[j].id ) {
        if( k == -1 ) k = j;
        else if( marker_info[k].cf < marker_info[j].cf ) k = j;
  }
}
if( k == -1 ) {
  argSwapBuffers();
  return;
}
```

Finally, the OpenGL transformation matrix between the marker and the camera is created. Only then can the solid cube be drawn. The final step is to swap the OpenGL buffers, thus rendering the whole thing on screen.

```
/* get the transformation between the marker and the real camera */
arGetTransMat(&marker_info[k], patt_center, patt_width, patt_trans);
/* draw the cude */
draw();
/* render */
argSwapBuffers();
```

Notice that the draw() function draws the cube using the call glutSolidCube(). As you can see, this is a GLUT helper function that doesn't exist in GLES. In Android, the cube will have to be drawn manually using GL API calls. This should be really simple.

Check out http://freeglut.sourceforge.net/docs/android.php for more information about GLUT.

Getting the ARToolKit Running on Android

As mentioned, there are three hurdles to getting the ARToolKit running in Android.

- It uses GLUT to control the life cycle of the application, including creating a window, creating a display surface, providing a main loop, and processing input events. GLUT is not available in Android.

- It uses OpenGL, not OpenGL ES, to draw virtual objects.

- It uses Video4Linux to access the hardware camera device at /dev/video0. This is possible in rooted devices only.

When I began looking into AR, I thought it would be neat to get the ARTK running on Android, so I began thinking about ways to overcome these caveats. Guess what? Somebody already beat me to it. The Project is called AndAR (short for Android Augmented Reality),[2] and it's an open source project based on the ARToolKit. Here is how the folks of AndAR overcome the limitations of the PC-based ARTK.

Getting a Video Feed

The PC version of the ARTK for Linux reads the video device directly from /dev/video0 using the Video4Linux API. Even though Android uses Video4Linux too, the video device is not accessible by normal applications (they require root access only). This makes it impossible to read the video feed unless you have a rooted device (which you don't have). To work around this, AndAR uses the Android Camera API and a surface view.

Using SurfaceView to Display Video

Listing 9-2 shows the CameraSurface class, which used the Android Camera API to render video on top a surface. Let's take a closer look.

Listing 9-2. Simple Surface View to Display Video

```
public class CameraSurface extends SurfaceView implements
  SurfaceHolder.Callback
{

  private static final String TAG = "Preview";

  private SurfaceHolder mHolder;

  public Camera camera;
```

---

[2]Android Augmented Reality available online at http://code.google.com/p/andar/.

```java
public CameraSurface(Context context) {
  super(context);
  // Install a SurfaceHolder.Callback so we get notified when the
  // underlying surface is created and destroyed.
  mHolder = getHolder();
  mHolder.addCallback(this);
  mHolder.setType(SurfaceHolder.SURFACE_TYPE_PUSH_BUFFERS);
}

@Override
public void surfaceChanged(SurfaceHolder holder, int format, int w, int h) {
  // 4 = RGB_565
  Log.d(TAG, "surfaceChanged Surface fomat=" + format + " w=" + w
      + " h=" + h);

  // Now that the size is known, set up the camera parameters and begin
  // the preview.
  Camera.Parameters parameters = camera.getParameters();

  Log.d(TAG,
      "surfaceChanged Preview size: " + parameters.getPreviewSize());

  // (17)- YCbCr_420_SP (NV21)
  Log.d(TAG,
      "surfaceChanged Preview format: " + parameters.getPreviewFormat());

  camera.startPreview();
}

@Override
public void surfaceCreated(SurfaceHolder holder) {
  Log.d(TAG, "surfaceCreated");

  camera = Camera.open();
  try {
    camera.setPreviewDisplay(holder);

    camera.setPreviewCallback(new Camera.PreviewCallback() {
      public void onPreviewFrame(byte[] data, Camera cam) {
        // Here we have a frame image in NV21 format
      }
    });
  } catch (IOException e) {
    e.printStackTrace();
  }

}
```

```
@Override
public void surfaceDestroyed(SurfaceHolder holder) {
    // Surface will be destroyed when we return, so stop the preview.
    // Because the CameraDevice object is not a shared resource, it's very
    // important to release it when the activity is paused.
    Log.d(TAG, "surfaceCreated Stop camera");

    camera.stopPreview();
    camera = null;

  }
}
```

> **Tip**   The Camera API requires a surface view to display a video feed. This surface view can then be assigned as the content view of the main activity, thus rendering the video feed in the application.

CameraSurface extends the Android base class SurfaceView,. It provides a dedicated drawing surface embedded inside of a view hierarchy. So, you can control the format of this surface and, if you like, its size; SurfaceView takes care of placing the surface at the correct location on the screen. The surface view also implements a SurfaceHolder.Callback. A client may implement this interface to receive information about changes to the surface such as surfaceCreated, surfaceChanged, and surfaceDestroyed.

surfaceCreated

surfaceCreated is called immediately after the surface is first created. It is commonly used to initialize rendering code. Note that only one thread can ever draw into a surface, so you should not draw into the surface here if your normal rendering will be in another thread. In Listing 9-2, this function performs the following steps:

1. It creates a new Camera object to access the first back-facing camera on the device. If the device does not have a back-facing camera, this returns null.

2. Next, it calls setPreviewDisplay to set the surface to be used for live preview. Either a surface or surface texture is necessary for preview, and preview is necessary to take pictures.

3. Finally, it installs a callback to be invoked for every preview frame in addition to displaying them on the screen. The callback will be repeatedly called for as long as preview is active. This method can be called at any time, even while preview is live, as seen in this code fragment:

```
camera = Camera.open();
camera.setPreviewDisplay(holder);
camera.setPreviewCallback(new Camera.PreviewCallback() {
  public void onPreviewFrame(byte[] data, Camera cam) {
    // Here we have a frame image in NV21 format
  }
});
```

> **Tip**   The default image format of the camera preview is YCbCr_420_SP (NV21). This is the format that will be received on the preview callback onPreviewFrame. Nevertheless, the format can be controlled by calling camera.setPreviewFormat(format). The image format constants are defined in the ImageFormat class.

surfaceChanged

surfaceChanged is called immediately after surfaceCreated. It receives a reference to the holder of the surface as well as the image format, plus width and height. In this case, this method starts capturing and drawing preview frames to the screen. Preview will not actually start until a surface is supplied with setPreviewDisplay(SurfaceHolder) or setPreviewTexture (SurfaceTexture), as shown in this code fragment:

```
Camera.Parameters parameters = camera.getParameters();
Log.d(TAG, "Preview size: " + parameters.getPreviewSize());
// Start preview:  Default pix format YCbCr_420_SP (NV21)
camera.startPreview();
```

surfaceDestroyed

surfaceDestroyed is called immediately before a surface gets destroyed. After returning from this call, you should no longer try to access this surface. If you have a rendering thread that directly accesses the surface, you must ensure that thread is no longer touching the surface before returning from this function. The following function must be used to stop the camera preview and dispose of resources:

```
camera.stopPreview();
camera = null;
```

With CameraSurface in place, the main application activity can then simply add this surface to its content view, thus rendering the video feed on screen (as shown in this fragment):

```
public void onCreate(Bundle savedInstanceState) {
    super.onCreate(savedInstanceState);
    setContentView(R.layout.main);

    mCameraSurface = new CameraSurface(this);

    FrameLayout preview = ((FrameLayout) findViewById(R.id.preview));
    preview.addView(mCameraSurface);
}
```

Hurdles of the Camera Surface and OpenGL

So you now know how to get a video feed to receive preview images that can be used by the ARTK to render virtual objects on top. However, because you need to render virtual shapes using OpenGL ES, common sense would suggest that you should start with an OpenGL (hardware accelerated) surface with a Camera object as a member function; then when this surface is created, it may initiate a Camera preview along with OpenGL draw operations overlaid on top. Hence, CameraSurface of Listing 9-2 could be rewritten to allow for GLES drawing, as shown in Listing 9-3.

Listing 9-3. CameraSurface Version 2

```
public class CameraSurface extends GLSurfaceView implements
  SurfaceHolder.Callback
{
  private static final String TAG = "GLPreview";

  public Camera camera;
  private GLThread mGLThread;
  private SurfaceHolder mHolder;

  public CameraSurfaceGL(Context context) {
    super(context);
    mHolder = getHolder();
    mHolder.addCallback(this);
    mHolder.setType(SurfaceHolder.SURFACE_TYPE_GPU);
  }

  public void setRenderer(Renderer renderer) {
    mGLThread = new GLThread(renderer, getHolder()); // mHolder);
    mGLThread.start();
  }
```

```java
@Override
public void surfaceChanged(SurfaceHolder holder, int format, int w, int h) {
  // Now that the size is known, set up the camera parameters and begin
  // the preview.
  Camera.Parameters parameters = camera.getParameters();

  Log.d(TAG," Preview size: " + parameters.getPreviewSize());

  camera.startPreview();
  mGLThread.onWindowResize(w, h);
}

@Override
public void surfaceCreated(SurfaceHolder holder) {
  Log.d(TAG, "surfaceCreated");

  camera = Camera.open();
  try {
    // THIS GIVES AN INVALID SURFACE ERROR!
    camera.setPreviewDisplay(holder);
    camera.setPreviewCallback(new Camera.PreviewCallback() {
        public void onPreviewFrame(byte[] data, Camera cam) {
        }
    });
  } catch (IOException e) {
    e.printStackTrace();
  }

  mGLThread.surfaceCreated();
}

@Override
public void surfaceDestroyed(SurfaceHolder holder) {
  // mGLThread.surfaceDestroyed();

  // Surface will be destroyed when we return, so stop the preview.
  // Because the CameraDevice object is not a shared resource, it's very
  // important to release it when the activity is paused.
  Log.d(TAG, "surfaceCreated Stop camera");

   camera.stopPreview();
   camera = null;

}

public void onWindowFocusChanged(boolean hasFocus) {
  super.onWindowFocusChanged(hasFocus);
  mGLThread.onWindowFocusChanged(hasFocus);
}
}
```

Listing 9-3 shows CameraSurface version 2 as a GL surface designed to use the preview display of a Camera object as well as being capable of doing GLES drawing operations. The caveat with this CameraSurface is that a GLES surface cannot set a Camera preview display and vice versa; a push buffer (Camera) surface cannot do GLES system calls to draw virtual objects on top. Take a look at Listing 9-3; when the camera surface constructor is called, the surface type is set to GPU (hardware).

```
mHolder.setType(SurfaceHolder.SURFACE_TYPE_GPU)
```

Whenever this surface attempts to set itself as the preview display of the camera with

```
camera.setPreviewDisplay(holder);
```

an exception will be thrown with the error "Invalid Surface" and the app will crash. Therefore, you cannot use this version of CameraSurface. To work around this caveat, AndAR uses two surfaces: a push buffer surface for the video feed, and an OpenGL ES surface to perform GL drawing calls, as seen in Figure 9-4.

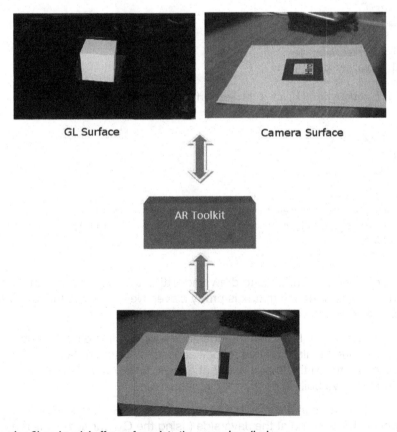

Figure 9-4. Merging GL and push buffer surfaces into the same view display

Thus you have two threads running simultaneously and accessing the same image buffer. When the onPreviewFrame fires on the camera surface, as shown in the following fragment, the image buffer can be sent via JNI to the ARTK for further work:

```
camera.setPreviewCallback(new Camera.PreviewCallback() {
  public void onPreviewFrame(byte[] data, Camera cam) {
     // Here we have a frame image in NV21 format
  }
});
```

As shown in Listing 9-1, with the image buffer, the ARTK can then detect any markers on the image, get a transformation matrix between the marker and the real camera, and draw the virtual object (as seen in the following code):

```
/* detect the markers in the video frame */
if( arDetectMarker(dataPtr, thresh, &marker_info, &marker_num) < 0 ) {
  cleanup();
  exit(0);
}

/* check for marker visibility */
k = -1;
for( j = 0; j < marker_num; j++ ) {
  if( patt_id == marker_info[j].id ) {
       if( k == -1 ) k = j;
       else if( marker_info[k].cf < marker_info[j].cf ) k = j;
  }
}
/* no markers ? */
if( k == -1 ) {
  return;
}

/* get the transformation between the marker and the real camera */
arGetTransMat(&marker_info[k], patt_center, patt_width, patt_trans);
/* draw GL stuff */
/* Swap buffers */
```

This technique of using two surfaces to draw and letting the ARTK handle the marker detection and the transformation matrix is pretty clever. Nevertheless, the following issues should be carefully considered:

- *Concurrency*: You have two threads accessing the same image buffer. Special care should be taken to lock access to shared data so only one thread can touch the image buffer at a given time. AndAR does this using the Java built-in concurrency mechanism.

- *OpenGL drawing in Java vs. the native side*: AndAR preforms all OpenGL ES drawing at the Java side (using the GL Surface). This may not be the best choice for a game that requires access to resources in the native side (for example, models, textures, etc.). It would be better to move all GL drawing to the native side, especially if you plan to reuse vast amounts of code from an existing game engine.

Using a Single Surface for Camera and GL Drawing

It turns out that is indeed possible to use a single surface to draw both camera video and OpenGL. As mentioned, the setPreviewDisplay (SurfaceHolder holder) method of the Camera API sets the surface to be used for live preview. Nonetheless, there is also the method setPreviewTexture (SurfaceTexture surfaceTexture), which sets a SurfaceTexture to be used for preview. SurfaceTexture captures frames from an image stream as an OpenGL ES texture. The image stream may come from either camera preview or video decode. A SurfaceTexture may be used in place of a SurfaceHolder when specifying the output destination of a Camera object. Doing so will cause all the frames from the image stream to be sent to the SurfaceTexture object rather than to the device's display.

There are two limitations when using a SurfaceTexture:

- The texture object underneath SurfaceTexture uses the GL_TEXTURE_ EXTERNAL_OES texture target, which is defined by the GL_OES_EGL_ image_external OpenGL ES extension. This limits how the texture may be used. Each time the texture is bound, it must be bound to the GL_TEXTURE_EXTERNAL_OES target rather than the GL_TEXTURE_2D target. Additionally, any OpenGL ES 2.0 shader that samples from the texture must declare its use of this extension using, for example, an #extension GL_OES_EGL_image_external : require directive. Such shaders must also access the texture using the samplerExternalOES GLSL sampler type.

- setPreviewTexture and SurfaceTexture are only available in API level 11 (Android 3.2) or later. This eliminates most of the Android devices out there (perhaps more than 90%). Thus, at this point in time, it is simply not feasible to use SurfaceTexture. Nevertheless, when Android 4 becomes the dominant version, I think SurfaceTexture will be the standard for capturing and processing video.

Drawing and Application Life Cycle

Drawing and the application life cycle are the second and third hurdles of using the ARTK in Android. As mentioned, the PC version of the ARTK uses OpenGL to draw. AndAR overcomes this by using a second surface for OpenGL ES drawing, as explained in the previous section. The tricky part is coordinating drawing between the two concurrent threads and using the ATK API calls to detect the markers and obtain a transformation matrix required to bind the virtual object to the marker.

The application life cycle is handled by Android itself via the onCreate method, thus removing the need for the GLUT API calls in the ARTK. The following code illustrates this by creating two surfaces, a camera surface described in Listing 9-2 and a GL Surface that renders two rotating cubes (using the scenes code from Chapter 2):

```
CameraSurface mCameraSurface;
GLSurface mGLSurface;

/** Called when the activity is first created. */
@Override
public void onCreate(Bundle savedInstanceState) {
  super.onCreate(savedInstanceState);
  setContentView(R.layout.main);

  mCameraSurface = new CameraSurface(this);
  mGLSurface = new GLSurface(this);

  mGLSurface.setRenderer(new CubeRenderer(true, false));
  FrameLayout preview = ((FrameLayout) findViewById(R.id.preview));

  preview.addView(mGLSurface);
  preview.addView(mCameraSurface);
}
```

Both surfaces are added to the application layout to produce the effect of the two rotating cubes from Chapter 2 on top of the videocam feed, as shown in Figure 9-5.

Figure 9-5. Two rotating cubes over a video feed

> **Tip** The source code for the two rotating cubes over video (shown in Figure 9-5) as well as the AndAR project that simulates the ARTK `simpleTest` program described in Figure 9-3 are included with the book's companion source code. Import the projects `ch09.Camera` and `ch09.AndAR` into your workspace and take a look at how the camera and GL surfaces are created and merged into the same content view. Remember that to run the AndAR test program you must print the pattern shown in Figure 9-2.

Other Toolkits Out There

Currently most of the AR projects use the ARTK as their base. Among the most remarkable are

- *Android Augmented Reality Viewer* (`http://code.google.com/p/android-ar-base/`): According to the authors, this project provides the base functionality for building an Android Augmented Reality application, including:

  - Camera marker tracking

  - A 3D game engine

  - A 3D sound support

  - An API for extending your AR apps

- *NyARToolKit for Android*: A Japanese project under the GNU public license, this is an AR toolkit for Android in C++. Digging through the source, it appears to be loosely based on the ARTK, although most of the code has been rewritten in C++. More information can be found at `http://nyartoolkit-for-android.soft112.com/`

You have taken the first step in learning about AR and how it can be applied to draw hardware accelerated objects that could be used in gaming. This section provided you with a foundation to build upon, but there is another new technology fighting to make it into your living room: Android TV. The next section looks at the evolution of this new technology and its implications in gaming.

Another very useful SDK is the Multi-Screen SDK, which provides developers with a set of API's and tools that enable multi-screen experiences for Games, Media Sharing, Social Collaboration and more.

The Multi-Screen application is divided into two applications. One application runs on a Samsung SMART TV, and the other application runs on a mobile device. The Multi-Screen SDK provides an API for your TV application and API's for Android, iOS, and JavaScript mobile applications.

The Multi-Screen APIs focus on three main features:

- *Discover*: The mobile APIs provide the ability to discover a compatible Samsung TV from your mobile application.

- *Connect*: The mobile applications can connect to your TV application. Connections are based on web sockets and provide bi-directional, reliable, and fast communication.

- *Communicate*: Once connected, each device has awareness of all other devices connected. This allows one device to send messages to any other device, or group of devices, including the TV.

To use the Multi-Screen SDK with Android you need:

- Your PC or Mac connected to the internet.

- Eclipse or Android Studio with the Android SDK installed.

- A text editor or suitable IDE for editing HTML, JavaScript, and CSS files for developing TV applications.

You can download the Multi-Screen SDK at `http://multiscreen.samsung.com/downloads/MultiScreenSDK-1.1.11.zip`.

Let's now discuss briefly the future of Google TV.

Google TV: The Beginning

With the rise of smart TVs, Google and others have taken the initiative to combine the best of the Web and TV into a single entertainment unit. Thus Google TV was born. Gaming consoles like the XBox and PlayStation had the upper hand, trying to become the main source of entertainment in the living room by providing games, e-mail, movies, and basic Internet services. Nevertheless, Internet TV is rising up to challenge consoles for living room dominance. It is worth mentioning that Google TV is not the only Internet TV offer available out there; there is also AppleTV, Roku, offerings by Samsung, and others. However, this section explores why you should develop for Google TV.

Google TV was built on top of Android 3.2. Here is what Google TV could do:

- Run on the Android operating system Honeycomb version 3.2.

- Provide the tools and APIs for developing applications in the Java programming language.

- Lack a touchscreen input device. Instead, applications are typically controlled with a remote control.

- Include a live TV Android application that displays the live TV signal.

- Have a Channel Listing content provider to offer a table of stations and channels for the configured signal provider.

- Support location services, USB, and Wi-Fi on the hardware side.

- Support OpenGL for Java including GLES 2.0 for hardware accelerated gaming.

On the other hand, GTV did **not**

- Support touch screens.

- Support the native development kit (NDK). This makes it difficult for native game development, although not impossible as you'll see later on.

- Support hardware including Bluetooth, camera, GPS, microphone, near field communications (NFC), and telephony.

Now, let's talk about the future of TV and Android.

Android TV: The Future

After the first Google TV experiment done in 2010 by Google together with Intel, Sony and Logitech, finally the new Android TV was launched. It had to compete with Apple TV and Amazon TV, which were also launched in the new market of hi-tech TV.

The most important characteristic of Android TV is the simplicity. This means basically two things. The first is that Google wants to make sure that the experience for the user to find interesting content will be as simple as possible suggesting TV programs based on the user's interests. Secondly, for Google, the simplicity of Android TV means the possibility to utilize other Android devices like smartphones, tablets and Wear to easily connect to the Android TV.

Finally, simplicity means that Android TV can be used with a lot of apps as well as allowing you to play Android games using it.

One of the most important features of Android TV is this gaming aspect, since it is fully integrated with the Google Play Games platform.

Here are some of the most important Android TV features:

- Familiar platform: apps used for Android TV utilize the same development platform used to develop other Android apps

- Simplicity: Simple to use and find content of interest

- Built-in voice search: Google's voice recognition technology can be used to send voice commands to Android TV

- TV control using Android phone and tablet: Android TV apps allow Android smartphones and tablets to be used as remote controls for Android TV

- Gaming: Android TV can be used to play Android games

- Mirroring: Android TV allows us to mirror Android smartphones and tablets

Here are the prerequisites you need to build an Android TV application:

- Use SDK tools version 23.0.5 or higher

- Use the SDK with Android 5.0.1 (API 21)

- Use Android TV libraries which include: v17 leanback, v7 recyclerview and v7 cardview

For more info about Android TV libraries please refer to `https://developer.android.com/training/tv/start/start.html#tv-libraries`.

The Android TV libraries included in the Android SDK Manager are shown in Figure 9-6.

Figure 9-6. *Android TV required libraries*

When using Android Studio you need to create a virtual Android TV emulator as shown in Figure 9-7.

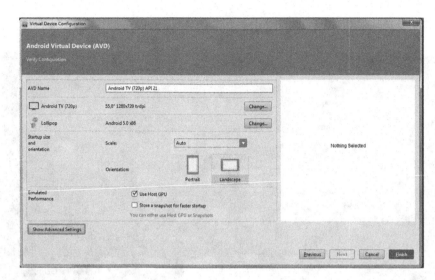

Figure 9-7. Creating an Android TV AVD emulator

The Android TV AVD emulator, once started, will look like the display in Figure 9-8.

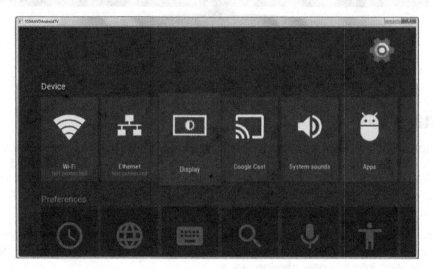

Figure 9-8. Android TV AVD emulator

For more information regarding Android TV refer to https://developer.android.com/tv/
index.html and http://www.android.com/tv/.

An example of a real Android TV is shown in Figure 9-9.

Figure 9-9. An example of a real Android TV

Summary

In this chapter you learned about two new and important technologies: augmented reality (AR) SDKs, and Toolkits. With AR, you learned the basics of rendering a video feed along with OpenGL objects using the Camera API and the ARToolKit. These tools provide you a foundation upon which to build not only AR-enabled games but all sorts of apps. AR is a new field in mobile development with a great potential for innovation.

You've also learned about Android TV and the integration with Android SDK version 5 and read briefly about some TV SDKs. And, you've been introduced to some resources for further information into this new gaming arena.

## Chapter 10

Deployment and Compilation Tips

This chapter offers tips to deploy your application, assist in compilation, and other time-saving goodies. Specifically, this chapter includes tips for the following:

- *Signing your application manually*: This is helpful if you use an automated build system to build and sign your apps. Keep in mind that applications must be signed before they can be distributed.

- *Creating a key store for signature of your application package*: This is required to sign your app either manually or using the workbench.

- *Signing your application using the workbench*: This will show you how to sign your app visually.

- *Install your signed application:* This will show how to install the signed application into the real Android device.

- *A JNI cheat sheet*: It includes the most important tips you should remember when building hybrid games that use both Java and C/C++.

Let's get started!

Signing Your Application

Before your application can be installed in any Android device, it must be signed using a Java key store. This section describes the steps you must follow to accomplish this task. You can find more details in the Android Developer's Guide.

In general you can sign your application in debug or release mode. For more information refer to `http://developer.android.com/tools/publishing/app-signing.html#debug-mode`.

> **Note**   Android developers, more information about signing your applications is available at
> `http://developer.android.com/guide/publishing/app-signing.html#setup`.

We'll show you first how to sign using the release mode. As first step, you need to create a key store. Let's start.

Creating a Key Store

A key store is a password-protected file that contains public/private key pairs used for JAR signatures. You can create a key store with the following command:

```
$ keytool -genkey -v -keystore my-release-key.keystore -alias alias_name -keyalg RSA
 -validity 10000 -storepass <password1> -keypass <password2>
```

Table 10-1 lists the possible arguments for the keytool command.

Table 10-1. Arguments for the keytool Command

Argument	Description
-genkey	Generate a public and private key pair.
-v	Use verbose output.
-keystore	Specify the name of the key store.
-alias <alias_name>	Add an alias for the key pair.
-validity <valdays>	Specify the validity period in days.
-storepass <password>	Add a password for the key store.
-keypass <password>	Add a password for the key.

> **Tip**   When you run your applications in the emulator, Android Studio will automatically sign the application using a debug key stored in `%USERPROFILE%\.android\debug.keystore` (in Windows) and `$HOME/.android/debug.keystore` (in Linux). Notice also that the debug key stored password is "android" and the key alias and password are androiddebugkey/android.

Let's now create a new key store file for use in signing the project.

Here are the steps:

1. Create a new directory to store your key store; for instance C:\mykeys

2. Run the command keytool to create the key store file (see Figure 10-1):

```
keytool -genkey -v -keystore c:/mykeys/myappkey.keystore -alias
mykeys -keyalg RSA -keysize 2048 -validity 10000
```

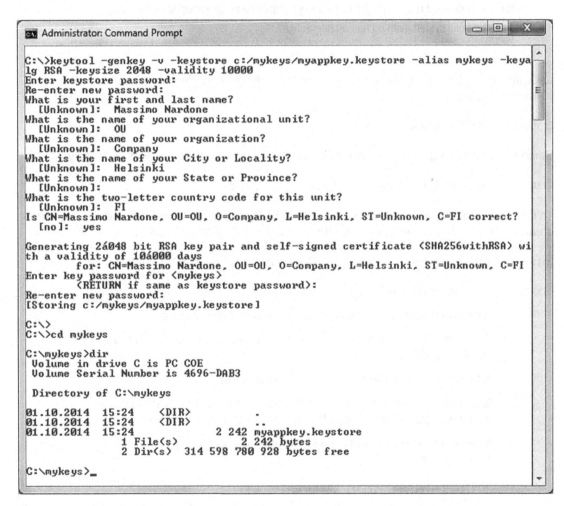

Figure 10-1. The keystore file creation output

Now the file myappkey.keystore in the directory C:\mykeys has been created successfully.

You'll now sign the application using the new key store file you just created.

Signing the Application

You have two choices when signing your application: manually, using the Java SDK jarsigner command; or visually, using Android Studio.

Signing Your APK Manually

> **Note**   Sometimes it may be desirable to sign your app manually, especially if you have an automated build system with no human interaction.

Let's suppose you want to sign a project named "MyFirstApp," which is located in the following directory:

`C:\Users\nardone\workspaceA\MyFirstApp`

Since you need to sign this project's APK file you'll locate it in the following directory:

`C:\Users\nardone\workspaceA\MyFirstApp\bin\MyFirstApp.apk`

To manually sign the APK file, you use the Java SDK jarsigner command and the key store created in the previous section to sign the packed application as follows:

`jarsigner -verbose -keystore <KEYSTORE-FILE> MyFirstApp.apk <KEYSTORE-ALIAS>`

The arguments are as follows:

- -verbose displays information about the files being signed.
- -keystore defines the location of the Java key store created in the previous section.
- MyFirstApp.apk is the application package to sign.
- KEYSTORE-ALIAS is the alias that represents the public/private key pair used for signature created in the previous section.
- As a bonus, you can verify the signatures are correct by using the command

   `jarsigner -verbose -verify <PATH-TO-THE-APK>`

> **Caution**   The keytool and jarsigner commands are part of the Java SDK, not the JRE. You will have to install a Java SDK and set up the paths in your system to be able to create a key store and sign your applications with jarsigner.

To sign the APK file, run the `jarsigner` command (see Figure 10-2):

```
jarsigner -verbose -keystore c:/mykeys/myappkey.keystore -storepass massimo -keypass massimo
C:\Users\nardone\workspaceA\MyFirstApp\bin\MyFirstApp.apk mykeys
```

```
Administrator: Command Prompt

  signing: res/drawable-xxhdpi/abc_ic_menu_share_holo_light.png
  signing: res/drawable-xxhdpi/abc_ic_search.png
  signing: res/drawable-xxhdpi/abc_ic_search_api_holo_light.png
  signing: res/drawable-xxhdpi/abc_ic_voice_search.png
  signing: res/drawable-xxhdpi/abc_ic_voice_search_api_holo_light.png
  signing: res/drawable-xxhdpi/abc_list_divider_holo_dark.9.png
  signing: res/drawable-xxhdpi/abc_list_divider_holo_light.9.png
  signing: res/drawable-xxhdpi/abc_list_focused_holo.9.png
  signing: res/drawable-xxhdpi/abc_list_longpressed_holo.9.png
  signing: res/drawable-xxhdpi/abc_list_pressed_holo_dark.9.png
  signing: res/drawable-xxhdpi/abc_list_pressed_holo_light.9.png
  signing: res/drawable-xxhdpi/abc_list_selector_disabled_holo_dark.9.png
  signing: res/drawable-xxhdpi/abc_list_selector_disabled_holo_light.9.png
  signing: res/drawable-xxhdpi/abc_menu_dropdown_panel_holo_dark.9.png
  signing: res/drawable-xxhdpi/abc_menu_dropdown_panel_holo_light.9.png
  signing: res/drawable-xxhdpi/abc_menu_hardkey_panel_holo_dark.9.png
  signing: res/drawable-xxhdpi/abc_menu_hardkey_panel_holo_light.9.png
  signing: res/drawable-xxhdpi/abc_spinner_ab_default_holo_dark.9.png
  signing: res/drawable-xxhdpi/abc_spinner_ab_default_holo_light.9.png
  signing: res/drawable-xxhdpi/abc_spinner_ab_disabled_holo_dark.9.png
  signing: res/drawable-xxhdpi/abc_spinner_ab_disabled_holo_light.9.png
  signing: res/drawable-xxhdpi/abc_spinner_ab_focused_holo_dark.9.png
  signing: res/drawable-xxhdpi/abc_spinner_ab_focused_holo_light.9.png
  signing: res/drawable-xxhdpi/abc_spinner_ab_pressed_holo_dark.9.png
  signing: res/drawable-xxhdpi/abc_spinner_ab_pressed_holo_light.9.png
  signing: res/drawable-xxhdpi/abc_tab_selected_focused_holo.9.png
  signing: res/drawable-xxhdpi/abc_tab_selected_holo.9.png
  signing: res/drawable-xxhdpi/abc_tab_selected_pressed_holo.9.png
  signing: res/drawable-xxhdpi/abc_tab_unselected_pressed_holo.9.png
  signing: res/drawable-xxhdpi/abc_textfield_search_default_holo_dark.9.png
  signing: res/drawable-xxhdpi/abc_textfield_search_default_holo_light.9.png
  signing: res/drawable-xxhdpi/abc_textfield_search_right_default_holo_dark.9.pn
g
  signing: res/drawable-xxhdpi/abc_textfield_search_right_default_holo_light.9.p
ng
  signing: res/drawable-xxhdpi/abc_textfield_search_right_selected_holo_dark.9.p
ng
  signing: res/drawable-xxhdpi/abc_textfield_search_right_selected_holo_light.9.
png
  signing: res/drawable-xxhdpi/abc_textfield_search_selected_holo_dark.9.png
  signing: res/drawable-xxhdpi/abc_textfield_search_selected_holo_light.9.png
  signing: res/drawable-xxhdpi/ic_launcher.png
  signing: classes.dex
jar signed.
```

Figure 10-2. Sign the MyFristApp.apk file

You can verify that the file `MyfirstApp.apk` is signed, using a command like this:

```
jarsigner -verbose -verify -certs MyFirstApp.apk
```

As very last step you align the final APK package using the `zipalign` tool, which ensures that all uncompressed data starts with a particular byte alignment relative to the start of the file, reducing the amount of RAM consumed by an app.

Run this command:

```
zipalign -v 4 MyFirstApp.apk ReadyMyFirstApp.apk
```

You have successfully signed the "MyFirstApp" Android app and the file ReadyMyFirstApp.apk can be now installed in your device.

If you wish, you can create a windows batch script to sign an APK manually, as shown in Listing 10-1.

Listing 10-1. Windows Batch Script to Sign the MyFirstApp Application Package (APK)

```
@echo off
rem Location of your JAVA SDK
set JAVA_HOME= C:\Program Files\Java\jdk1.8.0_20
rem Location of the APK to sign
set PKG= C:\Users\nardone\workspaceA\MyFirstApp\bin\MyFirstApp.apk

rem Sign it
"%JAVA_HOME%\bin\jarsigner" -verbose -keystore ar-release-key.keystore %PKG% android_radio

rem To verify that your .apk is signed, you can use a command like this
"%JAVA_HOME%\bin\jarsigner" -verbose -verify %PKG%
```

You may have to edit Listing 10-1 to set up the location of your Java SDK plus the location of the Android APK to sign.

Signing Your APK Visually

With Android SDK 1.5 or later, signing your package is much easier, provided you already have a key store; you don't need the jarsigner command in this instance. To sign the MyFirstApp project's package with the Android Studio, follow these steps:

1. Go into the Build menu and select **Generate Signed APK** (see Figure 10-3).

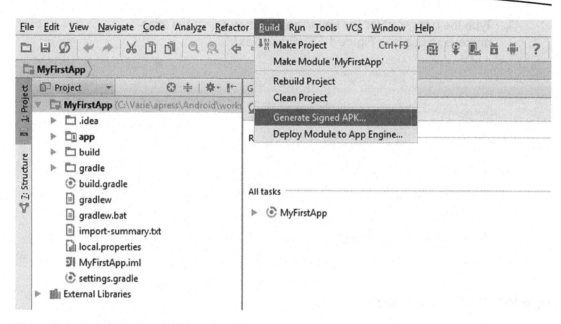

Figure 10-3. Generating a signed APK

2. Click **Choose existing...** to select the key store file
    myappkey.keystore to use (see Figure 10-4). Click Next.

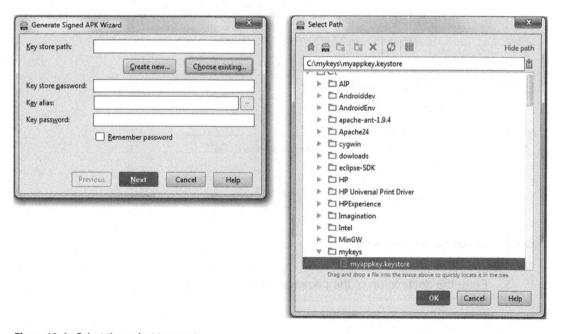

Figure 10-4. Select the project to export

3. Type the password for the key store and then select the alias
    mykeys to use (see Figure 10-5). Press Next.

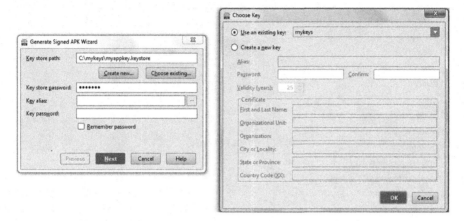

Figure 10-5. *The alias selection dialog*

4. Select the alias **mykeys** that represents the key pair to be used
    for the signature and enter the corresponding password
    (see Figure 10-6). Click Next.

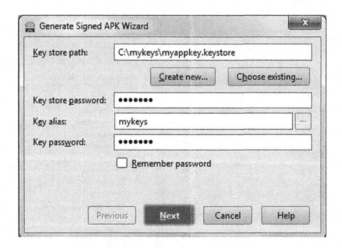

Figure 10-6. *The key alias selection dialog*

5. Enter the destination of the package, as shown in Figure 10-7.
    Click Next.

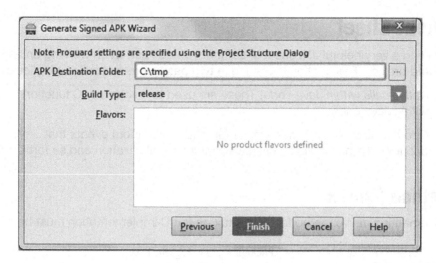

Figure 10-7. Choosing the destination folder for the application package

The file MyFirstApp.apk will be successfully created in the directory C:\tmp. See Figure 10-8.

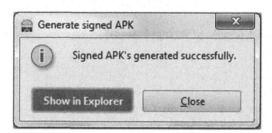

Figure 10-8. APK file successfully generated

Installing the APK File

Next, you'll see how to install the APK file you just created in the real Android device. Here are the steps to follow.

1. Make sure you enable "Unknown Sources" on your Android device.

2. Copy the file ReadyMyFirstApp.apk from the C\tmp directory to the download directory of your Android device.

3. Install the new application package.

4. Run the new application file.

You should see the result of the "MyFirstApp" application in your Android device.

JNI Cheat Sheet

Here you'll find a very helpful JNI cheat sheet that you can use when working on any type of JNI/C–related project. This section is divided in two basic communication pipelines:

- *Native calls within Java code*: These are used to invoke any C function within Java code.

- *C to Java callbacks*: These are useful to tell Java about events that occur on the native side, such as audio/video initialization and so forth.

JNI Method Syntax

When implementing native methods, the syntax on the C implementation must be

```
JNIEXPORT <RETURNTYPE> JNICALL Java_<PACKAGE>_<CLASS>_<METHOD>
  (JNIEnv * env, jclass cls, <ARGUMENTS>)
```

Note that any periods used in the Java names must be replaced with underscore characters. Thus the Java native method of

```
package native;
class Natives {
  public static native void GameMain(String[] args);
}
```

must be declared in C as

```
JNIEXPORT void JNICALL Java_native_Natives_GameMain
  (JNIEnv * env, jclass cls, jobjectArray jargv)
```

Take a look at the arguments. They are as follows:

- env: This is a C pointer to the JNI environment. It can be used to perform miscellaneous Java tasks within C such as:

  - Load classes, methods, exceptions, and more.

  - Invoke Java methods or exceptions.

- cls: This is an opaque reference to the class that is invoking the C function. It can be used to extract member variables, invoke methods or raise exceptions within the calling class.

- jargv: This is the most useful argument. In this case it represents the user defined string array sent by the caller (in this particular example, the startup arguments sent to the native layer). Note that this is a JNI object array, which is an opaque type representing a Java string array. It must be converted into a C array, which is shown in the next section.

Loading a Java Class as Global Reference

If you must keep a reference to a Java class (to invoke callbacks when certain events occur, for example), always use a global reference, as follows:

```
jclass clazz    = (*env)->FindClass(env, "quake/jni/Natives");
jclass globalCls = (jclass)(*env)->NewGlobalRef(env, clazz);
```

Here you have loaded the Java class quake.jni.Natives and created a global reference for it. This reference can be used anywhere to invoke C to Java callbacks. You must use a global reference to prevent the JVM garbage collector from removing the class from memory. The fact is that you don't know at which point the JVM will decide to get rid of the class. This is why you need a global reference.

Converting a Java Array to a C array

This can be really helpful if you are sending startup arguments to the native side. Java string arrays cannot simply be used within C; they must be converted. See the following examples.

- To get the length of the Java array jarray:

  ```
  (*env)->GetArrayLength(env, jarray);
  ```

- To extract a Java string from the Java array jarray at position i:

  ```
  jstring jrow = (jstring)(*env)->GetObjectArrayElement(env, jarray, i);
  ```

- To convert the string jrow into a C string:

  ```
  const char *row  = (*env)->GetStringUTFChars(env, jrow, 0);
  ```

Invoking Java Within C (Callbacks)

Remember from the preceding section that the Java class was loaded as a global reference? Here is where you use it. Callbacks are usually invoked from a different place than JNI functions (a game loop running in a separate thread, for example). Therefore, it is imperative that you attach to the current thread before doing any JNI API calls (if you don't, your app may crash).

```
(*g_VM)->AttachCurrentThread (g_VM,  &env, NULL)
```

- To load the Java static method OnInitVideo, which has two integer arguments, width and height:

  ```
  jmethodID mid = (*env)->GetStaticMethodID(env, jNativesCls,
  "OnInitVideo", "(II)V");
  ```

- To invoke the previous method (referenced by mid) using the global reference to the class loaded in the Global Reference section with two arguments:

  ```
  (*env)->CallStaticVoidMethod(env, jNativesCls, mid, width, height);
  ```

Summary

In this chapter you have learned how to deploy and compile an Android Application which included the following tasks:

- Creating a key store
- Signing your application
- Export the signed application
- Installing the APK file into Android Studio

In Chapter 11, which is the last chapter of this book, you'll learn how to write and compile a wearable application using the Android SDK Wear engine.

## Chapter 11

Discovering Android Wear

This chapter introduces you to Android Wear. You'll learn what you need to install and configure to develop your first Wear application using the Android SDK 5.0.1 API 21. More specifically we'll cover the following:

- *Understanding Android Wear*
- *Defining the Android libraries needed for the Wear Application*
- *Creating a Wear Emulator with Android AVD Manager*
- *Creating and running your first Wear application*

Let's get started!

What Is Android Wear?

Google officially announced in March 2014 that they were branching out into the world of wearables with the first version of a revised Android operating system especially designed for wearables. A few months later during the I/O event, Google launched two devices running Android Wear, such as the Samsung Gear Live and LG G Watch. This was the first step toward a new Android device called Android Wear.

Android Wear is the Google API for smart watches, Google Glass, and other wearable devices. Basically the Android Wear device communicates with any Android smartphone or tablet to get information to be shown on its screen.

Android Wear launch devices include:

- Motorola Moto 360
- LG G Watch
- Samsung Gear Live

- ASUS ZenWatch

- Sony Smartwatch 3

- LG Watch R

Figures 11-1 and 11-2 show what Samsung Gear Live looks like.

Figure 11-1. *The Samsung Gear Live Android Wear device*

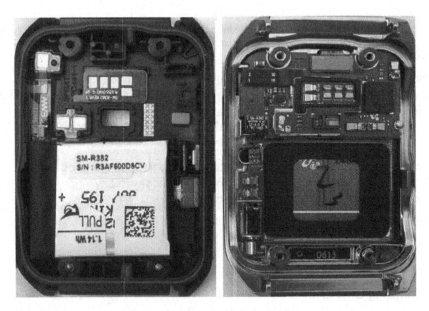

Figure 11-2. *The inside of a Samsung Gear Live Android Wear device*

Android Wear OS and User Interface (UI)

The Android Wear operating system uses Bluetooth to connect to a handheld device, which needs to run Android version 4.3 or higher. Once connected and paired with an Android smartphone or tablet, the Android Wear shows information or alerts, including apps like:

- Gmail
- Google Calendar
- Android phone notifications and calls
- Text messages

Conversely, Android Wear can also send commands to other Android devices it is connected to.

An Android wearable device might include the following features:

- Customizable Themes
- Changeable Bands
- Simple Interaction
- Personalized Fitness Manager

One of the greatest features of Android Wear is the vocal (voice) commands. You can actually execute tasks or retrieve information on your Android Wear just by giving a vocal command. All you need to do is to say, "Okay Google," and then say the command that you need.

You can also give vocal commands to your Android Wear to execute tasks on the Android smartphone or tablet it is connected to.

Using the vocal commands you might, for instance, execute the following tasks:

- *Launch an app on the paired smartphone or tablet*: For instance, "Open Gmail"
- *Take notes*: For example, "Take a note, buy bread and milk"
- *Get simultaneous answers to generic questions*: For example, "What is the capital of Italy?"
- *Send emails and texts*: For instance, "Send Massimo Nardone an email," and then dictate the email text

The Android Wear operating system is very different from what is normally used on smartphones and tablets. This mainly because Android Wear needs a user interface. Google had to develop a new OS and user interface for Android Wear. The interface has two main components: the Context Stream and the Cue Card.

Context Stream

The Android Wear OS is a card-based system, which means that the UI is a vertical stream of cards that appear automatically based on time, location, and many other user activities and interests.

When using your Android smartphone or tablet you see all the "Google Now" cards showing on your screen. With Android Wear, you see only one card at a time and you scroll only vertically between cards. Figure 11-3 shows some examples of Android Wear cards.

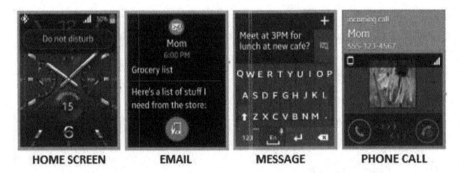

HOME SCREEN   EMAIL   MESSAGE   PHONE CALL

Figure 11-3. Samsung Gear Live Android Wear cards

You can develop full-screen apps for Android Wear; however, Google encourages developing apps that can be easily integrate with the Context Stream. This means that one of the starting points when developing for wearables is to learn how to incorporate the cards generated by your app into the existing Android Wear Context Stream. Let's consider how to do this.

Cue Card

As we said earlier you can give vocal commands to your Android wearable device by beginning with "Okay, Google" and then dictating the action you would like your wearable or connected smartphone/tablet to execute. When you use the "Okay, Google" vocal command you are actually using a "Cue Card."

The Cue Card recognizes and executes a certain task, based on a vocal command. Technically what happens is that the Cue Card understands the vocal command and searches for an app that can be matched to the command requested; it then executes that app.

Figure 11-4 shows how the "Okay, Google" command is sent to the Samsung Gear Live Android Wear device.

Figure 11-4. *Samsung Gear Live Cue Card*

On October 17, 2014, a new Android version 5.0 was released. Google announced that the newest version of Android 5.0 should be available to the Nexus 4, 5, 7 (2012 and 2013) and 10 in early November 2014,around the release date for the Nexus 6, Nexus 9, and Nexus Player.

Let's now develop our first Wear application.

Developing an Android Wear App

In this section you'll learn now how to develop two types of Android wearable applications. As first step, you'll see a how to run a wearable timer application using the Android AVD emulator. Then you'll learn how to configure an Android smartphone or tablet to send notification to the developed Android emulator Wear device.

> **Note**   Android Wear development information can be found at: `https://developer.android`
> `.com/wear/index.html`

You'll want consider these characteristics of the wearable operating system before you start to develop an Android wearable app:

■ The wearable device's system enforces a timeout period, which means that if you don't do anything when an activity is displayed, the device will go into sleep mode. When it wakes back up, the Wear home screen is displayed instead of your activity.

■ Consider the very small size of Wearable devices when designing a wearable app.

■ Remember that users will not download apps directly onto the wearable. Instead, you bundle the wearable app inside the Android smartphone or tablet app. So, for instance, when users install a certain app on their smartphone, the system automatically installs the wearable app as well. Of course, for testing you can install the developed app directly into the wearable device or emulator.

Let's start by setting up the wearable environment.

Setting Up the Environment

Before you start to set up the wearable app environment, keep in mind that wearable apps can access a lot of the available standard Android APIs, but they do not support the following APIs:

■ `android.webkit`

■ `android.print`

■ `android.app.backup`

■ `android.appwidget`

■ `android.hardware.usb`

> **Note** If you want to check whether your wearable device supports a certain feature, you can call `hasSystemFeature()` before trying to use an API.
>
> Google recommends using Android Studio for Android Wear development because it provides project setup, library inclusion, and packaging conveniences that aren't available in ADT.

Notice that all the code included in this chapter was developed, compiled and tested using Eclipse IDE for Java Developers (eclipse-java-luna-SR1a-win32-x86_64.zip).

Your first step is to install the Android Wear system image and support packages needed by your wearable app.

To do this, open the Android SDK Manager and check that you have the latest versions of the following three packages:

- SDK Tools

- Platform tools

- Build tools

Figure 11-5 shows what the Android SDK Manager looks like.

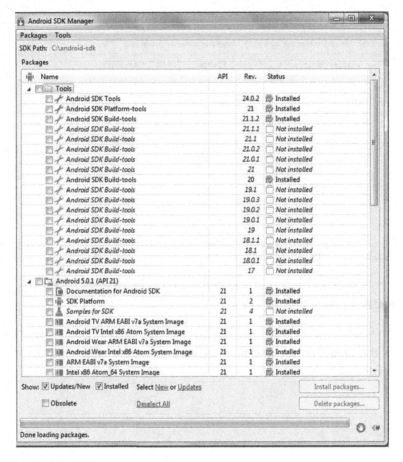

Figure 11-5. Android SDK Manager

Creating a Wear Emulator

Let's follow these steps to create an Android Wear emulator.

1. Start the Android AVD: Windows ➤ Android Virtual device Manager (see Figure 11-6)

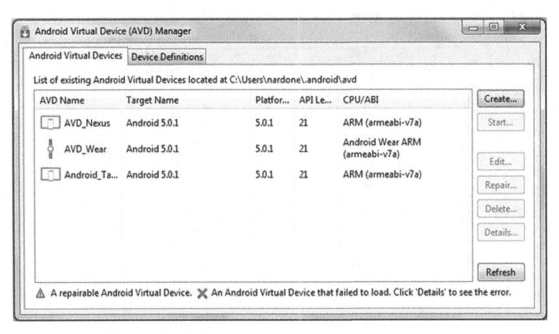

Figure 11-6. Android Virtual Device (AVD) Manager

2. Click the Create button and then create the Android Wear emulator (see Figure 11-7)

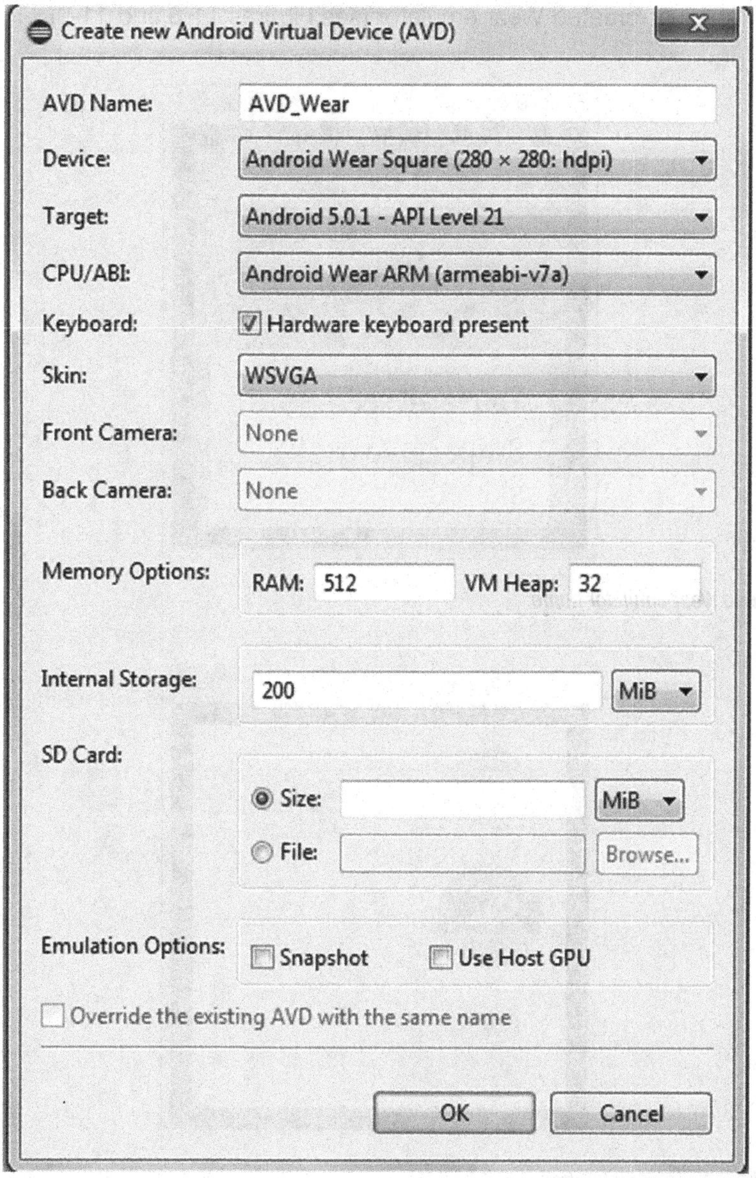

Figure 11-7. Android Wear emulator creation Wizard

3.   Start the just-created Wear emulator (see Figures 11-8 and 11-9)

Figure 11-8. Android Wear emulator home

Figure 11-9. Android Wear emulator menu

Now you are ready to test your Wear emulator with a simple timer application that will not need to interact with any Android smartphone or tablet.

1.   Download the Timer Wear application from the Android development site: `http://developer.android.com/samples/Timer/index.html`.

2.   Install, compile and run the application with the new Android SDK version 5.0.1 API 21. The result of this simple timer application is shown in Figure 11-10.

Figure 11-10. *Android Wear Timer Application*

Creating an Android Support Wearable Application

So far we've covered how to configure Android Wear, and we also tested a simple application. The next task is how to develop an application to connect your real Android smartphone or tablet to the Wear emulator we just created.

To create an Android Wear project, you need the Android Wear Support library (android.support.wearable), which you can manually extract from Google Support Repository and add to your workspace.

Follow these steps to configure the wear Application:

1. Find the wearable support library file named wearable-1.0.0.aar. This is normally located in the Android SDK folder you installed, such as <YourSDK Directory>/extras/google/m2repository/com/google/ android/support/wearable/1.0.0/wearable-1.0.0.aar.

   In my case, the file is found in C:\eclipse-SDK\adt-bundle- windows-x86_64-20140702\sdk\extras\google\m2repository\com\ google\android\support\wearable\1.0.0.

2. Copy the wearable-1.0.0.aar to a new location; for instance: C:\eclipse-SDK\wear.

3. Rename this file as a zip file, such as wearable-1.0.0.zip.

4. Extract it in the just-created directory.

5. Create a new directory named libs and copy classes.jar into that directory. See Figure 11-11.

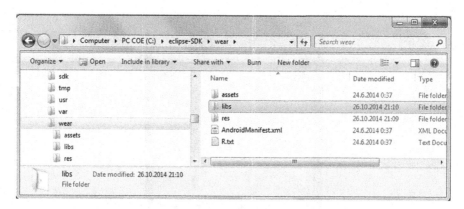

Figure 11-11. Wear Support libraries

Adding a Support Library The next thing to do is to add this Android Wear Support library to your Eclipse workspace. Here are the step to do that. First, let's create a new Android application project named Wear.

1. In Eclipse, click the New Android Project icon on the main toolbar or press CTRL-N and select Android ➤ Android project. This opens the New Android Project dialog box.

2. In the dialog box, enter a project name (Wear in this example).

3. Enter an application name (wear in this example).

4. Enter a package name (chap11.wear in this example).

5. Specify the SDK versions to be used and click Next.
    (see Figure 11-12)

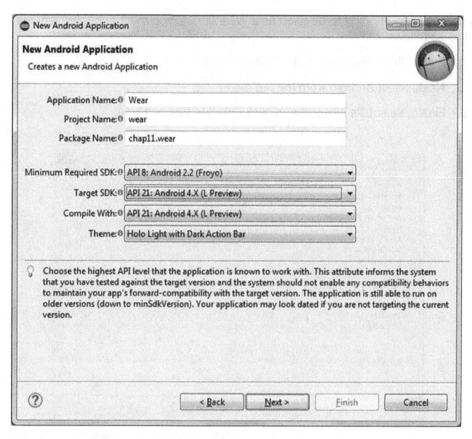

Figure 11-12. Create Wear Support libraries project Wear

6. Create an activity with the name "MainActivity" and click Finish (see Figure 11-13).

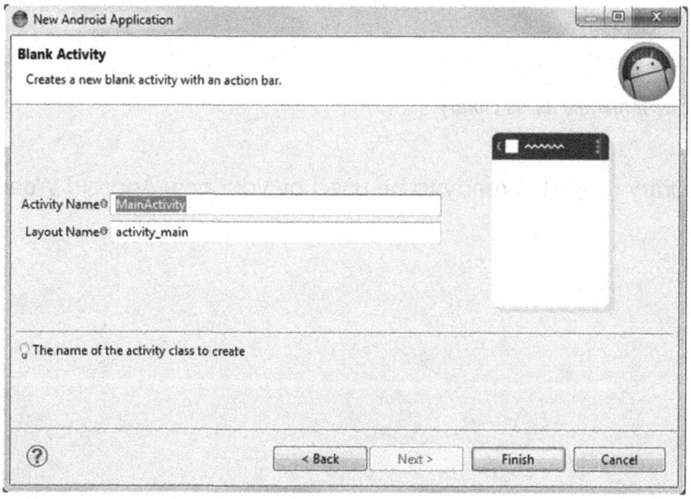

Figure 11-13. New Wear activity

Because this library is going to be used as a Wear library, you must configure it in the project properties as follows:

1. Right-click the project and select Properties.

2. Next, select Android from the left menu

3. Finally, select "Is Library" and click OK. See Figure 11-14.

Figure 11-14. Project wear marked as "Is Library"

Now your Wear library project is ready to be used by your new Android Wear application.

Connecting a Wear App

Now that you have created the wear support library project, you can proceed with creating the new wear app that will connect your Android smartphone or tablet to the Wear emulator you just created, and will then receive a text to display.

Let's create a new Android application project named wear:

1. In Eclipse, click the New Android Project icon on the main toolbar or press CTRL-N and select Android ➤ Android project. This opens the New Android Project dialog box.

2. In the dialog box, enter a project name (ch11.Project in this example).

3. Enter an application name (Ch11.Project in this example).

4. Enter a package name (ch11.project in this example).

5. Specify the SDK versions to be used and click Next. (see Figure 11-15)

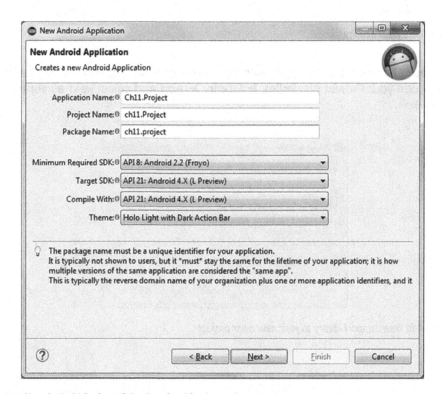

Figure 11-15. New Android Project dialog box for this chapter's example

6. Create an activity by giving it the name "MainActivity" and click Finish (see Figure 11-16).

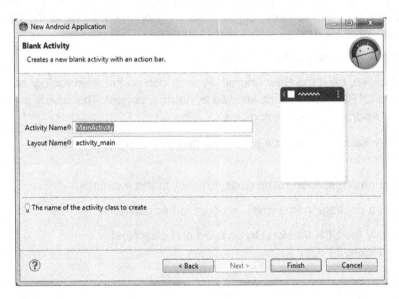

Figure 11-16. New Wear activity

The next step is to make sure the app uses the wear library project you created as library. To do that, open your Project properties ➤ Library ➤ Add and select wear as library. See Figure 11-17).

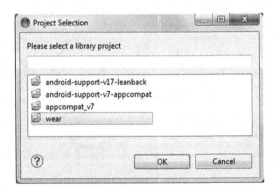

Figure 11-17. Add Wear support library to your new wear project

The application is now ready to be connect to your Android smartphone or tablet. Run this project to see the result in the Wear emulator you created earlier. See Figure 11-18.

Figure 11-18. Project result in the AVD Wear emulator

> **Note**   The cloud icon beside the battery icon means that your Android Wear is not paired/connected to any real Android devices.

Understanding the Code

Let's look closely now at what you need to add to your wearable application and how it should be configured.

Listing 11-1 shows the source code for the AndroidManifest.xml file for ch11.project.

Listing 11-1. AndroidManifest.xml file

```
<?xml version="1.0" encoding="utf-8"?>
<manifest xmlns:android="http://schemas.android.com/apk/res/android"
    package=" ch11.project"
    android:versionCode="1"
    android:versionName="1.0" >
```

```
<uses-sdk
    android:minSdkVersion="20"
    android:targetSdkVersion="21" />

<application
    android:allowBackup="true"
    android:icon="@drawable/ic_launcher"
    android:label="@string/app_name"
    android:theme="@style/AppTheme" >
    <activity
        android:name=".MainActivity"
        android:label="@string/app_name" >
        <intent-filter>
            <action android:name="android.intent.action.MAIN" />
            <category android:name="android.intent.category.LAUNCHER" />
        </intent-filter>
    </activity>
</application>

</manifest>
```

The AndroidManifest.xml file contains information about the SDK version used and all the rest of the specifications regarding the project, such as label, theme, and icon.

Next, let's have a look at the MainActivity component of our wearable project.

The file ch11.project.MainActivity.java is created by the wizard, and it is the entry point to the phone application. Listing 11-2 shows the code for this file. There are some remarkable things to note about this file.

As you probably know, when the application starts, the method onCreate(Bundle savedInstanceState) will be invoked by Android, which will load the native library using System.loadLibrary(name).

Listing 11-2. Main Activity for This Chapter's Example

```
package ch11.project;

import android.app.Activity;
import android.os.Bundle;
import android.support.wearable.view.WatchViewStub;
import android.widget.TextView;

public class MainAvtivity extends Activity {

        private TextView mTextView;

        protected void onCreate(Bundle savedInstanceState) {
                super.onCreate(savedInstanceState);
                setContentView(R.layout.activity_main);
                final WatchViewStub stub = (WatchViewStub) findViewById(R.id.watch_view_stub);
```

```
        stub.setOnLayoutInflatedListener(new WatchViewStub.
        OnLayoutInflatedListener() {
                public void onLayoutInflated(WatchViewStub stub) {
                        mTextView = (TextView) stub.findViewById(R.id.text);
                }
        });
    }
}
```

You updated the `ProjectActivity.java` file by adding the wearable library:

```
import android.support.wearable.view.WatchViewStub;
```

Now you need to call the `onCreate` method so that the screen content will be updated with the new value.

```
mTextView = (TextView) stub.findViewById(R.id.text
```

Every time you add a wearable support library to the project, a file will be automatically added to the project as well. In this case it is called `R.java`. Listing 11-3 shows the code for this file.

Listing 11-3. R.java for This Chapter's Example

```
/* AUTO-GENERATED FILE.  DO NOT MODIFY.
 *
 * This class was automatically generated by the
 * aapt tool from the resource data it found.  It
 * should not be modified by hand.
 */
package android.support.wearable;

public final class R {
        public static final class attr {
                public static final int circle_border_color = 0x7f010005;
                public static final int circle_border_width = 0x7f010004;
                public static final int circle_color = 0x7f010001;
                public static final int circle_padding = 0x7f010006;
                public static final int circle_radius = 0x7f010002;
                public static final int circle_radius_pressed = 0x7f010003;
                public static final int layout_box = 0x7f010000;
                public static final int rectLayout = 0x7f010009;
                public static final int roundLayout = 0x7f01000a;
                public static final int shadow_width = 0x7f010007;
                public static final int update_interval = 0x7f010008;
        }
        public static final class color {
                public static final int black = 0x7f040000;
                public static final int blue = 0x7f040001;
                public static final int dark_blue = 0x7f040002;
                public static final int disabled_text_light = 0x7f040003;
                public static final int dismiss_close = 0x7f040004;
```

```
        public static final int dismiss_close_pressed = 0x7f040005;
        public static final int dismiss_overlay_bg = 0x7f040006;
        public static final int green = 0x7f040007;
        public static final int grey = 0x7f040008;
        public static final int light_grey = 0x7f040009;
        public static final int orange = 0x7f04000a;
        public static final int primary_text_dark = 0x7f04000b;
        public static final int primary_text_light = 0x7f04000c;
        public static final int red = 0x7f04000d;
        public static final int secondary_text_light = 0x7f04000e;
        public static final int semitransparent_grey = 0x7f04000f;
        public static final int white = 0x7f040010;
    }
    public static final class dimen {
        public static final int card_content_padding_rect_left = 0x7f050000;
        public static final int card_content_padding_rect_right = 0x7f050001;
        public static final int card_content_padding_rect_top = 0x7f050002;
        public static final int close_button_diameter = 0x7f050003;
        public static final int dismiss_padding = 0x7f050004;
    }
    public static final class drawable {
        public static final int card_background = 0x7f020000;
        public static final int card_frame = 0x7f020001;
        public static final int card_frame_pressed = 0x7f020002;
        public static final int close_button = 0x7f020003;
        public static final int confirmation_animation = 0x7f020004;
        public static final int generic_confirmation_00163 = 0x7f020005;
        public static final int generic_confirmation_00164 = 0x7f020006;
        public static final int generic_confirmation_00165 = 0x7f020007;
        public static final int generic_confirmation_00166 = 0x7f020008;
        public static final int generic_confirmation_00167 = 0x7f020009;
        public static final int generic_confirmation_00168 = 0x7f02000a;
        public static final int generic_confirmation_00169 = 0x7f02000b;
        public static final int generic_confirmation_00170 = 0x7f02000c;
        public static final int generic_confirmation_00171 = 0x7f02000d;
        public static final int generic_confirmation_00172 = 0x7f02000e;
        public static final int generic_confirmation_00173 = 0x7f02000f;
        public static final int generic_confirmation_00174 = 0x7f020010;
        public static final int generic_confirmation_00175 = 0x7f020011;
        public static final int generic_confirmation_00176 = 0x7f020012;
        public static final int generic_confirmation_00177 = 0x7f020013;
        public static final int generic_confirmation_00178 = 0x7f020014;
        public static final int generic_confirmation_00179 = 0x7f020015;
        public static final int generic_confirmation_00180 = 0x7f020016;
        public static final int generic_confirmation_00181 = 0x7f020017;
        public static final int generic_confirmation_00182 = 0x7f020018;
        public static final int generic_confirmation_00183 = 0x7f020019;
        public static final int generic_confirmation_00184 = 0x7f02001a;
        public static final int generic_confirmation_00185 = 0x7f02001b;
        public static final int generic_confirmation_00186 = 0x7f02001c;
        public static final int generic_confirmation_00187 = 0x7f02001d;
        public static final int generic_confirmation_00188 = 0x7f02001e;
```

```
public static final int generic_confirmation_00189 = 0x7f02001f;
public static final int generic_confirmation_00190 = 0x7f020020;
public static final int generic_confirmation_00191 = 0x7f020021;
public static final int generic_confirmation_00192 = 0x7f020022;
public static final int generic_confirmation_00193 = 0x7f020023;
public static final int go_to_phone_00156 = 0x7f020024;
public static final int go_to_phone_00157 = 0x7f020025;
public static final int go_to_phone_00158 = 0x7f020026;
public static final int go_to_phone_00159 = 0x7f020027;
public static final int go_to_phone_00160 = 0x7f020028;
public static final int go_to_phone_00161 = 0x7f020029;
public static final int go_to_phone_00162 = 0x7f02002a;
public static final int go_to_phone_00163 = 0x7f02002b;
public static final int go_to_phone_00164 = 0x7f02002c;
public static final int go_to_phone_00165 = 0x7f02002d;
public static final int go_to_phone_00166 = 0x7f02002e;
public static final int go_to_phone_00167 = 0x7f02002f;
public static final int go_to_phone_00168 = 0x7f020030;
public static final int go_to_phone_00169 = 0x7f020031;
public static final int go_to_phone_00170 = 0x7f020032;
public static final int go_to_phone_00171 = 0x7f020033;
public static final int go_to_phone_00172 = 0x7f020034;
public static final int go_to_phone_00173 = 0x7f020035;
public static final int go_to_phone_00174 = 0x7f020036;
public static final int go_to_phone_00175 = 0x7f020037;
public static final int go_to_phone_00176 = 0x7f020038;
public static final int go_to_phone_00177 = 0x7f020039;
public static final int go_to_phone_00178 = 0x7f02003a;
public static final int go_to_phone_00185 = 0x7f02003b;
public static final int go_to_phone_00186 = 0x7f02003c;
public static final int go_to_phone_00187 = 0x7f02003d;
public static final int go_to_phone_00188 = 0x7f02003e;
public static final int go_to_phone_00189 = 0x7f02003f;
public static final int go_to_phone_00190 = 0x7f020040;
public static final int go_to_phone_00191 = 0x7f020041;
public static final int go_to_phone_00192 = 0x7f020042;
public static final int go_to_phone_00193 = 0x7f020043;
public static final int go_to_phone_00194 = 0x7f020044;
public static final int go_to_phone_00195 = 0x7f020045;
public static final int go_to_phone_00196 = 0x7f020046;
public static final int go_to_phone_00197 = 0x7f020047;
public static final int go_to_phone_00198 = 0x7f020048;
public static final int go_to_phone_00199 = 0x7f020049;
public static final int go_to_phone_00200 = 0x7f02004a;
public static final int go_to_phone_00210 = 0x7f02004b;
public static final int go_to_phone_00211 = 0x7f02004c;
public static final int go_to_phone_00212 = 0x7f02004d;
public static final int go_to_phone_00213 = 0x7f02004e;
public static final int go_to_phone_00214 = 0x7f02004f;
public static final int go_to_phone_00215 = 0x7f020050;
public static final int go_to_phone_00216 = 0x7f020051;
public static final int go_to_phone_00217 = 0x7f020052;
```

```
            public static final int go_to_phone_00218 = 0x7f020053;
            public static final int go_to_phone_00219 = 0x7f020054;
            public static final int go_to_phone_00220 = 0x7f020055;
            public static final int go_to_phone_00221 = 0x7f020056;
            public static final int go_to_phone_00222 = 0x7f020057;
            public static final int go_to_phone_00223 = 0x7f020058;
            public static final int go_to_phone_00224 = 0x7f020059;
            public static final int go_to_phone_animation = 0x7f02005a;
            public static final int ic_full_cancel = 0x7f02005b;
            public static final int ic_full_sad = 0x7f02005c;
    }
    public static final class id {
            public static final int action_error = 0x7f080006;
            public static final int action_success = 0x7f080008;
            public static final int all = 0x7f080000;
            public static final int animation = 0x7f080009;
            public static final int bottom = 0x7f080001;
            public static final int dismiss_overlay_button = 0x7f08000c;
            public static final int dismiss_overlay_explain = 0x7f08000b;
            public static final int error_message = 0x7f080007;
            public static final int left = 0x7f080002;
            public static final int message = 0x7f08000a;
            public static final int right = 0x7f080003;
            public static final int text = 0x7f08000d;
            public static final int title = 0x7f08000e;
            public static final int top = 0x7f080004;
    }
    public static final class layout {
            public static final int confirmation_activity_layout = 0x7f030001;
            public static final int dismiss_overlay = 0x7f030002;
            public static final int watch_card_content = 0x7f030005;
    }
    public static final class style {
            public static final int CardContent = 0x7f060000;
            public static final int CardText = 0x7f060001;
            public static final int CardTitle = 0x7f060002;
            public static final int DismissOverlayText = 0x7f060003;
            public static final int TextAppearance_Wearable_Large = 0x7f060004;
            public static final int TextAppearance_Wearable_Medium = 0x7f060005;
            public static final int TextAppearance_Wearable_Small = 0x7f060006;
            public static final int TextView_Large = 0x7f060007;
            public static final int TextView_Large_Light = 0x7f060008;
            public static final int TextView_Medium = 0x7f060009;
            public static final int TextView_Medium_Light = 0x7f06000a;
            public static final int TextView_Small = 0x7f06000b;
            public static final int TextView_Small_Light = 0x7f06000c;
            public static final int Theme_Wearable = 0x7f06000d;
            public static final int Theme_Wearable_Modal = 0x7f06000e;
    }
```

```
public static final class styleable {
        public static final int[] BoxInsetLayout = { 0x7f010000 };
        public static final int BoxInsetLayout_layout_box = 0;
        public static final int[] CircledImageView = { 0x01010119, 0x7f010001,
        0x7f010002, 0x7f010003, 0x7f010004, 0x7f010005, 0x7f010006, 0x7f010007 };
        public static final int CircledImageView_android_src = 0;
        public static final int CircledImageView_circle_border_color = 5;
        public static final int CircledImageView_circle_border_width = 4;
        public static final int CircledImageView_circle_color = 1;
        public static final int CircledImageView_circle_padding = 6;
        public static final int CircledImageView_circle_radius = 2;
        public static final int CircledImageView_circle_radius_pressed = 3;
        public static final int CircledImageView_shadow_width = 7;
        public static final int[] DelayedConfirmationView = { 0x7f010008 };
        public static final int DelayedConfirmationView_update_interval = 0;
        public static final int[] WatchViewStub = { 0x7f010009, 0x7f01000a };
        public static final int WatchViewStub_rectLayout = 0;
        public static final int WatchViewStub_roundLayout = 1;
    }
}
```

This file mainly define all the classes like class layout and class style, which are used when rendering the layout and style of the wearable application.

The next step is to look at the project.properties file. Since you used the wear reference library wear created earlier, the project.properties file should look like this:

```
target=android-21

android.library.reference.1=../wear
```

Now you can take a look at the files under the folder "res" of the project. The first change you want to make is to the file styles.xml, which will look like this:

```
<resources>

    <!-- Application theme. -->
    <style name="AppTheme" parent="android:Theme.DeviceDefault">
        <!-- All customizations that are NOT specific to a particular API-level can go here. -->
    </style>

</resources>
```

Please refer to http://developer.android.com/guide/topics/ui/themes.html for more information about styles and themes.

By utilizing this code, you'll use the default application theme for your project. Next, we'll take a look at the activity_my.xml file. Listing 11-4 shows the code for this file.

Listing 11-4. Activity_my.xml

```xml
<?xml version="1.0" encoding="utf-8"?>
<android.support.wearable.view.WatchViewStub xmlns:android="http://schemas.android.com/apk/
res/android"
    xmlns:app="http://schemas.android.com/apk/res-auto"
    xmlns:tools="http://schemas.android.com/tools"
    android:id="@+id/watch_view_stub"
    android:layout_width="match_parent"
    android:layout_height="match_parent"
    app:rectLayout="@layout/rect"
    app:roundLayout="@layout/round"
    tools:context="ch11.project.MainActivity"
    tools:deviceIds="wear" >

</android.support.wearable.view.WatchViewStub>
```

The most important thing to check about this file is the layout style, which in this case is rectangular:

```
app:rectLayout="@layout/rect"
```

Also check the reference to the wear library:

```
tools:deviceIds="wear" >
```

Every time you create a new wear project, two layout files are created, such as rect.xml and round, which are used depending on whether the wear device is rectangular or rounded.

Listings 11-5 and 11-6 show the code for these files.

Listing 11-5. rect.xml

```xml
<?xml version="1.0" encoding="utf-8"?>
<LinearLayout xmlns:android="http://schemas.android.com/apk/res/android"
    xmlns:tools="http://schemas.android.com/tools"
    android:layout_width="match_parent"
    android:layout_height="match_parent"
    android:orientation="vertical"
    tools:context="ch11.project.MainActivity"
    tools:deviceIds="wear_square" >

    <TextView
        android:id="@+id/text"
        android:layout_width="wrap_content"
        android:layout_height="wrap_content"
        android:text="@string/hello_square" />

</LinearLayout>
```

Listing 11-6. round.xml

```
<?xml version="1.0" encoding="utf-8"?>
<RelativeLayout xmlns:android="http://schemas.android.com/apk/res/android"
    xmlns:tools="http://schemas.android.com/tools"
    android:layout_width="match_parent"
    android:layout_height="match_parent"
    tools:context="ch11.project.MainActivity"
    tools:deviceIds="wear_round" >

    <TextView
        android:id="@+id/text"
        android:layout_width="wrap_content"
        android:layout_height="wrap_content"
        android:layout_centerHorizontal="true"
        android:layout_centerVertical="true"
        android:text="@string/hello_round" />

</RelativeLayout>
```

The last layout file to check is the `string.xml` file. Listing 11-7 shows the code for this file.

Listing 11-7. strings.xml

```
<?xml version="1.0" encoding="utf-8"?>
<resources>

    <string name="app_name">ch11.Project</string>
    <string name="hello_round">My first Wear App</string>
    <string name="hello_square">My first Wear App</string>

</resources>
```

This file, which is based on the type of wearable (such as rounded or rectangular), defines the string to be displayed. In our case the string is "My First Wear App."

Now that you've seen all the code you need for this simple wearable application, let's run and test it.

Connecting an Android Device to the AVD Emulator

So far you've created the Android Wear emulator and the project that allows the emulator to be connected to a real Android device. Remember that you will need an Android device running on Android OS 4.3+ and above to connect to the Wear emulator.

Let's now see how to connect your Android smartphone or Tablet to the Wear emulator just created in your project.

The first step is to install the "Android Wear App" from the Google Play store: https://play.google.com/store/apps/details?id=com.google.android.wearable.app (see Figure 11-19)

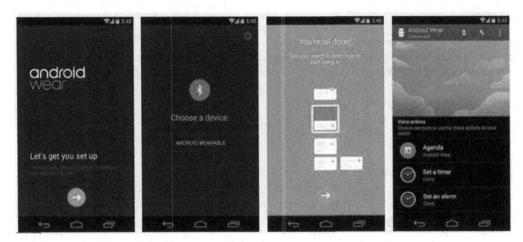

Figure 11-19. Google's Android Wear App for Android devices

Once you've installed the Android Wear app onto your Android device, you follow these steps:

1. Enable USB debugging on your handheld device.

2. Connect your Android device to the computer using a USB cable.

3. To test that your Android device is successfully connected to the computer, run the following command:

    ```
    ./adb devices
    ```

The result is shown in Figure 11-20.

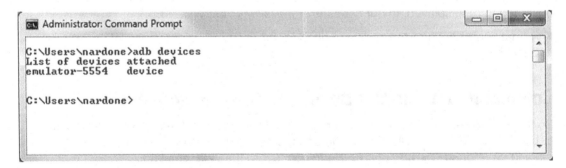

Figure 11-20. Android AVD active device

4. Open the TCP port 5601 on your computer so that the Android Wear emulator can use it to communicate with your Android device.

5. Finally, to connect your Android Wear emulator to your Android device run the following command:

```
adb -d forward tcp:5601 tcp:5601
```

Now your Android Wear emulator is connected to your Android device. See Figure 11-21.

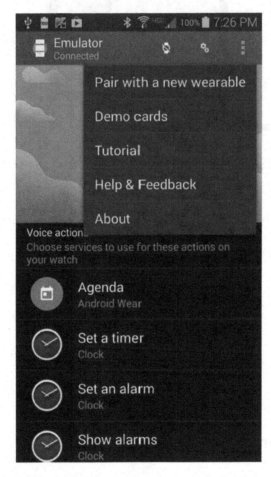

Figure 11-21. Android device connected to the Wear emulator

As you can see, the cloud icon is no longer shown because the emulator is already connected to your Android device. See Figure 11-22.

Figure 11-22. Wear emulator connected to the Android device

To complete the app, let's now run the project chap11 created earlier. The result will be show in Figure 11-23.

Figure 11-23. Wear emulator receives the text from the Android device

This Application was also tested with a real Android wearable device.

Congratulations! You've now completed your first Wear application.

This app was a simple one, of course, but other Android Wear apps can be just as easily implemented, now that you know the basics.

Final Thoughts

I hope that you have enjoyed *Pro Android 4 Games, Third Edition*. I wrote this book to show you the things that can be done with Java and C, two powerful languages. I've demonstrated how one person can bring a complex PC game to Android with little effort in record time by using these two great languages.

I've also provided examples in this book about new features available in OpenGL ES 3.1, and included information for new applications such as Android TV and Android Wear. During the writing of this manuscript the Android SDK version 5.0.1 API 21 was released, which made this book even easier to update since a lot of previous limitations were solved.

All in all, with the release of Android SDK version 5.0.1, OpenGL ES 3.1 and NDK, Android may become a serious contender with iOS for gaming. Android has a ways to go to catch up, but the platform development seems to run at a tremendous pace. Android vs. iOS—I can't wait to see who wins. At the moment, my heart is with Android.

Index

Get the eBook for only $10!

Now you can take the weightless companion with you anywhere, anytime. Your purchase of this book entitles you to 3 electronic versions for only $10.

This Apress title will prove so indispensible that you'll want to carry it with you everywhere, which is why we are offering the eBook in 3 formats for only $10 if you have already purchased the print book.

Convenient and fully searchable, the PDF version enables you to easily find and copy code—or perform examples by quickly toggling between instructions and   applications. The MOBI format is ideal for your Kindle, while the ePUB can be utilized on a variety of mobile devices.

Go to www.apress.com/promo/tendollars to purchase your companion eBook.